The Family Law Act 1996

with annotations by

Professor Michael Freeman

*Professor of English Law at University College London,
a barrister of Gray's Inn*

LONDON
SWEET & MAXWELL
1996

Published in 1996 by
Sweet & Maxwell Limited of
100 Avenue Road
London NW3 3PF
Typeset by MFK Information Services Ltd.,
Hitchin, Herts
Printed and bound in Great Britain by
Butler & Tanner Ltd, Frome and London

A CIP catalogue record for this book is available
from The British Library

ISBN 0–421–55100–3

The Family Law Act 1996

AUSTRALIA
LBC Information Services
Brisbane • Sydney • Melbourne • Perth

CANADA
Carswell
Ottawa • Toronto • Calgary • Montreal • Vancouver

AGENTS:
Steimatzky's Agency Ltd., Tel Aviv;
N. M. Tripathi (Private) Ltd., Bombay;
Eastern Law House (Private) Ltd., Calcutta;
M.P.P. House, Bangalore;
Universal Book Traders, Delhi;
Aditya Books, Delhi;
MacMillan Shuppan KK, Tokyo;
Pakistan Law House, Karachi

To my sister-in-law, Judith Corré, who has experienced most of the problems of this Act and borne them with fortitude and good humour.

CONTENTS

INTRODUCTION

New divorce laws are seldom uncontroversial and this one was brimful with controversy. Not until the last moment could the government be certain that its Family Law Bill would pass, and it only passed then as a result of eleventh hour concessions. The passage of the Bill was haunted by the ghost of the previous year's Family Homes and Domestic Violence Bill which was cruelly killed by a cabal of high priests of the "Right" swept into action by the frenzy of William Oddie and other *Daily Mail* columnists. The opposition to the Family Law Bill was more temperate but no less real. At least the target of the attack this time was divorce reform: last November the opponents were to a large extent tilting at windmills, opposing provisions some of which had been law for almost twenty years.

It had a stormy passage but it did eventually pass into law. It may not be in operation until 1999: there is a lot of work still to do. Much of the Act is a framework waiting for detailed rules and regulations: on matters as central as mediation the details thus far vouchsafed are sketchy.

The Act is in fact two Acts: one which reforms the law of divorce; a second which improves the available remedies for use in the battle to conquer domestic violence. The two are uncomfortable bedfellows, not because they are not related—in perhaps one-third of divorces there has been violence—but because of the dissonance between a new divorce law which proclaims the end of the matrimonial offence and a revamped code on domestic violence which recognises that we are no nearer eliminating "domestic hooliganism" than we were when Sir George Baker, then President of the Family Division, coined the phrase in 1978 in the first great domestic violence case. One reflection of this dissonance is the way references to domestic violence and child abuse permeate the new divorce structure and processes.

A question often asked is whether under the new divorce law, divorce will be easier to obtain or more difficult to secure. Certainly, many of the opponents of the new law resisted its passage because they thought it made divorce easy. But could divorce, "quickie divorce" as it was called throughout the debates inside and outside Parliament, have been any easier than it became under a Special Procedure (to which incidentally Parliament never gave authority) with 75 per cent of divorces being based on adultery or unreasonable behaviour, but with these offences attracting barely a semblance of judicial scrutiny? Certainly, divorce will now be a lengthier process, even longer where there are children of the family under 16. There will be no need to prove fault, but there is no guarantee, quite the reverse, that mud will not be slung in the counselling and mediation sessions that most couples will face, or that reflection on the past and consideration about future arrangements will be a non-recriminatory rite of passage. It is difficult to see how the new period for reflection and consideration is not at least in part a social control mechanism, even a punishment for marital failure, though this would be denied, when couples are forced to reflect and consider even when they have already done so, as surely many will. The reflection and consideration period can be extended: it can never be abridged, not even in cases of the grossest moral turpitude or serious violence or where delay will harm children.

With the end of the matrimonial offence—divorce is now reduced to the anodyne statement of marital breakdown—the burden has to some extent shifted to what the "other party" (as the respondent is now called) has to prove to secure an "order preventing divorce". The old defence of "grave financial or other hardship" bit only on the divorce based on five years' separation, and its bark was immeasurably worse than its bite. The new defence has stronger teeth: the hardship need only be "substantial" and it extends also to that suffered by children of the family. We can be certain that initially this new defence will be used. Whether it will be any more successful than the previous model, which at best was a bargaining counter, we can only wait and see. Expectations are not high, though it has to be said that the intention is that some divorces will be frustrated. Of greater significance may be the provisions which build into the divorce process opportunities for the reluctant divorcee to obstruct and delay divorce. Though minimum distress and cheapness of process are proclaimed as goals—one of the novelties of the legislation is its announcement in s.1 of "General Principles"—it may be wondered whether such ideals will be attained in the kind of prolonged negotiations which this Act countenances.

Though much of this Act is a divorce reform measure, it does not have, as previous divorce reform legislation has had, the title "Matrimonial Causes Act" or "Divorce Reform Act". In part this is because the Act covers so much other ground. More significantly, it is because ideologically this Act is committed to an ideal of marriage rather than to mechanisms for bringing marriages to an end. The Act proclaims at its outset that "the court and any person, in exercising functions under or in consequence of Part II and III, shall have regard to the following general principles—(a) that the institution of marriage is to be supported...". In terms of the Act, this leads to an emphasis on mediation, on counselling, on reflection, on anything in fact which will lead to reconciliation or at least the salvaging of relationships so that they can continue and detrimentally affect the parties and their children as little as possible.

But on another level, state commitment to the institution of marriage packs messages about rights and responsibilities, about model relationships, about the relationship of the state to the family. It privileges and prioritises in ways reminiscent of Lord Penzance's famous definition of marriage in *Hyde v. Hyde* in 1866. So being married is better than not being married, marriage is a better arrangement than cohabitation, monogamy is preferable to polygamy, staying married is better than getting divorced, heterosexuality is on a higher plain than homosexuality. The Lord Chancellor was clear that counselling was intended to save marriages, not "alternative lifestyles". However, the Act, perhaps because it is two Acts, is not totally consistent. Many of the remedies relating to occupation of the matrimonial home and to domestic violence extend to cohabitants and former cohabitants. Indeed, this is the first Act to use that concept. However, an attempt to extend the summary procedure in s.17 of the Married Women's Property Act 1882 to cohabitants—it was extended to engaged couples in 1970—failed. It was sacrificed on the altar of prejudice, for no discernible principle can justify imposing a more costly procedure for determining property disputes upon those who have not agreed to marry. Gay couples are, somewhat surprisingly, included within the rubric of "associated persons" and thus qualify for domestic violence remedies, a victory for "Sister George" that few can have anticipated and one which the "moral majority" (and even the *Daily Mail*) can surely not have noticed.

At the centre of the new model of divorce is mediation. The Act itself spells out no details about this. It is one of the things that parties will learn about at the information meetings they must attend not less than three months before making a statement which initiates the divorce process. Solicitors are likely, under rules to be made, to have the duty to inform parties of the availability of mediation and to give them details of persons qualified to help in connection with mediation. We know that mediation will not, as some feared might have been the case, be compulsory. We know legal aid funding will be available for mediation where it appears to the mediator suitable to the dispute and the parties and all the circumstances. It is also clear from the Act—how could it be otherwise in an Act which also targets domestic violence—that the government is more sensitive to the dangers of using mediation where violence has wrecked a marriage: "killing us softly" is how one critic put it. But its awareness of the dangers of "violence or other harm" does not extend to an understanding that power imbalances can distort the process of mediation. There must be a fear that mediation will be appropriate to far fewer cases than is optimistically anticipated.

Mediation is part of a retreat from law and lawyers. It looks to assist the parties to find a resolution to their problems, rather than imposing one upon them. It does not measure behaviour—as such it is a natural concomitant of the sweeping away of the matrimonial offence. And it looks to the future rather than the past, to the restructuring of relationships rather than to recrimination or blame for failures. But the future requires that full attention is not just to the long-term welfare of children but also to such matters as property, financial assets, financial provision, tax and pensions. How many mediators will be qualified to dispense advice on this range of questions? And if mediators are not so qualified, will not negotiated agreements favour the more resourceful? Is this yet another "divorce revolution" out of which men will profit and women lose? If the same amount of state funding—or as some fear, less—is to be available to fund information meetings, counselling and mediation as well as legal assistance as now goes into legal aid, how many women in particular will have access to solicitors? How will the courts react to negotiated agreements? Will consent orders be made as readily? Mediation poses more questions than it answers. The danger is that, having identified problems with legal processes, the alternative may create greater ones. Family Law Acts are the last places to throw out babies with the bathwater.

There is much more to this Act than the overhaul of divorce. There is the prospect of pension-splitting. This equitable division of assets has been persistently rejected by the government, despite the support of the Pensions Management Institute, amongst others, for the concept. "Prospect" is the operative word, for people who divorce will have to wait until the next century for the change to take effect. The State Earnings Related Pension Scheme will be included, but probably not pension rights built up overseas. Nor will pension-splitting, it seems, cover those who have already reached separation orders or divorce settlements.

The domestic violence reforms will be generally welcomed. The recognition that children may apply for an occupation order or non-molestation order in their own right is important, if only symbolically. That those under 16 require leave is unnecessarily cautious, but in the light of its model (the Children Act 1989) not surprisingly so. The ability of the police and possibly other organisations—yet again the details are to be specified in rules—to seek such orders on behalf of victims of domestic violence (it is not clear whether this will include children as well as adult victims) is more contentious. It divided the Law Commission and the Home Affairs Select Committee, the former favouring, the latter opposing such proactivity. The government did not favour this extension of police powers and the provision, open-ended in that it is not stated who will have the powers, was sneaked into the Act very late in its passage through Parliament. The case for and against giving third parties, particularly the police, this power is neatly balanced. Anything which makes our law enforcement agencies take domestic violence more seriously is to be welcomed, but if it leads to their transferring their attention from a criminal law response to one using civil law resources the clock may be turned back to the days when domestic violence was not regarded as real police work at all. Even more significantly, there is the concern that in taking autonomy away from victims you re-victimise them: a form of public "violence" aggravates private violence. Before pronouncing on this any further we will need to see the rules to discover what scope for consultation or attention to victims' wishes there will be.

Perhaps the most suspect aspect of the domestic violence provisions is the concept of "associated persons", which the Act uses to restrict eligibility to seek remedies. The concept was invented by the Law Commission, which rejected the idea that injunctive relief, of the type it proposed and the Act adopts, should be generally available. The list of "associated persons" is broad—there are seven categories and these include persons who live or have lived in the same household, otherwise than merely by reason of one of them being the other's employee, tenant, lodger or boarder and thus it includes gay partners and former partners. But the government omitted, contrary to Law Commission advice, persons who have had a sexual relationship. This may have been wise: "sexual relationship" may have been difficult to define. However, the steady stream of cases where romantic interest or infatuation leads to unwanted attention and unwarranted harassment, as well as the new attention given to "stalking", suggest here was a nettle waiting to be grasped. Given the problems that the law of tort has had to confront—the contours of the tort of harassment remain fuzzy—a more generalised criterion, such as exists in Australian states, might have been a more positive response.

Of new powers, that to oust child abusers by adding exclusion orders to interim care orders and emergency protection orders is to be warmly welcomed. It was surely a mistake, as the *Nottingham* litigation demonstrated, to omit such powers from the Children Act in 1989. Their inclusion now should obviate the need for local authorities to use more draconian powers, exactly Nottingham's concern, but the limited duration of such exclusion orders may continue to pose problems.

The concern for children exemplified here is to the fore in a plethora of other provisions in the Act. Little of this concern was in the original Bill. Thus, provision may now be made for the separate representation of children in a range of civil proceedings, including marital proceedings and applications for occupation orders and non-molestation orders but not Children Act proceedings, which is an unfortunate omission.

Until children can be separately represented in all proceedings, and there is a strong argument for including mediation within this, we will continue to be in breach of the United Nations Convention on the Rights of the Child, Art. 12, para. 2 of which requires that the child 'be provided the opportunity to be heard in any judicial and administrative proceedings affecting the child, either directly, or through a representative or an appropriate body . . .'. Attempts to strengthen the status and participatory rights of children were resisted. *Looking To The Future*, the blueprint of the divorce part of this Act, was an adult-focused document. Children featured in it as objects of concern. The report made no reference to important research evidence about the ability of children to participate in decision-making about their lives. The image of children it conveyed was of them as victims. The voice of victims is rarely listened to. Even when victims are not blamed—which is an all-too-common occurrence—they are rarely given any autonomy.

The powerlessness of children caught in the crossfire of divorce will not be mitigated by a mediation process which objectifies them. Like the home, money and pension arrangements, they are to be negotiated about. That the bargaining is to be civilised—or that this is the hope and the ideal—does not detract from the fact that children are an object of bargaining. Nor does the fact (or is it a fiction?) that their welfare is the dominant concern. They are not there, and they are not being listened to. There is the beginnings of a recognition of this in the Act. Thus the mediation code will require the mediator to have arrangements designed to ensure that the parties are 'encouraged to consider' the welfare, wishes and feelings of children and 'whether and to what extent each child should be given the opportunity to express his or her wishes and feelings in the mediation'. This may prove a tame concession.

There remains an assumption that the best interest of children will be secured by a facilitation of agreement between their parents. This overlooks the fact that what parents agree may be what is in their interests, rather than their child's interests. And where they are in agreement, how much mediation will take place? Who will put the child's case? *Looking To The Future* was clear: not only do mediators not act for either party, but they do not act for the child. The second assumption refuses to acknowledge that any of this could be a problem for it postulates the 'reasonable' parent who is a 'responsible' parent. So wedded is our law to the normative concept of parental responsibility that there is a refusal to acknowledge that parents often act with selfish disregard for the rights and needs of their children.

It is important that the 'satisfaction' provision, diluted by the Children Act and tucked away in a schedule of that Act, is now embodied in Part II of this Act. It is important also that, before a court makes a decision that it cannot make a divorce or separation order because it is not in a position to exercise its powers under the Children Act, for example to make a residence order, it is to have regard to the wishes and feelings of the child and that this consideration is placed first (as it was in the Children Act) in the checklist. But, though it is a precondition of divorce and separation that financial arrangements are satisfied, even, where the parties are Jews who married in a synagogue, that steps have been taken to dissolve the marriage religiously, the court, as before, is not required to be satisfied that the arrangements made for the children's future are satisfactory.

The Act is thus far from an unqualified success. But it will be welcomed by victims of domestic violence, by the mediation profession, by children's welfare organisations, by those who want to see a fairer distribution of pensions, by Jewish organisations concerned with the plight of women denied a religious divorce and by all who saw the reliance on the matrimonial offence as unseemly.

Its pro-marriage stance may be greeted more sceptically. The 'moral Right' will appreciate the acknowledgement, in surely one of the oddest provisions ever put into a statute, to the effect that cohabitation does not involve the same commitment as marriage.

The police may welcome their additional powers. The gay certainly ought to be gratified that domestic violence remedies now extend to them. But the move away from law and lawyers, the emphasis on mediation, information meetings (which ought to last a week if proper coverage is to be given to the listed matters!), the length of time it will now take to secure a divorce and the opportunities for delay built into the new process of reflection and consideration are less likely to be applauded. We legislate on divorce and now domestic violence once in a generation. When we return to these subjects in 2020, are we likely to find fewer divorces, more marriages saved, less domestic violence? It is my confident prediction that none of these goals will be achieved.

This book could not have been produced without the assistance of Rebekah Williams. I am most grateful to her.

Michael Freeman
August 1, 1996

TABLE OF CASES

References are to the Introduction or the General Note to the specified section, Part or Schedule.

Table of Cases

Table of Cases

TABLE OF STATUTES

References are to the Introduction or the General Note to the specified section, Part or Schedule.

TABLE OF STATUTORY INSTRUMENTS

References are to the Introduction or the General Note to the specified section, Part or Schedule.

FAMILY LAW ACT 1996*

(1996 c. 27)

ARRANGEMENT OF SECTIONS

PART I

PRINCIPLES OF PARTS II AND III

---

* Professor Michael Freeman, Professor of English Law at University College London, a barrister of Gray's Inn.

An Act to make provision with respect to: divorce and separation; legal aid in connection with mediation in disputes relating to family matters; proceedings in cases where marriages have broken down; rights of occupation of certain domestic premises; prevention of molestation; the inclusion in certain orders under the Children Act 1989 of provisions about the occupation of a dwelling-house; the transfer of tenancies between spouses and persons who have lived together as husband and wife; and for connected purposes. [4th July 1996]

PARLIAMENTARY DEBATES
Hansard, H.L. Vol. 567, cols. 700–790; Vol. 568, cols. 277–313, 325–354, 802–898, 908–968, 982–1026, 1129–1178, 1188–1224, 1382–1444; Vol. 569, cols. 1145–1157, 1173–1202, 1610–1670, 1681–1716; Vol. 570, cols. 10–73, 77–146, 618–675, 692–730; H.C. Vol. 274, cols. 738–806; Vol. 276, cols. 443–543; Standing Committee E Official Report, cols. 1–384; Vol. 279, cols. 535–658; H.L. Vol. 573, cols. 1059–1120.
 Part IV of the Act was also debated (briefly) in 1995 when the Family Homes and Domestic Violence Bill was before Parliament. The debates can be found as follows: *Hansard*, H.L. Vol. 561, cols. 1254–1272, 1586; Public Committee, cols. 3–28; Vol. 564, cols. 1061–1076; Vol. 565, cols. 220–226. H.C. Second Reading Committee, cols. 3–6; Vol. 262, col. 798; Standing Committee B, cols. 3–4. See also proceedings of the Special Public Committee with Evidence, H.L. Paper 55 (London: H.M.S.O. April 24, 1995).

INTRODUCTION AND GENERAL NOTE

The Family Law Act 1996—in effect two disparate though related Acts, one reforming the law and process of divorce, the other the law relating to domestic violence—proved the most difficult and controversial of this period of government. What is now Pt. IV of this Act began life as the Family Homes and Domestic Violence Bill in 1995. It proceeded with relatively little notice being taken of it—it had moved swiftly through the House of Lords under the new Jellicoe procedure—when it was sabotaged by a small number of Conservative M.P.s who were concerned that, in, as they judged it, improving the rights of cohabitants, the Bill was undermining the institution of marriage. That some of the provisions they identified had been the law since 1976 either escaped their attention or was deemed irrelevant. The Bill was lost at the eleventh hour.

Most of that Bill has been retrieved and is to be found in Pt. IV of this Act. But there are significant omissions and changes: for example, the 1995 Bill would have extended the summary procedure in s.17 of the Married Women's Property Act 1882 (c. 75) to cohabitants, but there is no place for this provision in the new Act. An understanding of the difference between the two models of domestic violence legislation can readily be gauged by a glance at s.41 of the Act which directs courts, when considering the nature of cohabitants' relationships, "to have regard to the fact that they have not given each other the commitment involved in marriage".

The lost Bill of 1995 has been tagged on to major divorce legislation. The Act thus contains the first major divorce reform since the Divorce Reform Act 1969 (c. 55) (which has been operative since 1971). Irretrievable breakdown is finally established as the sole ground for divorce (and for separation). The compromise of 1969, under which irretrievable breakdown was the only ground for divorce but the issue was not left at large because irretrievable breakdown was deemed non-justiciable (with the consequence that five facts, three of which were fault-based, were retained as pre-conditions for the establishment of irretrievable breakdown), has finally been rejected. As a result of the 1996 Act divorce will become a lengthier, more tortuous process, but the intention is that it will be conducted in a more civilised, less distressful, less recriminatory way. Central to the new divorce law is the obligation on the parties to reflect and consider. They are to reflect on whether their marriage can be saved (reconciliation is a key to the understanding of the new law): they are to consider what arrangements should be made for the future.

Although this Act reforms the law and process of divorce and the law relating to domestic violence remedies, as a subtext it is really about the institution of marriage. The general principles set out in s.1 underline, we are told, Pts. II and III of the Act (dealing with divorce and mediation), but in reality the ideology of the whole Act is informed by these principles. This is a divorce Act which is pro-marriage: it encourages counselling, mediation, reconciliation, the promotion of good continuing relationships; it disdains the conventional "quickie" divorce; and it rejects the idea that questions relating to children (residence and contact), to the matrimonial home and to money are, as we have come to call them, "ancillary". They are, the Act recognises, integral to the divorce process, to be solved before divorce is finalised. It is also a domestic violence Act saturated with messages about the respective institutions of marriage and cohabitation.

The Act had a rough passage through Parliament. Until the very last moment no one could be certain whether we would get an Act at all. There were premonitions that the Bill "Mark 2" might be wrecked as "Mark 1" was. The final Act differs markedly from the Family Law Bill published in November 1995. It is a package: it contains compromises and concessions. A number of these were wrung from an unwilling Government at the last moment. Notable amongst these are the provisions on pensions splitting in ss.16 and 17 of the Act. Hardly less significant is the power, the details of which have been left to Rules of Court, to enable others to seek injunctive relief on behalf of victims of domestic violence (see s.60). The Law Commission had recommended this (see *Domestic Violence and Occupation of the Matrimonial Home*, Law Com. No. 207 (1992), paras. 5.18–5.23), but the innovation did not find favour with the House of Commons Home Affairs Committee (see *Domestic Violence*, H.C. 245–I, 1993) or with the Government. Also of great importance is the extension of separate representation for children into civil proceedings (see s.64).

COMMENCEMENT

Section 65 (the power to make rules, orders and regulations by statutory instrument) came into force on July 4, 1996 (see s.67(2)). The remainder of the Act will come into force on such day or days as the Lord Chancellor may by order appoint (see s.67(3)).

TRANSITIONAL PROVISIONS
These are set out in Sched. 9 (see s.66(2)).

EXTENT
The whole Act (except s.17, on the division of pension assets in Scotland) applies to England and Wales (s.67(4)).
Section 17 extends only to Scotland (s.67(4)).
Amendments to the Judicial Proceedings (Regulations of Reports) Act 1926 (c. 61) and the repeal (in Sched. 10) of s.2(1)(b) of the Domestic and Appellate Proceedings (Restriction of Publicity) Act 1968 (c. 63) extend to Scotland.
Amendments of s.38 of the Family Law Act 1986 (c. 55) extend to Northern Ireland.
Amendments of the Maintenance Orders Act 1950 (c. 37), the Civil Jurisdiction and Judgments Act 1982 (c. 27), the Finance Act 1985 (c. 54), and ss.42 and 51 of the Family Law Act 1986 extend to both Scotland and Northern Ireland.
These amendments are in Sched. 8.

PART I

INTRODUCTION TO PARTS I, II AND III
Part II of the Act reforms the law and restructures the process of divorce and of separation. Part III deals with legal aid for mediation in family matters. Part I sets out general principles which are to govern the operation of both Pts. II and III. As already indicated, to some extent these principles are imbricated in the whole Act.
The origins of this Part of the Act are in *Looking To The Future: Mediation and the Ground for Divorce*. This was first published as a Consultation Paper in December 1993 (Cm. 2424) and subsequently as the Government's Proposals in April 1995 (Cm. 2799). In the Foreword to the former—it is slightly shortened in the latter—the Lord Chancellor encapsulates divorce reform within his religious ideals. In an unprecedented statement, an affirmation of a credo, he says:
"I personally believe strongly in the value of the institution of marriage and I believe that it is a divinely appointed arrangement fundamental to the well-being of our community" (p.iii).
This is reflected in the General Principles in s.1. But the origins go deeper. Research studies, such as that by Davis and Murch (*Grounds for Divorce*, O.U.P. 1988), were voicing criticism of the reformed divorce law from the early 1980s. The unsatisfactory nature of this compromise between offence-based facts and the breakdown principle had been accentuated by the introduction of the Special Procedure for divorce in 1977 (on this, see Waite L.J. in *Pounds v. Pounds* [1994] IFLR 775, 778). In 1988 the Law Commission published *Facing The Future* (Law Com. No. 170). Of the reformed law it said:
"The present law does not, nor could it reasonably be expected to, buttress the stability of marriage by preventing determined parties from obtaining a speedy divorce. Because of the compromise nature of the 1969 Act, the benefits ... have been brought at the price of incoherence and increased confusion for litigants. Thus the law is neither understandable nor respected and there is evidence of not considerable consumer dissatisfaction. Attaining the aims of maximum fairness and minimum bitterness has been rendered impossible by the retention of the fault element. The necessity of making allegations in the petition "draws the battle-lines" at the outset. The ensuing hostility makes the divorce more painful, not only for the parties but also for the children, and destroys any chance of reconciliation and may be detrimental to post-divorce relationships. Underlying all these defects is the fact that whether or not the marriage can be dissolved depends principally upon what parties have done in the past. In petitions relying on fault-based facts, the petitioner is encouraged to "dwell on the past" and to recriminate.
At the same time, the present divorce process may not allow sufficient opportunity for the parties to come to terms with what is happening in their lives. A recent study of the process of "uncoupling" points out that one party has usually gone far down that path before the other one discovers this, by which time it may be too late. Once the divorce process had been started it may have a "juggernaut" effect, providing insufficient opportunity for the parties to re-evaluate their positions. Thus, there is little or no scope for reconciliation, conciliation or renegotiation of the relationship. It is clear that both emotionally and financially it is much less costly if ancillary matters can be agreed between the parties. Where antagonism is created or exacerbated by the petition, or their respective bargaining power distorted, the atmosphere is not conductive to calm and sensible negotiations about the future needs of the parties and their children. Above all, the present law fails to recognise that divorce is not a final product but part of a massive transition for the parties and their children. It is crucial in the interests of the children (as well as the parties) that the

transition is as smooth as possible, since it is clear that their short and long-term adjustment depends to a large extent on their parents' adjustment and in particular on the quality of their post-divorce relationship with each parent. Although divorce law itself can do little actively to this end, it can and should ensure that the divorce process is not positively adverse to this adjustment. As Lord Hailsham has said, 'though the law could not alter the facts of life, it need not unnecessarily exaggerate the hardships inevitably involved'. There seems little doubt that the present law is guilty of just this." (paras. 3.48–3.50).

Two years later (*The Ground for Divorce* (1992), Law Com. No. 192) the Law Commission proposed "divorce after a period for the consideration of future arrangements and for reflection" (in the Draft Bill attached to the Report). It was this initiative which the Government took up. As Cretney has noted (see "Divorce Reform in England: Humbug and Hypocrisy Or a Smooth Transition?" in M. Freeman (ed.), *Divorce: Where Next?* (Dartmouth, 1996), p.39 at p.44), it was the first time this century that government had itself contemplated initiating legislation to change the ground of divorce.

The Consultation Paper (Cm. 2424) published by the Government in 1993 set out its objectives for a better divorce process (see para. 4.1 and also para. 3.5 in the Government's Proposals). These were:

"to support the institution of marriage; to include practicable steps to prevent the irretrievable breakdown of marriage; to ensure that the parties understood the practical consequence before taking any irreversible decision; where divorce is unavoidable, to minimise the bitterness and hostility between the parties and reduce the trauma for the children; and to keep to the minimum the cost to the parties and the taxpayer."

These objectives are addressed, to a greater or lesser extent, in the Act. Whilst it would be unfair to call the Act a cost-cutting measure, a comment on the last of these objectives, particularly in the light of proposed legal aid reforms, is called for. With no more public money committed to divorce than heretofore, it must follow that, with the same (or less) money having to fund information meetings, mediation and legal advice, there will be less money to resource legal aid and advice for divorcing couples. Accordingly, there must be concern that there will be less legal protection for poorer people, and especially for women.

A Summary of Parts I, II and III

Part I sets out the general principle underlying Pts. II and III of the Act.

Section 1 sets out the general principle to which the court and any person exercising functions under, or in consequence of, Pts. II and III shall have regard. These are the support of the institution of marriage, the encouragement to save marriage, the ideal (dating back to *Field of Choice* in 1966 (Cmnd. 3123), one of the sources of the 1969 reform) that divorce should be organised to cause the minimum of distress, as well as in such a way as to promote continuing relationships and so as not to incur unreasonable expenditure and with the removal or diminution of the risk of violence to the parties and to any children. The violence consideration was not in the original Bill: it was added by the House of Commons (*Hansard*, H.C. Vol. 279, cols. 600–601). A similar clause had failed to pass at Committee stage after a lengthy debate (cols. 55–119).

Part II of the Act deals with the circumstances in which separation and divorce orders may be made. The terminology should be noted: "order" replaces decree and judicial separations are now to be called "separations".

Section 2 provides that a court may give a divorce order which has the effect of dissolving a marriage, or a separation order which provides for the separation of the parties to a marriage.

Section 3 requires the court, on application, to make a divorce or separation order if the requirements listed, including those of s.8 relating to information meetings, and s.9 as regards arrangements for the future, are satisfied. A divorce order may not be made if an order preventing divorce is in force.

Section 4 requires the court, on application, to convert a separation order into a divorce order, provided that the parties have been married for at least two years, and there is not an order in force preventing divorce.

Section 5 provides that a marriage is to be taken to have broken down irretrievably if, but only if, there is a statement of belief by one or both parties that the marriage has broken down, the period for reflection and consideration has ended and there is a declaration that the applicant believes the marriage cannot be saved.

Section 6 requires the party or parties making the statement to state that they are aware of the purpose of the period for reflection and consideration and that they wish to make arrangements for the future. It provides for other requirements yet to be made (by Rules). It also lays down circumstances in which a statement will be ineffective.

Section 7 provides that a period of nine months must pass (commencing on the fourteenth day after a statement of marital breakdown is received by the court) before an application for a divorce or separation order which relates to that statement can be made to the court. This period is to be one of reflection (on whether the marriage can be saved, with an opportunity to effect a reconciliation) and consideration (of which arrangements should be made for the future). A statement cannot be made until the parties have been married for one year (see s.7(6)): the existing one year absolute bar on divorce is thus preserved. The period of nine months is extended by a further six months if there is a child of the family who is under 16 years when the application is made (s.7(11), (13)).

Section 8 sets out the requirements relating to attendance at information meetings. A statement cannot be made unless the maker of that statement has attended an information meeting not less than three months before making the statement (s.8(2)).

Section 9 sets out the requirements as to arrangements for the future. There must be produced to the court one of the following: a court order dealing with financial arrangements (this includes a consent order); a negotiated agreement as to financial arrangements; a declaration by both parties that they have made their financial arrangements; a declaration by one that he has no significant assets and does not intend to apply for financial provision, that he believes the other has no significant assets and does not intend to make an application for financial provision and that there are therefore no financial arrangements to be made. Matters relating to the welfare of children (see s.11) must also have been considered. This section also contains the so-called *get* clause, following precedents in New York and Ontario. The court may direct that there be produced to the court a declaration by both parties that he has given, and she has received, a *get* (see s.9(3)).

Section 10 allows the court to make an order preventing a marriage from being dissolved if satisfied that it would cause substantial financial or other hardship to the other party or to a child of the family, and would be wrong in all the circumstances. These include the conduct of the parties and the interests of any child of the family.

Section 11, the result of a House of Commons' amendment, gives the court the power not to make a divorce order or separation order where it appears it ought to exercise its powers under the Children Act 1989 (c. 41) (for example, to make a residence order under s.8 of that Act) but is not in a position to do so without giving further consideration to the case, and there are exceptional circumstances which make it desirable in the interests of the child that it should not make the divorce or separation order. The section applies principally, but not exclusively, to children under 16 years (see s.11(5)).

Section 12 gives the Lord Chancellor power to make procedural rules.

Section 13 enables the court, after it has received a statement of marital breakdown, to direct that the parties attend a meeting explaining mediation and providing them with an opportunity to make use of mediation. It may make this direction at any time, including in the course of proceedings connected with the breakdown of the marriage. This is broadly defined (see s.25).

Section 14 deals with the power of the court to adjourn proceedings connected with the breakdown of a marriage. The maximum period of an adjournment will be prescribed by the rules.

Section 15, together with Sched. 2, provides that financial provision under the Matrimonial Causes Act 1973 (c. 18) may be made before a divorce or separation order, but that the 1973 Act's position regarding the annulment of marriage is retained. Schedule 2 makes minor and consequential amendments to the 1973 Act connected with these changes.

Section 16 amends the Matrimonial Causes Act 1973 so as to give the court power to divide pensions on divorce.

Section 17 amends the Family Law (Scotland) Act 1985 (c. 37) so as to give Scottish courts the power to divide pensions on divorce.

Section 18 amends the Domestic Proceedings and Magistrates Courts Act 1978 (c. 22), providing that behaviour and desertion are no longer to be grounds on which an application for a financial provision order may be made.

Section 19 deals with the circumstances in which the courts in England and Wales have jurisdiction to make a divorce or separation order. The law on the stay of proceedings is also amended (see Sched. 3).

Section 20 provides that the date on which the court receives a statement of marital breakdown is, as a general rule, to be treated as the date when marital proceedings commence. It also provides definitions of the end of marital proceedings.

Section 21 provides that, where a separation order is in force and one of the parties dies intestate, property devolves as if the surviving spouse had died before the intestacy occurred.

Section 22 gives to the Lord Chancellor power, with the approval of the Treasury, to make grants in connection with marriage support services, and to fund research into the causes of, and ways of preventing, marital breakdown.

Section 23, the result of a House of Commons' amendment, provides for the funding of marriage counselling for those who would not be required to make any contribution towards the cost of mediation provided for them under the Legal Aid Act 1988 (c. 34), Pt. III A.

Section 24 contains definitions and other interpretative provision.

Section 25 sets out the proceedings which will be proceedings connected with the breakdown of a marriage.

Section 26 amends the Legal Aid Act 1988 by inserting a new s.13A. It provides definitions of "family matters", "mediation" and "mediator".

Section 27 amends the Legal Aid Act 1988 by inserting a new s.13B. This allows the Legal Aid Board to secure the provision of mediation to persons where financial resources make them eligible for mediation under regulations. It also provides that mediation should be funded only if it appears to a mediator that mediation is suitable, and sets out provisions which must be included in any contract for the provision of mediation entered into by the Legal Aid Board. There is to be a Code of Practice and this will require the mediator to institute arrangements designed to ensure, *inter alia*, that parties participate in mediation willingly and are not influenced by the fear of violence or other harm, and that parties are encouraged to consider the welfare, wishes and feelings of children.

Section 28 amends the Legal Aid Act 1988 by inserting a new s.13C. It provides that, under regulations, contributions will be payable to the Legal Aid Board in respect of mediation. It further provides that regulations may be made giving the Legal Aid Board a first charge on property recovered or preserved as a result of mediation. It also amends s.16 of the 1988 Act, so that regulations may provide that the costs of mediation are included in the charge created by that section in favour of the Legal Aid Board.

Section 29 amends s.15 of the Legal Aid Act 1988 so as to provide that, for the purposes of determining whether to grant representation for the purposes of proceedings relating to family matters, mediation is to be considered more appropriate than taking proceedings, except where a mediator has certified that mediation does not appear to be suitable, for prescribed descriptions of proceedings or in prescribed circumstances.

PRINCIPLES OF PARTS II AND III

The general principles underlying Parts II and III

1. The court and any person, in exercising functions under or in consequence of Parts II and III, shall have regard to the following general principles—

(a) that the institution of marriage is to be supported;

(b) that the parties to a marriage which may have broken down are to be encouraged to take all practicable steps, whether by marriage counselling or otherwise, to save the marriage;

(c) that a marriage which has irretrievably broken down and is being brought to an end should be brought to an end—

(i) with minimum distress to the parties and to the children affected;

(ii) with questions dealt with in a manner designed to promote as good a continuing relationship between the parties and any children affected as is possible in the circumstances; and

(iii) without costs being unreasonably incurred in connection with the procedures to be followed in bringing the marriage to an end; and

(d) that any risk to one of the parties to a marriage, and to any children, of violence from the other party should, so far as reasonably practicable, be removed or diminished.

DEFINITIONS
"court; the": s.24(1).
"party": s.24(1).

GENERAL NOTE
Section 1 lays down general principles which are to govern Pts. II and III of this Act. Principles are not rules. They have a dimension of weight that rules may lack. Principles may conflict with each other. The importance of principles may depend upon context. So may their meaning. Behind principles are values. The values being supported by the general principles listed in s.1 are pro-marriage, pro-children and anti-violence. The principles are important as much for what they imply and for what they do not say, as for what they actually state. Principles wax and wane.

The emphasis on saving marriage (see s.1(b)) is not novel: it can be traced back to the Denning Committee and to earlier legislation with its emphasis on reconciliation. The emphasis on a minimum of distress has been implicit in our thinking about divorce since the late 1960s, though it is notable that the intention is now to cause as little distress to the children as possible. The importance attached to continuing relationships emerged with the emphasis in the 1970s on conciliation rather than reconciliation. The publication of the American study by Judith Waller-stein and John Kelly, *Surviving The Breakup* (Free Press, 1980, and see the article by M.D.A. Freeman, "How Children Cope with Divorce", (1981) 11 Fam. Law. 105) gave this a boost by showing that the children who came out of divorce best are those able to interact with both parents after divorce, though doubt has been cast on this since (see F. Furstenberg *et al* (1987) 52 American Sociological Rev. 695). The Children Act 1989 affirms this by leaving both parents after divorce with parental responsibility. Recognition that there is violence and abuse in the family came only in the mid-1960s (as far as children are concerned) and into the 1970s in the case of women. Only now is it coming to be recognised that domestic violence is a form of child abuse (see Audrey Mullender and Rebecca Morley, *Children Living with Domestic Violence* (Whiting and Birch 1994). Support for the institution of marriage could have been found in any official family law document since Victorian times but it has never been embodied in legislation before. The principle is not novel: the felt need to articulate it is. Nor at face-value is it controversial, but the message it packs is. For support for the institution of marriage inevitably prioritises that relationship over alternative lifestyles such as cohabitation. It also puts heterosexuality onto a pedestal with the inevitable downgrading and discrimination that this entails for gay and lesbian relationships. And, although the Act does not say so, the implication is that it is the institution of monogamous marriage that deserves the support of the courts and other institutions.

Any person. For example, mediator, marriage counsellor.

In exercising functions under or in consequence of Pts. II and III. The general principles do not apply to other Parts of the Act. Marriage and cohabitation are, however, treated differently in Pt. IV of the Act: see, in particular, s.41 (where the court is required to consider the nature of cohabitants' relationships, it is to have regard to the fact that they have not given each other the commitment involved in marriage).

Shall have regard. There is a mandatory obligation.

Institution of marriage. It is the institution of marriage that is stressed, not this particular marriage. Marriage in these terms is an ideological enclosure which confers identity and meaning, *per* Carol Smart, *The Ties that Bind* (RKP, 1984, p.143). "Marriage" clearly means "marriage" and not (what is erroneously called) "common law marriage". It means monogamous marriage and it means marriage between parties who are respectively male and female (in a biological sense), thus ruling out "marriage" involving a transsexual. It clearly also privileges heterosexuality over homosexuality, and marriage over cohabitation. Marriage becomes the prescribed relationship against which all else is measured, and in comparison to which all else is usually found wanting.

Marriage counselling. One of the purposes of the information meeting is to give the party or parties the opportunity of having a meeting with a marriage counsellor and of encouraging that party or those parties to attend that meeting (see s.8(6)(b)).

Or otherwise. For example, by mediation.

Save the marriage. Although a divorce reform measure, it will be noted that the buttressing of marriage remains a primary objective.

Minimum distress. The language is very reminiscent of that of the Law Commission in *Field of Choice* (Cmnd. 3123) 1966, when reference was made to burying empty shells with the least bitterness, distress and humiliation (see para. 15). The language of *Field of Choice* did not find its way into the 1969 legislation. In the late 1960s the emphasis was on the minimum distress to the parties: in 1996 "the children affected" are also included.

As good a continuing relationship. This is usually thought particularly important where children are affected. Thus the Children Act 1989 allows for joint parenting arrangements (see s.11(4)). And there is a presumption of contact between the child and the non-residential parent. But there is mixed evidence on the significance of contact with the non-resident parent: Amato and Keith (1991) 110(1) Psychological Bulletin 26 offer a corrective to the Wallerstein and Kelly Study, *Surviving The Breakup*, and Furstenberg *et al* ((1987) 52 American Sociological Review 695) were unable to find a set of conditions in which the quality of the children's relationship with their non-residential parent significantly affected the children's well-being. In contrast, there is little if any doubt that children's relationship with their residential parent is crucial in mediating the impact of divorce. Research shows that the resident parent's well-being and effectiveness, and positive relationships between resident parents and their children, are amongst the most significant factors in mitigating negative outcomes for children (see L. Burghes, *Lone*

Parenthood and Family Disruption: The Outcomes For Children, Family Policy Studies Centre, 1994; T.L. Thiriot and E.T. Buckner (1991) 17(1/2) *Journal of Divorce and Remarriage* 27). There is also evidence of contact being used as an opportunity to perpetuate a relationship disfigured by domestic violence (M. Hester and L. Radford (1992) Journal of Social Welfare and Family Law 57; M. Hester *et al* in Audrey Mullender and Rebecca Morley (eds), *Children Living With Domestic Violence* (Whiting and Birch, 1994, p.102).

Risk of violence. See references to Marianne Hester's work in the previous note. See also the finding that there is a higher incidence of child sexual abuse in families involved in residence and contact disputes than in the general population (see N. Thoennes and P.G. Tjaden (1990) 14 Child Abuse and Neglect 151).

PART II

DIVORCE AND SEPARATION

Court orders

Divorce and separation

2.—(1) The court may—

(a) by making an order (to be known as a divorce order), dissolve a marriage; or

(b) by making an order (to be known as a separation order), provide for the separation of the parties to a marriage.

(2) Any such order comes into force on being made.

(3) A separation order remains in force—

(a) while the marriage continues; or

(b) until cancelled by the court on the joint application of the parties.

DEFINITIONS
"court; the": s.24(1).
"divorce order": s.24(1) (referring back to s.2(1)(a)).
"separation order": s.24(1) (referring back to s.2(1)(b)).

GENERAL NOTE
This section provides that the court may make a divorce order, which has the effect of dissolving a marriage; or a separation order, which provides for the separation of the parties to a marriage. Orders come into force immediately (the nisi/absolute distinction is rejected). A separation order lasts as long as the marriage continues, that is until the order is converted into a divorce order or one of the parties dies, or until cancelled on a joint application.

Subs. (1)
This subsection spells out the two orders that can be made.
The court may. It retains a discretion not to make the order.
Order...divorce order. No longer a divorce decree.
On circumstances, see s.3(1).
On orders preventing divorce see s.10.
Dissolve a marriage. The order comes into force immediately. See s.2(2).
Note: How Long To Get A Divorce. Before the court may make a divorce order, the following steps need to have been fulfilled.

1. The parties must have attended an *information meeting* or meetings.

2. A *statement* of *marital breakdown* initiating marital proceedings must be made to the court. This cannot be done until three months after the information meeting.

3. The statement is served on the other party by the court and after 14 days the *period for reflection and consideration* begins. This lasts for nine months, but is extended by another six months in two cases: first, where one party applies to the court, within the initial period, for time for further reflection; and secondly, where there was a child of the family under 16 years at the date of the statement. The court may refuse to extend the period where satisfied that delaying the making of a divorce order would be significantly detrimental to the welfare of any child of the family. There can be no extension where there exists a non-molestation order or occupation order.

It will be observed that the minimum period of time from attending an information meeting to a divorce order is 54 weeks (three months and nine months + 14 days) and this may be extended to 80 weeks. In addition, it should be noted that a statement cannot be made before the first anniversary of the marriage. However, there is nothing stopping a party attending an information meeting during the first year of marriage, though no point in so doing before nine months of the marriage have been enjoyed/endured. The earliest a marriage without children can be dissolved is therefore after 93 weeks: the earliest a marriage with children (who may have been born or conceived before marriage) may be dissolved is after 119 weeks (nearly two years, four months).

Separation order.
On duration, see s.2(3).
On when it comes into force, see s.2(2).
On circumstances, see s.3(1).
On concurrent applications for separation and divorce, see s.3(3).
On conversion to a divorce order, see s.4.
On effect on intestacy, see s.21.

Provide for the separation. An application may be made immediately after marriage; there is no bar on applications during the first year of marriage. The effect of the order is to relieve the spouses from the duty of cohabiting with each other. If the respondent refuses to leave, the applicant may need to seek an occupation order and/or a non-molestation order (on which see Pt. IV).

Subs. (2)
Orders come into force immediately.
Comes into force. In the case of divorce, the order dissolves the marriage (there is no longer a nisi/absolute distinction); in the case of separation, it relieves the parties from the obligation of cohabitation. A divorce order cannot be rescinded, but a separation order can be cancelled (see s.2(3)(b)).

Subs. (3)
Separation orders last as long as the marriage unless cancelled upon a joint application.
While the marriage continues. A separation order may be converted into a divorce order (see s.4(3)). It may not be converted until the marriage has lasted two years (s.4(1)).
Until cancelled ... joint application. Cancellation cannot be at the request of one party.

Circumstances in which orders are made

3.—(1) If an application for a divorce order or for a separation order is made to the court under this section by one or both of the parties to a marriage, the court shall make the order applied for if (but only if)—
   (a) the marriage has broken down irretrievably;
   (b) the requirements of section 8 about information meetings are satisfied;
   (c) the requirements of section 9 about the parties' arrangements for the future are satisfied; and
   (d) the application has not been withdrawn.
   (2) A divorce order may not be made if an order preventing divorce is in force under section 10.
   (3) If the court is considering an application for a divorce order and an application for a separation order in respect of the same marriage it shall proceed as if it were considering only the application for a divorce order unless—
   (a) an order preventing divorce is in force with respect to the marriage;
   (b) the court makes an order preventing divorce; or
   (c) section 7(6) or (13) applies.

DEFINITIONS
   "court; the": s.24(1).
   "divorce order": s.2(1)(a).
   "order preventing divorce": s.10(2).
   "separation order": s.2(1)(b).

GENERAL NOTE
   This section details the pre-conditions that must be satisfied before a court makes a divorce or separation order:
      i There must still be an application
      ii The marriage must have broken down irretrievably

   iii Information meetings must have been attended

   iv There must not be an order preventing divorce in force

   v The statement to commence proceedings must not have been made before the first anniversary of the marriage.

If there is an order preventing divorce (see iv) or the court makes one (see s.3(3)(b)) or if the statement was made before the first anniversary of the marriage (see v), the court may still make a separation order. It may also make a separation order where the time for reflection and consideration has been extended (by virtue either of an application or there being a child under 16 years) and this extended period has not been exhausted.

There is no reference in s.3 to the interests of children. An attempt to move an amendment which would have added another paragraph to s.3(1) failed at Committee stage in the House of Commons (see Standing Committee E, cols. 120–121). However, reference should be made to s.10(2) and to s.11(2). Under s.10(2) an order preventing divorce may be made where dissolution would result in substantial financial or other hardship to a child of the family and dissolution would be wrong when all the circumstances, including the interests of any child of the family, were considered. Under s.11(2), where the court is not in a position to exercise its powers under the Children Act 1989 (for example, to decide on the child's living arrangements) and there are exceptional circumstances, the court may direct that an order (including a separation order) shall not be made.

Subs. (1)

This subsection lists the pre-conditions for divorce and separation orders. See further the General Note on this section.

An application. This must have been preceded by a statement of marital breakdown. The statement and the application do not have to be made by the same party (see s.5(2)). It must also be preceded by the period for reflection and consideration (s.7). There must also be produced to the court arrangements for the future (s.9).

One or both of the parties. It was the Booth committee in 1985 which first suggested this, or is given the credit for so doing. Actually, Lord Gardiner suggested as much (see *Hansard*, H.L. Vol. 303, col. 1375) and the case was argued in 1971 (see M. Freeman, 24 Current Legal Problems 178, 194). See now *The Ground For Divorce* (1992) Law Com. No. 192, para. 5.10. A joint application is a joint acknowledgement and this should assist an amicable resolution of the practical matters involved.

Shall make the order. This would seem to preclude any exercise of discretion but this is embedded within the interpretation of the circumstances set out.

If (but only if). The circumstances are pre-conditions. No order can be made unless they are satisfied.

Broken down irretrievably. This is now the sole "ground" for divorce and separation. Hitherto, for divorce, irretrievable breakdown has had to be established in conjunction with one of five facts and courts have refused divorces where no fact can be proved although the marriage has irretrievably broken down (see *Richards v. Richards* [1972] 1 W.L.R. 1073; *Buffery v. Buffery* [1988] 2 F.L.R. 365; *Stringfellow v. Stringfellow* [1976] 1 W.L.R. 645). Previously, for judicial separation, it was not necessary to prove irretrievable breakdown at all, but merely one of the five facts (Matrimonial Causes Act 1973, s.17). It should be noted that the statement of marital breakdown attests to a belief that the marriage has broken down: until the period of reflection has elapsed it is too early to believe in irretrievable breakdown. An application must be accompanied by a declaration in terms set out in s.5(1)(d). It cannot be made more than one year after the end of the period for reflection and consideration (see s.5(3)(b)).

Information meetings. See s.8.

Parties' arrangement for the future. See s.9.

Has not been withdrawn. The hope (but surely not the expectation) is that there will be withdrawals because reflection, coupled with counselling and mediation, persuades parties to reconcile.

Subs. (2)

The court cannot make a divorce order if there is an order preventing divorce in force. Such orders, which are expected to be very rare, are rooted in the concept of substantial hardship.

Order preventing divorce. See s.10. If there is also an application for a separation order, this may be made instead (see s.3(3)(a)).

Subs. (3)

Concurrent applications for divorce and separation are to be treated as applications for a divorce order unless there is an order preventing divorce in force or the court makes one or the statement on marital breakdown antedated the first anniversary of the marriage or the period of reflection and consideration has been extended.

Divorce order. See s.2(1)(a).
Separation order. See s.2(1)(b).
Proceed ... only ... divorce order. This application takes precedence.
Order preventing divorce. See s.10.
Is in force. But the court can also make one (see s.3(2)(b)).
Section 7(b) or (13) applies. Section 7(b) applies when the applicant "jumped the gun" and made a statement of marital breakdown before the first anniversary of the marriage. Section 7(13) applies where the other party has applied for time for further reflection and the period has been extended by six months as a result.

Conversion of separation order into divorce order

4.—(1) A separation order which is made before the second anniversary of the marriage may not be converted into a divorce order under this section until after that anniversary.

(2) A separation order may not be converted into a divorce order under this section at any time while—
   (a) an order preventing divorce is in force under section 10; or
   (b) subsection (4) applies.

(3) Otherwise, if a separation order is in force and an application for a divorce order—
   (a) is made under this section by either or both of the parties to the marriage, and
   (b) is not withdrawn,
the court shall grant the application once the requirements of section 11 have been satisfied.

(4) Subject to subsection (5), this subsection applies if—
   (a) there is a child of the family who is under the age of sixteen when the application under this section is made; or
   (b) the application under this section is made by one party and the other party applies to the court, before the end of such period as may be prescribed by rules of court, for time for further reflection.

(5) Subsection (4)—
   (a) does not apply if, at the time when the application under this section is made, there is an occupation order or a non-molestation order in force in favour of the applicant, or of a child of the family, made against the other party;
   (b) does not apply if the court is satisfied that delaying the making of a divorce order would be significantly detrimental to the welfare of any child of the family;
   (c) ceases to apply—
        (i) at the end of the period of six months beginning with the end of the period for reflection and consideration by reference to which the separation order was made; or
        (ii) if earlier, on there ceasing to be any children of the family to whom subsection (4)(a) applied.

DEFINITIONS
   "child of the family": s.24(1).
   "court; the": s.24(1).
   "divorce order": s.2(1)(a).
   "non-molestation order": s.42(1).
   "occupation order": s.39.
   "order preventing divorce": s.10.
   "party": s.24(1).
   "separation order": s.2(1)(b).

GENERAL NOTE
   This section deals with the circumstances under which a separation order may be converted into a divorce order, and the circumstances in which it may not be converted. It may be converted on an application for a divorce order by either or both of the parties. If it is not then

withdrawn, a divorce order is to be granted provided the provisions of s.11 (dealing with the welfare of children) can be met (see s.4(3)). It may not be converted if the second anniversary of the marriage has not been reached (s.4(1)), or if an order preventing divorce is in force (s.4(2)(a)), or if the time for reflection and consideration has been extended either on the other party's application or because there is a child of the family under 16 years (s.4(4)), but these restrictions (that is, those in s.4(4)) do not apply if there is an occupation or non-molestation order in force, or if delaying the order would be significantly detrimental to the welfare of any child of the family (s.4(5)(a) and (b)). These restrictions cease to apply when the extended period for reflection and consideration is up and when there are no longer any relevant children of the family.

There is no provision allowing for the court to refuse to convert on the hardship grounds set out in s.10. *Looking to the Future* (1995, Cm. 2799), para. 4.50 envisaged that such a provision would be made.

Subs. (1)

Conversions are postponed until after the second anniversary of the marriage. Since a marriage without children can be dissolved after 93 weeks of marriage, it follows that, if the separation route is initially that pursued, a further 11 weeks and a day wait is required (the Act says "after that anniversary").

Separation order ... before. The earliest time that a separation order can be made is after 54 weeks of marriage, provided there are no children.

Subs. (2)

This subsection proscribes conversions when there is an order preventing divorce or the period for reflection and consideration has been extended, by reason either of an application so to do or the presence of children of the family under 16 years.

Subs. (3)

This subsection mandates that the requirements of s.11 (dealing with the welfare of children) must be satisfied before a conversion can be made. Either or both or the parties may apply for a conversion.

Otherwise. There are thus no other restrictions on a conversion save those in s.4(2) and (4), and subject to the requirements of s.11 being met. This is significant. It means that the hardship bar in s.10 can be outflanked by applying for a separation order and then asking for it to be converted into a divorce order. The court cannot make an order preventing divorce at the conversion stage. In addition, it means that the "get" hurdle in s.9(3) can also be surmounted by applying for a separation order (it is difficult to see how a court could direct that a declaration be produced stating that required steps to dissolve the marriage have been taken) and subsequently applying for the separation order to be converted into a divorce order.

Is in force. On which, see s.2(3).

Either. It is important to note that conversion can take place on the initiative of one of the parties, particularly in the light of the note on "otherwise".

Not withdrawn. On which, see s.24(2), (3).

Requirements of s.11. I.e. those relating to the welfare of children.

Subs. (4)

Following on from subs. (2), this subsection prevents a conversion into a divorce order where the additional six months added to the period for reflection and consideration have not passed, or the end of the period by which the court extended the period for reflection and consideration has not been completed.

Child of the family. See s.7(13).

Time for further reflection. See s.7(10).

Subs. (5)

This subsection limits the previous one. Accordingly, the court may convert a separation order into a divorce order where there is an occupation or non-molestation order in force, where a delay in making the divorce order would be significantly detrimental to the welfare of any child of the family and where the reasons for not converting in subs. (4) no longer exist.

Significantly detrimental. The addition of the adjective "significantly" to qualify "detrimental" indicates that reliance on this provision should be sparing.

Welfare of any child .... "Welfare" is not defined (nor was it in the Children Act 1989). It has been said to be:

> "an all encompassing word. It includes material welfare, both in the sense of adequacy of
> resources to provide a pleasant home and a comfortable standard of living and in the sense

of adequacy of care to ensure that good health and due personal pride are maintained. However, while material considerations have their place they are secondary matters. More important are the stability and security, the loving and understanding care and guidance, the warm and compassionate relationships that are essential for the full development of the child's own character, personality and talents" *per* Hardie Boys J. in *Walker v. Walker and Harrison* [1981] N Z Recent Law 257, and cited by the Law Commission in *Review of Child Law: Custody*, Working Paper No. 96 (1985), para. 6.10.

Marital breakdown

Marital breakdown

5.—(1) A marriage is to be taken to have broken down irretrievably if (but only if)—
  (a) a statement has been made by one (or both) of the parties that the maker of the statement (or each of them) believes that the marriage has broken down;
  (b) the statement complies with the requirements of section 6;
  (c) the period for reflection and consideration fixed by section 7 has ended; and
  (d) the application under section 3 is accompanied by a declaration by the party making the application that—
        (i) having reflected on the breakdown, and
        (ii) having considered the requirements of this Part as to the parties' arrangements for the future,
      the applicant believes that the marriage cannot be saved.

(2) The statement and the application under section 3 do not have to be made by the same party.

(3) An application may not be made under section 3 by reference to a particular statement if—
  (a) the parties have jointly given notice (in accordance with rules of court) withdrawing the statement; or
  (b) a period of one year ("the specified period") has passed since the end of the period for reflection and consideration.

(4) Any period during which an order preventing divorce is in force is not to count towards the specified period mentioned in subsection (3)(b).

(5) Subsection (6) applies if, before the end of the specified period, the parties jointly give notice to the court that they are attempting reconciliation but require additional time.

(6) The specified period—
  (a) stops running on the day on which the notice is received by the court; but
  (b) resumes running on the day on which either of the parties gives notice to the court that the attempted reconciliation has been unsuccessful.

(7) If the specified period is interrupted by a continuous period of more than 18 months, any application by either of the parties for a divorce order or for a separation order must be by reference to a new statement received by the court at any time after the end of the 18 months.

(8) The Lord Chancellor may by order amend subsection (3)(b) by varying the specified period.

DEFINITIONS
  "order preventing divorce": s.10(2).
  "party": s.24(1).
  "period for consideration and reflection": s.7(1), (2).
  "statement": s.24(1).
  "withdrawing": s.24(2), (3).

GENERAL NOTE
  This section erects an irrefutable presumption of marital breakdown when a statement has been made by one or both parties to that effect in accordance with the requirements of s.6, the

period for reflection and consideration has ended, and the party applying for an order (or the other party: see s.5(2)) makes a declaration that, having reflected on the breakdown and considered the requirements as to arrangements in the future in s.9, s/he believes the marriage cannot be saved.

Subs. (1)

This subsection sets out the circumstances in which a marriage is taken to have broken down irretrievably: see the General Note to this section, above.

Taken to have broken down irretrievably. It seems there is an irrefutable presumption.

If (but only if). The list in (a) to (d) constitutes essential pre-conditions.

A statement. That is, a statement of marital breakdown (see s.6). This statement cannot be made until the first anniversary of the marriage.

By one (or both) of the parties. The statement and the application do not have to be made by the same party.

The marriage has broken down. Not broken down "irretrievably", because it is too early categorically to state that.

The period...has ended. It usually lasts for nine months but extensions are provided for in s.7:
    i It may be extended in cases of inordinate delay in service of the statement (s.7(4)).
    ii It stops running when parties notify the court that they are attempting a reconciliation and require extra time, only resuming when notice is given that the attempted reconciliation is unsuccessful (s.7(8)).
    iii It is extended by six months in all cases (subject to the proviso where there is an occupation or non-molestation order and delay in the divorce order would be significantly detrimental to a child's welfare: s.7(12)) where there is a child of the family under 16 years (s.7(11), (13)).
    iv It is extended also by six months if the other party applies for time for further reflection (s.7(10), (13)). This is also subject to the violence/welfare proviso in s.7(12).

An application under s.3. I.e. for a divorce order or separation order.

The applicant believes. It is irrelevant what the other party (who may have made the statement) believes.

Reflected. See s.7(1)(a).

Considered. See s.7(1)(b) and s.9.

Subs. (2)

The statement of marital breakdown and the application for a divorce order or separation order do not need to be made by the same party to the marriage. A statement could also be made by one or both and an application made by one or both parties.

Subs. (3)

In two circumstances an application for a divorce or separation order cannot follow from a statement of marital breakdown. First, where the parties jointly withdraw the statement. Secondly, where the period of reflection and consideration ended a year or more ago.

Jointly given notice. It must be a joint notice even if it was a statement of one party.

One year...has passed. The statement lapses and the whole process, if desired, will have to begin again. One reason for inaction will be that the parties are attempting a reconciliation and this is catered for in the section (see s.5(5)): in such a case the specified period resumes running when notice is given that the attempted reconciliation has been unsuccessful, though it can only last a maximum of 18 months (s.5(7)). But it is thought that there will be many cases, although the number is impossible to predict, where inaction will be the result of just "not getting round to it". To stop the clock running, such parties will need to pretend they are attempting a reconciliation and give notice to that effect. All this presumes that the parties will know the detailed rules and, even if the information meeting gives this sort of information, how many will remember it? Even with the knowledge and the necessary pretence, after 18 months the whole process lapses.

The specified period. For when it stops running, see s.5(6)(a). For when it resumes running, see s.5(6)(b). The Lord Chancellor has the power to order a variation of the specified period (see s.5(8)).

Subs. (4)

A period of time during which there is an order preventing divorce on hardship grounds does not count towards the one year after during which an application for divorce or separation may not be made.

An order preventing order. See s.10.

Specified period. One year (but the Lord Chancellor has the power to amend this (see s.5(8))).

Subs. (5)
This provides a mechanism for the 12 month clock to stop and to start again. A joint notice that reconciliation is being attempted must be given to the court.
Specified period. One year (see s.5(3)(b)).
Jointly give notice. It must be a joint notice. A notice by one party is insufficient.
Additional time. The maximum additional time is 18 months (see s.5(7)). In effect two-and-a-half years may elapse from the end of the period of reflection and consideration before the whole process is halted, provided there is notice that reconciliation is still being attempted. Where a couple have children the divorce process could continue for more than four years (without them, for more than three-and-a-half years).

Subs. (6)
The one year period after the end of the period for reflection and consideration is halted by a *joint* notice that reconciliation is being attempted, and begins again when *either* party gives notice that this has been unsuccessful.
Stops ... received by the court. It is receipt of the joint notice that brings the period to a halt.
Resumes ... either ... gives notice. It is the giving of notice (not its receipt) that starts the period running again.

Subs. (7)
The maximum period allowed for interruption of the divorce process after the year for reflection and consideration has ended is 18 months. If desired, the process has to begin all over again and may do so at any time.
Specified period. See s.5(3)(b).
New statement ... at any time. Since the new statement may be received at any time, it must follow that this statement (*cf* the original one) need not be preceded by attendance at an information meeting again. Common sense would also seem to dictate this conclusion.

Subs. (8)
The specified period of one year may be varied by the Lord Chancellor.
Order. See s.65.

Statement of marital breakdown

6.—(1) A statement under section 5(1)(a) is to be known as a statement of marital breakdown; but in this Part it is generally referred to as "a statement".
(2) If a statement is made by one party it must also state that that party—
(a) is aware of the purpose of the period for reflection and consideration as described in section 7; and
(b) wishes to make arrangements for the future.
(3) If a statement is made by both parties it must also state that each of them—
(a) is aware of the purpose of the period for reflection and consideration as described in section 7; and
(b) wishes to make arrangements for the future.
(4) A statement must be given to the court in accordance with the requirements of rules made under section 12.
(5) A statement must also satisfy any other requirements imposed by rules made under that section.
(6) A statement made at a time when the circumstances of the case include any of those mentioned in subsection (7) is ineffective for the purposes of this Part.
(7) The circumstances are—
(a) that a statement has previously been made with respect to the marriage and it is, or will become, possible—
(i) for an application for a divorce order, or

(ii) for an application for a separation order,
to be made by reference to the previous statement;
(b) that such an application has been made in relation to the marriage and
has not been withdrawn;
(c) that a separation order is in force.

DEFINITIONS
"divorce order": s.2(1)(a).
"party": s.24(1).
"separation order": s.2(1)(b).

GENERAL NOTE
This section further explains what is involved in a statement of marital breakdown. A party
(or parties) making such a statement must state that they are aware of the purpose of the period
of reflection and consideration and that they wish to make arrangements for the future. Com-
pliance with rules yet to be made under s.12 is also required.

Subs. (1)
Statement under s.5(1)(a). The maker of the statement believes that the marriage has broken
down.

Subss. (2) and (3)
These list what statements of marital statement must also state, *viz* awareness of the purpose
of the period for reflection and consideration and a willingness to make arrangements for the
future.

Subs. (4)
Requirements of rules. See s.12(1)(a)–(d). The rules are yet to be made.

Subs. (5)
Under that section. I.e. s.12.

Subss. (6) and (7)
This provides for the circumstances in which a statement will be ineffective. These are:
(i) when there is already in existence an operative statement;
(ii) when there is an application for a divorce or separation order that has not been withdrawn; and
(iii) that there is a separation order in force (which can, under s.3, be converted into a divorce order).
Withdrawn. See s.24(2).
Separation order is in force. See s.2(2) and (3).

Reflection and consideration

Period for reflection and consideration

7.—(1) Where a statement has been made, a period for the parties—
(a) to reflect on whether the marriage can be saved and to have an opportunity to effect a reconciliation, and
(b) to consider what arrangements should be made for the future,
must pass before an application for a divorce order or for a separation order
may be made by reference to that statement.
(2) That period is to be known as the period for reflection and
consideration.
(3) The period for reflection and consideration is nine months beginning
with the fourteenth day after the day on which the statement is received by
the court.
(4) Where—
(a) the statement has been made by one party,
(b) rules made under section 12 require the court to serve a copy of the
statement on the other party, and
(c) failure to comply with the rules causes inordinate delay in service,

the court may, on the application of that other party, extend the period for reflection and consideration.

(5) An extension under subsection (4) may be for any period not exceeding the time between—

(a) the beginning of the period for reflection and consideration; and

(b) the time when service is effected.

(6) A statement which is made before the first anniversary of the marriage to which it relates is ineffective for the purposes of any application for a divorce order.

(7) Subsection (8) applies if, at any time during the period for reflection and consideration, the parties jointly give notice to the court that they are attempting a reconciliation but require additional time.

(8) The period for reflection and consideration—

(a) stops running on the day on which the notice is received by the court; but

(b) resumes running on the day on which either of the parties gives notice to the court that the attempted reconciliation has been unsuccessful.

(9) If the period for reflection and consideration is interrupted under subsection (8) by a continuous period of more than 18 months, any application by either of the parties for a divorce order or for a separation order must be by reference to a new statement received by the court at any time after the end of the 18 months.

(10) Where an application for a divorce order is made by one party, subsection (13) applies if—

(a) the other party applies to the court, within the prescribed period, for time for further reflection; and

(b) the requirements of section 9 (except any imposed under section 9(3)) are satisfied.

(11) Where any application for a divorce order is made, subsection (13) also applies if there is a child of the family who is under the age of sixteen when the application is made.

(12) Subsection (13) does not apply if—

(a) at the time when the application for a divorce order is made, there is an occupation order or a non-molestation order in force in favour of the applicant, or of a child of the family, made against the other party; or

(b) the court is satisfied that delaying the making of a divorce order would be significantly detrimental to the welfare of any child of the family.

(13) If this subsection applies, the period for reflection and consideration is extended by a period of six months, but—

(a) only in relation to the application for a divorce order in respect of which the application under subsection (10) was made; and

(b) without invalidating that application for a divorce order.

(14) A period for reflection and consideration which is extended under subsection (13), and which has not otherwise come to an end, comes to an end on there ceasing to be any children of the family to whom subsection (11) applied.

DEFINITIONS

"child of the family": s.24(1).
"court; the": s.24(1).
"non-molestation order": s.42(1).
"occupation order": s.39(1).
"party": s.24(1).
"statement": s.6(1).

GENERAL NOTE

This provides that a period of nine months and 14 days must pass between a statement of marital breakdown being received by the court and an application for a divorce or separation order which relates to that statement. This period is one of reflection (as to whether the marriage can be saved) and consideration (of the arrangements that can be made for the future). It is extended in certain circumstances, in particular where there is a child of the family under 16 years (where it is extended by six months).

The original Family Law Bill (cl. 7) stipulated a period of one year, following the Law Commission recommendations (see *The Ground for Divorce* (1992) Law Com. No. 192, paras. 5.27, 5.69 and 5.79). The Law Commission, however, rejected the proposition that the period should be longer if there were children (see para. 5.28). Although the Act stipulates nine months and 14 days, and not one year, no statement of marital breakdown may be made fewer than three months after attendance at an information meeting, and, according to the Lord Chancellor, "it was always the intention that the extra three months given to parties to consider the information that they had received should not extend the overall period for reflection and consideration" (*Hansard*, H.L. Vol. 573, col. 1092).

Subss. (1)–(3)

The period for reflection and consideration is at the heart of the divorce reform. According to the Law Commission:

"The lapse of a substantial period of time provides solid evidence of a permanent break-down in the marital relationship. It restrains hasty or rash applications and ensures that the couple have given some consideration to what the future will hold before finally committing themselves to a divorce. It provides an opportunity to reflect upon the children's best interests and to explore the possibility of reconciliation." (*The Ground for Divorce* (1992) Law Com. No. 192, para. 3.26).

An application for a divorce or separation order cannot be made until the period for reflection and consideration (nine months and 14 days where there are no children of the family under 16 years) and 15 months and 14 days (where there are) has passed.

A statement. I.e. a statement of marital breakdown (see ss.5 and 6).

Reflect on whether the marriage can be saved. With the assistance of counselling and mediation.

Arrangements for the future. See s.9.

Must pass. According to *Looking To The Future* (para. 4.16), the parties "will be required to spend time reflecting on whether their marriage can be saved, and if not, to face up to the consequences of their actions and to make arrangements to meet their responsibilities ...". The Act can mandate the passage of time: it cannot mandate reflection and consideration. It is difficult to see what this provision will achieve, given that it is unenforceable. As a symbolic affirmation of responsibility, it is laudable: as a measure likely to effect social change it is, one suspects, risible. Cretney's comment that some may "prefer to spend their time on the far more pleasurable activity of conceiving—necessarily illegitimate—babies", or "seeking means of exploiting their emotional or financial advantage, or brooding on grievances and perhaps using the available legal procedure as a way of seeking satisfaction for the wrongs they have suffered" (see "Divorce Reform: Humbug and Hypocrisy or a Smooth Transition?" in M. Freeman (ed.), *Divorce: Where Next?* (Dartmouth, 1996, p.39 at p.52) is very much to the point.

An application. This needs to be made by the party making the statement (see s.5(2)).

Nine months. But where there is a child of the family under 16 years this is extended to 15 months (s.7(11), (13)). Other circumstances where the period may be extended are listed in s.7(4), (7) and (10).

Subs. (4)

Failure by a party making a statement to comply with rules relating to service of that statement (these rules have yet to be made) may lead the court to extend the period for reflection and consideration.

Inordinate delay. Given the time frame of 9 months and 15 months, it is submitted that a delay of more than a week could be inordinate.

The court may. There is no obligation on the court to extend, but, within the court's definition of "inordinate", complete discretion.

Subs. (5)

An extension under subs. (4) is not to exceed the gap between the beginning of the period for reflection and consideration and the time service is effected, but it may be for a lesser period.

Subs. (6)

This subsection in effect preserves the one year absolute bar on divorce. A statement cannot be made before the first anniversary of the marriage to which it relates.

The bar (formerly three years and discretionary) is rooted in a 1930s compromise. The Law Commission dodged the issue (see *The Ground for Divorce* (1992) Law Com. No. 192, para.

5.82). *Looking To The Future* (para. 4.42) thought it would help "to protect couples rushing into re-marriage too soon without having had time to think why their previous marriage was so short-lived".

A statement. But the information meeting can be attended during the first year of marriage.

Divorce order. The bar does not apply to applications for separation orders.

Subss. (7) and (8)

Parties can *jointly* notify the court that they are attempting reconciliation and need additional time. Time then stops and only resumes when *either* of them notify the court that the attempt has been unsuccessful. If the period of attempted reconciliation exceeds 18 months, a new statement of marital breakdown is required (see s.7(9)).

Jointly give notice. It must be a joint notice.

Notice is received by the court. Receipt of notice is required.

Resumes ... either gives notice to the court. It is the giving of notice, not its receipt, that starts the clock going again.

Subs. (9)

A new statement of marital breakdown is required if the period for reflection and consideration is interrupted under the previous subsection by a continuous period of more than 18 months.

Subs. (10)

This provides for a six month extension for further reflection when the non-applicant applies to the court and the arrangements for the future (ignoring for these purposes the marginal "get" issue in s.9(3)) are satisfied.

Application for a divorce order. Not a separation order.

Within the prescribed period. The period has not yet been prescribed.

The requirements of s.9. That is, relating to arrangements for the future.

Subs. (11)

Where there is a child of the family under 16 years, the period for reflection and consideration is extended by six months (to 15 months, but beginning only on the 14th day after the day on which the statement is received by the court). An amendment (described by Lord Simon of Glaisdale, its sponsor, as an "exploratory amendment" *Hansard*, H.L. Vol. 568, col. 827) to prohibit divorce where there was a child of the family under 16 years did not attract support (see *Hansard*, H.L. Vol. 568, cols. 803–827). The present provision was not in the Law Commission report, *Looking To The Future* or the original Family Law Bill. It was added by the House of Commons after a long and diffuse debate at Committee stage (see *Hansard*, H.C. Vol. 276, cols. 491–543).

Application for a divorce order. This does not apply to applications for separation orders.

Child of the Family. This means in relation to the parties to a marriage:
  "(a) a child of both of those parties; and
   (b) any other child, not being a child who is placed with those parties as foster parents by a
       local authority or voluntary organisation, who has been treated by both of those parties
       as a child of their family."

This definition is in s.52(1) of the Matrimonial Causes Act 1973, to which this Act refers (see s.24(1)). It is also in the Children Act 1989, s.105(1). There is no reported case where any child other than a step-child has been held to be a child of the family under paragraph (b).

If there is an occupation or non-molestation order in force or the delaying of the making of a divorce order would be significantly detrimental to a child of the family, this extension provision does not apply.

When the application is made. The extension comes to an end if there cease to be any children of the family under 16 years.

Subs. (12)

The period for reflection and consideration is not to be extended where there is an occupation or non-molestation order or the court is satisfied that delaying the divorce order would be significantly detrimental to the welfare of any child of the family.

Occupation order ... non-molestation order. These do not have to have powers of arrest attached to them.

Child of the family. See note on subs. (11) above. It is difficult to see why a provision whose object is the protection of children should only extend in the case of step-children to those "treated" as a child of the family, but that is the effect of the provision.

Is satisfied. On a balance of probabilities.

Significantly detrimental. Not merely "detrimental"; "significantly" suggests sparing use of this provision is intended.

Subs. (13)
The extension does not invalidate the application for the divorce order; it merely postpones it.

Subs. (14)
The attainment of the age of 16 by any children of the family brings to an end an extended period for reflection and consideration, which has not otherwise come to an end.

Attendance at information meetings

8.—(1) The requirements about information meetings are as follows.

(2) A party making a statement must (except in prescribed circumstances) have attended an information meeting not less than three months before making the statement.

(3) Different information meetings must be arranged with respect to different marriages.

(4) In the case of a statement made by both parties, the parties may attend separate meetings or the same meeting.

(5) Where one party has made a statement, the other party must (except in prescribed circumstances) attend an information meeting before—
   (a) making any application to the court—
        (i) with respect to a child of the family; or
        (ii) of a prescribed description relating to property or financial matters; or
   (b) contesting any such application.

(6) In this section "information meeting" means a meeting organised, in accordance with prescribed provisions for the purpose—
   (a) of providing, in accordance with prescribed provisions, relevant information to the party or parties attending about matters which may arise in connection with the provisions of, or made under, this Part or Part III; and
   (b) of giving the party or parties attending the information meeting the opportunity of having a meeting with a marriage counsellor and of encouraging that party or those parties to attend that meeting.

(7) An information meeting must be conducted by a person who—
   (a) is qualified and appointed in accordance with prescribed provisions; and
   (b) will have no financial or other interest in any marital proceedings between the parties.

(8) Regulations made under this section may, in particular, make provision—
   (a) about the places and times at which information meetings are to be held;
   (b) for written information to be given to persons attending them;
   (c) for the giving of information to parties (otherwise than at information meetings) in cases in which the requirement to attend such meetings does not apply;
   (d) for information of a prescribed kind to be given only with the approval of the Lord Chancellor or only by a person or by persons approved by him; and
   (e) for information to be given, in prescribed circumstances, only with the approval of the Lord Chancellor or only by a person, or by persons, approved by him.

(9) Regulations made under subsection (6) must, in particular, make provision with respect to the giving of information about—
   (a) marriage counselling and other marriage support services;
   (b) the importance to be attached to the welfare, wishes and feelings of children;

    (c) how the parties may acquire a better understanding of the ways in
which children can be helped to cope with the breakdown of a
marriage;

    (d) the nature of the financial questions that may arise on divorce or sep-
aration, and services which are available to help the parties;

    (e) protection available against violence, and how to obtain support and
assistance;

    (f) mediation;

    (g) the availability to each of the parties of independent legal advice and
representation;

    (h) the principles of legal aid and where the parties can get advice about
obtaining legal aid;

    (i) the divorce and separation process.

    (10) Before making any regulations under subsection (6), the Lord Chan-
cellor must consult such persons concerned with the provision of relevant
information as he considers appropriate.

    (11) A meeting with a marriage counsellor arranged under this section—

    (a) must be held in accordance with prescribed provisions; and

    (b) must be with a person qualified and appointed in accordance with pre-
scribed provisions.

    (12) A person who would not be required to make any contribution
towards mediation provided for him under Part IIIA of the Legal Aid Act
1988 shall not be required to make any contribution towards the cost of a
meeting with a marriage counsellor arranged for him under this section.

    (13) In this section "prescribed" means prescribed by regulations made by
the Lord Chancellor.

DEFINITIONS

    "child of the family": s.24(1) (and see note on s.8(11)).
    "marital proceedings": s.20.
    "party": s.24(1).
    "statement": s.61(1).

GENERAL NOTE

    This section outlines the provisions relating to information meetings.

    The origins of the information interview are in *Looking To The Future* (see chapter 8 of the
Consultation Paper and chapter 7 of the White Paper). In the White Paper several advantages of
a single first port of call were identified:

    "It provides an opportunity to consider whether divorce is the right course of action; it
ensures that all persons obtain the same access to information about the divorce process
and related matters; and it raises awareness of support services, and encourages couples to
consider family mediation rather than arms length negotiations through lawyers or litigation." (para. 7.7).

    What was originally envisaged was a "one-to-one" interview, but this became a group session.
Indeed, the Family Law Bill called it an information "session", rather than "meeting", as it has
now become (see *Hansard*, H.L. Vol. 570, col. 21). The intention has been to draw a clear line
between the functions of providing information—to give an impartial view of the available services—and the giving of advice. There was also an original plan for the person conducting the
interview to take decisions about access to public funding. But the functions of giving information and determining eligibility for legal aid or funded mediation were separated in the White
Paper (see paras. 6.15, 7.13–7.28).

Subs. (1)

    This subsection introduces information meetings: they are intended to be on a one-to-one
basis, not by means of group sessions.

    Information meetings. See s.8(6).

Subs. (2)

    It is a necessary pre-condition to making a statement of marital breakdown that an infor-
mation meeting has been attended three months or nine months before. Provision is made for
exceptions to be prescribed. The Lord Chancellor indicated (see *Hansard*, H.L. Vol. 568, cols.
983–984) that the range of exceptions would include the "housebound", the "disabled", those

who risked violence by going to a particular place and those in custody. Alternative arrangements will be "prescribed".
Prescribed. See s.8(13).
Information meeting. See s.8(6).

Subs. (3)
The concept of the group session is finally rejected: each marriage must have its own information meeting. Unless the number of divorces drops substantially, it is difficult to see how this can really happen, even with video presentations.

Subs. (4)
Where both parties make a statement they can receive the information together or separately. It may be assumed that most parties in a position to make a joint statement will also attend the same meeting. Where they do not, the problem identified in the note on subs. (3) will be accentuated.

Subs. (5)
Where one party makes a statement, the other is not allowed to make an application regarding a child of the family or regarding property or financial matters or contest any such application before s/he attends an information meeting. It is faintly amusing that "contest" should reappear!
Prescribed circumstances. For the sort of circumstances likely to be prescribed, see the note on subs. (2) above.
Prescribed description. See s.8(13).

Subs. (6)
The purpose of the information meeting is dual: information-providing and the route to a meeting with a marriage counsellor. Subsection (9) lists matters on which information must be given.
Marriage counsellor. See also s.8(9)(a).

Subs. (7)
The information meeting must be conducted by a qualified and impartial person.
Prescribed. See s.8(13).

Subs. (8)
This provides for regulations to be made relating to the giving of information. Information may be given in writing (see s.8(8)(b)) and may be given otherwise than at information meetings where exemptions (see the note to subs. (2) above) are prescribed.

Subs. (9)
Nine areas which information meetings must cover are highlighted. The reality is that the attention given to each of these important areas can only be cursory at best.
Marriage counselling. See further s.23. Useful accounts are David Clark and Douglas Haldane, *Wedlocked?* (Polity Press, 1990) and Jane Lewis, David Clark and David Morgan, *Whom God Hath Joined Together* (Routledge, 1992).
The importance to be attached ... children. If this is a normative assertion that parents are to attach importance to the welfare, wishes and feelings of children, it is a welcome addition to the law (a comparison between s.1 of the Children Act 1989 and Art. 3 of the United Nations Convention on the Rights of the Child or with the Children (Scotland) Act 1995, s.6 is worth making). More likely—since such a radical change in the law is not to be expected through the backdoor—it is telling parents that courts, by law (and see further s.11 of this Act), and other institutions, as a matter of good practice, do attach importance to the welfare, wishes and feelings of children.
The ways ... children can be helped to cope. The evidence is that parental conflict may cause as much, if not more, distress to children than parental separation. See A.J. Cherlin *et al* (1991) 252 Science 1386; J. Elliott and M. Richards (1991) 5 International Journal of Law and the Family 258. Making divorce more difficult or lengthening the process—as this Act does—may not benefit children at all.
Nature of the financial questions ... services to help. Much here depends on the socio-economic status of the parties. For some it will be advice on the millionaires' defence (see *Van G v. Van G* [1995] 1 F.L.R. 328), on Duxbury calculations, lump sums, pension splitting and accountants; for others it will be directions to the local D.S.S. office. But how long is the information meeting to last? How detailed is the written information to be? Will *Rayden* be handed out? Will the poor be given the *National Welfare Benefit Handbook*? Will the dispensers of information have the legal expertise?

Protection available against violence. This means not just legal protection as found in Pt. IV of this Act, but the resources of the police, social services, refuges. Presumably also, information about rehousing and about claiming compensation from the Criminal Injuries Compensation Board.

Mediation. What are they to be told about mediation? *Looking To The Future* claims that mediation "enables spouses to accept responsibility for the breakdown, to accept the responsibility for the ending of marriage, to address face to face the questions of fault and blame," and that, where conduct is an issue, mediation "offers an opportunity to address what went wrong with the marriage" (see para. 7.5). But Walker, McCarthy and Timms in a recent authoritative study (*Mediation: The Making and Remaking of Co-operative Relationships* (1994)), found that "not addressing the past is much appreciated by clients who are feeling guilt. For them it came as a relief to discover that the mediators were not judgmental and that fault was not an issue" (p.62). Under the scheme envisaged by this Act mediators—most without legal qualifications— will be negotiating financial agreements. What will the courts' attitude to these agreements be? Hoffmann L.J.'s remarks in *Pounds v. Pounds* [1995] 1 F.L.R. 775, 791 are worth quoting:

> "The agreement may be held to be binding, but whether it will be can be determined only after litigation and may involve ... examining the quality of the advice which was given by the party who wishes to resile. It is then understandably a matter for surprise and resentment on the part of the other party that one should be able to repudiate an agreement on account of the inadequacy of one's own legal advisers, over whom the other party had no control and of whose advice he has no knowledge."

Will courts be involved in the fairness of agreements negotiated in mediation or will the reluctance to do so evinced since *Edgar v. Edgar* [1980] 1 W.L.R. 1410 be all the more marked because both parties have participated in the mediation process? What is the information meeting to tell them?

The availability ... of independent legal advice and representation. In the light of legal aid reorganisation and cuts, this may reflect an ideal rather than reality.

The principles of legal aid. Presumably this would involve an introduction to the "merit" and "means" test (or whatever there is when the Family Law Act 1996 is operative).

The divorce and separation process. I.e., a short introduction to the stages set out in this Act.

Subs. (10)
There is a duty on the Lord Chancellor—which is open-ended in that he can choose whom he consults—to consult persons concerned with the provision of information before he makes regulations.

Subs. (11)
This provision is directed at the concern (see for example *Hansard*, H.L. Vol. 570, cols. 21–22) that unauthorised and untrained marriage counsellors will offer themselves at information meetings.

Subs. (12)
A person eligible for totally-funded mediation (see Pt. III of the Act) is similarly qualified for marriage counselling.

Arrangements for the future

9.—(1) The requirements as to the parties' arrangements for the future are as follows.

(2) One of the following must be produced to the court—

(a) a court order (made by consent or otherwise) dealing with their financial arrangements;

(b) a negotiated agreement as to their financial arrangements;

(c) a declaration by both parties that they have made their financial arrangements;

(d) a declaration by one of the parties (to which no objection has been notified to the court by the other party) that—

(i) he has no significant assets and does not intend to make an application for financial provision;

(ii) he believes that the other party has no significant assets and does not intend to make an application for financial provision; and

(iii) there are therefore no financial arrangements to be made.

(3) If the parties—

(a) were married to each other in accordance with usages of a kind mentioned in section 26(1) of the Marriage Act 1949 (marriages which may be solemnized on authority of superintendent registrar's certificate), and

(b) are required to co-operate if the marriage is to be dissolved in accordance with those usages,

the court may, on the application of either party, direct that there must also be produced to the court a declaration by both parties that they have taken such steps as are required to dissolve the marriage in accordance with those usages.

(4) A direction under subsection (3)—

(a) may be given only if the court is satisfied that in all the circumstances of the case it is just and reasonable to give it; and

(b) may be revoked by the court at any time.

(5) The requirements of section 11 must have been satisfied.

(6) Schedule 1 supplements the provisions of this section.

(7) If the court is satisfied, on an application made by one of the parties after the end of the period for reflection and consideration, that the circumstances of the case are—

(a) those set out in paragraph 1 of Schedule 1,

(b) those set out in paragraph 2 of that Schedule,

(c) those set out in paragraph 3 of that Schedule, or

(d) those set out in paragraph 4 of that Schedule,

it may make a divorce order or a separation order even though the requirements of subsection (2) have not been satisfied.

(8) If the parties' arrangements for the future include a division of pension assets or rights under section 25B of the 1973 Act or section 10 of the Family Law (Scotland) Act 1985, any declaration under subsection (2) must be a statutory declaration.

DEFINITION
"party": s.24(1).

GENERAL NOTE
Section 9 has to be read together with Sched. 1. It sets out the requirements as to arrangements for the future. The requirements relating to the welfare of children (in s.11) must always be satisfied. In addition, financial arrangements (a court order, a negotiated agreement, a declaration that financial arrangements have been made or a declaration that, in the light of absence of significant assets, there are no financial arrangements to be made) must be produced in the court. If the arrangements include a division of pension assets or rights the declaration must be a statutory declaration. Schedule 1 contains exemptions from the duty to produce to the court financial arrangements.

The section also contains (in subss. (3), (4)) the so-called "get" clause moved during the Third Reading in the House of Lords by Lord Meston (see *Hansard*, H.L. Vol. 570, cols. 663–665). This is directed at a problem within the Jewish community: although the ordinary civil law of divorce applies to Jews, the husband must in addition give his wife a bill of divorcement (a *get*) and she must accept it. If he refuses so to do she acquires the status of an *agunah* (literally "chained woman") and cannot remarry according to orthodox Jewish law, although he can. Section 9(3) is an attempt to offer a way out of this problem: whether it succeeds is dubious, as is shown in the note on subss. (3) and (4) below.

Subss. (1) and (2)
Subject to certain exemptions (see s.9(7) and Sched. 1), the courts cannot make a divorce or a separation order unless the parties have settled, whether by agreement or adjudication, their financial arrangements. It was nevertheless recognised (see *Looking To The Future*, para. 4.29) that this could "play into the hands of an unreasonable, spiteful or malicious spouse or provide a formidable bargaining chip for the more powerful or determined party". The Government said also that it wished to ensure that "weaker or vulnerable parties and their children are sufficiently protected" (para. 4.30). Some attempt to do this is found in Sched. 1; (see particularly, paras. 1 and 4).

There must be produced to the court one of the following:
— a court order (it can be a consent order)
— a negotiated agreement
— a declaration (which need not be statutory) by *both* parties that they have made their financial arrangements
— a declaration (which need not be statutory) that the applicant has no significant assets and does not intend to apply for financial provision and s/he believes the other party has none either, so that there are no financial arrangements to be made.

Financial arrangements. If these include pension splitting arrangements the declaration must be a statutory declaration.

No significant assets. Of course, what is "significant" depends upon individual interpretation. There is no room for the court to question this interpretation.

Believes. The section does not say "reasonably" believes.

Subss. (3) and (4)
These subsections contain the so-called "get" clause. The *get* is a consensual divorce: the Rabbinical Court (Beth Din) supervises the procedure for the consensual delivery and acceptance of the bill of divorce (see further S. Maidment (1974) 37 M.L.R. 611 and D. Gordon, *Foreign Divorces: English Law and Practice* (Gower, 1988). A *get* delivered in England will not dissolve a marriage, nor will one written in England but delivered in Israel (see *Berkovits v. Grinberg (Attorney-General Intervening)* [1995] 2 All E.R. 683, following *R v. Secretary of State for Home Department ex p. Fatima* [1986] A.C. 527 and holding that to constitute an overseas divorce, all proceedings must take place in the same foreign jurisdiction).

There are about 275 *gittim* (gets) in the UK annually (see Board of Deputies of British Jews: Annual Statistics). These do not dissolve the marriages but are regarded by most Jews as a necessary pre-condition to remarriage. This is certainly the view of the orthodox rabbinical authorities who represent (at least nominally) three-quarters of the Jewish community (there are about 300,000 Jews in Britain). In the majority of cases the husband willingly gives his wife a *get* and she receives it. But in about 10 per cent of cases there is a refusal so to do. Formerly, nearly all refusals were by husbands: there are now a substantial number of women who refuse to accept a *get*. Until the eleventh century a husband could divorce his wife against her will. Rabbinical reform changed this: it also gave the wife power to demand a divorce in certain circumstances (see I. Haut, *Divorce In Jewish Law and Life* (1983)). These include the possession of certain physical defects, such as a loathsome disease or revolting disfigurement, being engaged in a malodorous occupation, impotence or sterility, refusal to support, habitual unfaithfulness and apostasy. It has been argued convincingly that this list can be extended by analogy to physical and sexual violence (see M. Frishtik (1991) 9 Jewish Law Annual 145). Today, a husband must still grant the divorce of his own free will, but the *Beth Din* may apply coercion in cases in which the wife is by Jewish law (*halakhically*) entitled to a divorce: the use of coercion is justified by employing the legal fiction of constructive consent (see I. Haut, *Divorce In Jewish Law and Life* (1983) pp.23–24). In the view of the twelfth century scholar Maimonides, the recalcitrant husband really desires to comply with Jewish law, but is prevented from so doing by his evil disposition. The doctrine of constructive consent is limited to coercion by a Beth Din and to situations where a *get* is halakhically required. Thus, secular courts may not force a husband to give a *get*: if they do, the *get* which results is invalid (*me' useh*). If, however, a secular court compels a husband to comply with a Beth Din in order that a *get* shall be given, the resulting *get* is valid.

Despite these reforms, the position of Jewish women remains inferior to that of men for two reasons. First, under certain conditions the husband can invoke a procedure which enables him to remarry (in effect polygamously) despite the absence of a *get*. No such procedure is available to the wife. Secondly, the consequence of violating Jewish law, and remarrying without first complying with the get requirement, are much more severe for the wife than for the husband. If a wife is separated from the husband and has not received a *get*, she is regarded as an *agunah*, a chained woman, a "hostage to a dead marriage" (*per* S.D. Glick (1993) 31 J. Fam Law 885 and see, further, J.N. Porter, *Women In Chains* (Aronson, 1995)). She is still married to her husband and cannot remarry in religious form until she obtains a *get* from her husband. If she cohabits with a man other than her husband, whether the man is married or not, she and her partner are guilty of adultery. Any children from such a union are *mamzerim* (translated not entirely accurately as "bastards"). She forfeits her alimony rights and, even if her husband subsequently gives her a *get*, she is barred from marrying her partner. But the husband who is separated from his wife without granting her a *get* is not similarly stigmatised. If he cohabits with another woman, he does not commit adultery: he is technically guilty of "polygamy". Any resulting children are not *mamzerim*. Furthermore, if he subsequently delivers a *get* to his wife, he can marry the woman with whom he has been cohabiting.

There is thus a problem. It is one created by Jewish law. We are usually told that this cannot be changed, although, as we have seen, it was changed in the eleventh century. But there is a difference between change and interpretation. Contemporary interpretations of Jewish law violate fundamental principles of *halakhic* ethics (see E. Berkovits, *Jewish Women In Time and Torah* (1990). It is a sad commentary on our times that women are treated by Jewish law today worse than they were in the twelfth century. Certainly, rabbis up to and including Moses Maimonides saw the need to facilitate divorce for a wife who found her husband repulsive. He wrote: "they force him to divorce her immediately because she is not like a captive woman who must have sexual relations with one whom she hates." It is a sad reflection upon the dilemma of a religious minority that, having forgotten its liberal heritage, it has to call upon the dominant culture to bale it out. The Jewish community should not have to go cap in hand to legislatures in countries in which they live, when, by rediscovering their own sources and interpreting these creatively and dynamically they can solve problems which their interpretations have created. The *halakha* seen in its "best light" (*cf.* R. Dworkin, *Law's Empire* (1986)) unquestionably offers remedies long neglected, and this is recognised by leading rabbinical scholars, such as Eliezer Berkovits.

But the Jewish community has pressed for legislative interpretation since the early 1980s. Earlier than this the Court of Appeal in *Brett v. Brett* [1969] 1 All E.R. 1007 had attempted to intervene by increasing the lump sum it ordered the husband to pay in default of his delivery of a *get*. But this ruling, though acceptable to British rabbinical authorities in 1969, is no longer acceptable. They now regard such a *get* as coerced and therefore *me' useh* (a demonstration of how interpretation can change!).

There was an attempt to tackle the *get* problem by legislation in 1984 when the Matrimonial and Family Proceedings Bill was before Parliament. This used the New York model and in essence would have prevented a decree nisi being made absolute before religious barriers to remarriage were removed. The proposal was criticised by the Solicitor General and made no headway. By October 1986 the then Lord Chancellor, Lord Hailsham, was amenable to legislation but insisted it required a private member's initiative and none was forthcoming. With a former Chief Rabbi now in the House of Lords (Lord Jakobovits) and the willingness of Lord Meston to move an amendment, there is now legislation.

Contemporaneously, the rabbinical authorities have taken the initiative to introduce the pre-nuptial agreement as a way of promoting a solution to the *get* problem. There are two models for this agreement, one which contains an arbitration clause and which in the first four months (April–July 1996) has not been agreed to by anyone (indeed, any prospective bride and groom prepared to sign this model are advised to seek advice from a solicitor first). The other model, which is also flawed, initially had a minimal take-up but is now being agreed to by about half of those who are marrying in orthodox synagogues in London. The pre-nuptial agreement is only in operation where the writ of the London Beth Din extends: it is thought that if and when the Manchester Beth Din introduces the concept it will insist on the arbitration model. Further understanding of the concept of the pre-nuptial agreement may be sought in B. Herring and K. Auman, *The Pre-Nuptial Agreement* (Aronson, 1996).

The parties were married. Despite the past tense, there is a presumption against retrospective legislation. The better view is that this provision only applies to marriage after this Act comes into operation.

Married ... in accordance with usages. That is, married under the auspices of a synagogue authority. This provision accordingly has no application where Jews marry in a register office or abroad, though in both instances a *get* is required as a pre-condition to remarriage and all the consequences described in the General Note to these subsections are equally applicable.

Are required to co-operate. Read superficially, this may be thought to impose a normative requirement (that those who married according to Jewish usages co-operate). But this is not what the provision says: it merely describes Jewish law and practice which is to the effect that if a marriage is to be dissolved according to Jewish law the parties must co-operate with the rabbinical authorities. Even if interpreted as a normative obligation, the word "co-operate" is so weak that it is difficult to see what it means or how any such obligation could be enforced.

The court may. The court has a discretion. This is to be exercised in accordance with subs. (4), so that the direction should only be given where it is "just and reasonable" to give it. It seems likely that the courts will only make the direction sought when the parties have agreed to take their matrimonial disputes to the Beth Din, that is have signed one of the two pre-nuptial agreements.

Application of either party. I.e., not necessarily the applicant for the divorce or separation order.

There must also be produced to the court a declaration. This does not adopt the New York approach (or the strategy that was employed in 1984 and has been argued for subsequently). It does not prevent a divorce order being made in default of a *get* being granted and accepted. It merely requires—should the court exercise its discretion so to direct—a declaration. If the declaration is given fraudulently or if any remaining steps are not subsequently taken, a divorce order is not revoked. The party failing to comply will be in contempt of court, but the penal sanctions for this (up to two years' imprisonment) will not assist the marital status problems of the other party. A declaration by a husband with Israeli domicile, nationality and residence that he will give a *get* under the auspices of the Israeli rabbinical authorities will only suffice if the *get* is delivered in Israel (see *Berkovits v. Grinberg* [1995] 2 All E.R. 983).

By both parties. It is important that the declaration is by both parties, since the wife must receive the *get*. One problem which the provision does not tackle—it is difficult to see how it could—is of the spouse who has simply disappeared or abandoned the other spouse. Clearly, it will be impossible to obtain a declaration from such a spouse. If he is the husband, the wife is likely to remain an *agunah*.

Just and reasonable. It is thought the courts are more likely to exercise their discretion to make a direction when there is a pre-nuptial agreement. If so, the "get" provision will only bite on marriages celebrated under the auspices of the London Beth Din since April 1996 and then only on those in which there is such an agreement (hitherto about half).

May be resolved. Lord Meston said that the power of revocation was a "safeguard" (*Hansard*, H.L. Vol. 570, col. 664), but it is difficult to contemplate circumstances in which a court might wish to revoke a direction, other than the discovery that the conditions for a direction (*e.g.* marriage in accordance with Jewish usages) were not met.

Subs. (6)
This gives effect to Sched. 1, which provides exemptions to s.9(2). See the Note on Sched. 1.

Subs. (7)
If the court is satisfied that the conditions for an exemption from s.9(2) are met, it may make a divorce or separation order, even though the conditions in s.9(2) are not satisfied.
Satisfied. I.e., on a balance of probabilities.
May make a divorce ... separation order. It retains a discretion not to do so.

Subs. (8)
Declaration about pension-splitting must be statutory declarations.

Orders preventing divorce

Hardship: orders preventing divorce

10.—(1) If an application for a divorce order has been made by one of the parties to a marriage, the court may, on the application of the other party, order that the marriage is not to be dissolved.

(2) Such an order (an "order preventing divorce") may be made only if the court is satisfied—

   (a) that dissolution of the marriage would result in substantial financial or other hardship to the other party or to a child of the family; and

   (b) that it would be wrong, in all the circumstances (including the conduct of the parties and the interests of any child of the family), for the marriage to be dissolved.

(3) If an application for the cancellation of an order preventing divorce is made by one or both of the parties, the court shall cancel the order unless it is still satisfied—

   (a) that dissolution of the marriage would result in substantial financial or other hardship to the party in whose favour the order was made or to a child of the family; and

   (b) that it would be wrong, in all the circumstances (including the conduct of the parties and the interests of any child of the family), for the marriage to be dissolved.

(4) If an order preventing a divorce is cancelled, the court may make a divorce order in respect of the marriage only if an application is made under section 3 or 4(3) after the cancellation.

(5) An order preventing divorce may include conditions which must be satisfied before an application for cancellation may be made under subsection (3).

(6) In this section "hardship" includes the loss of a chance to obtain a future benefit (as well as the loss of an existing benefit).

DEFINITIONS
    "child of the family": s.24(1) (and see note on s.7(11)).
    "divorce order": s.2(1)(A).
    "party": s.24(1).

GENERAL NOTE
    This section provides for the court to make orders preventing divorce on hardship grounds. The previous law (in the Matrimonial Causes Act 1973, s.5) provided a hardship defence but this was limited to divorces based on five years separation (see s.1(2)(e) of the 1973 Act) and limited to grave financial or other hardship likely to be suffered by the respondent (who, since it was a s.1(2)(e) divorce, was being divorced without her/his consent). The provision of s.10 is wider:
    (i) it applies to all applications for divorce orders;
    (ii) hardship includes hardship to a child of the family;
    (iii) the hardship to qualify now needs to be "substantial", not "grave", a lesser standard to satisfy.
    On the other hand, an order preventing divorce may be cancelled (see s.10(3)). Section 5 of the 1973 Act was designed to meet the small number of cases in which the divorce itself would cause more hardship than the marital breakdown had already done (*Field of Choice*, para. 41). In most cases, it is the breakdown and the separation, the problems of running two households rather than one, which causes financial hardship, often to both of the parties (see *Mathias v. Mathias* [1972] Fam. 287; *Talbot v. Talbot* [1971] 115 S.J. 870). In practice it has been found that the only significant hardship which may flow from the divorce itself is the potential loss of an occupational widow's pension for which the husband is unable to provide sufficient compensation (*cf Julian v. Julian* [1972] 116 S.J. 763 and *Johnson v. Johnson* [1981] 12 Fam. Law 116 (the only reported cases in which the bar was imposed) with *Parker v. Parker* [1972] 2 W.L.R. 21, *Le Marchant v. Le Marchant* [1977] 1 W.L.R. 559 and *Reiterbund v. Reiterbund* [1975] Fam. 99). The bar was rarely invoked and even more rarely successful. No divorce was ever refused on the grave other hardship ground (in *Lee v. Lee* [1973] 117 S.J. 616, it was initially refused because the wife needed accommodation for the disabled son, but after a change in the circumstances, it was granted on appeal). Cases in which it was refused—in each case social stigma in an ethnic community being the issue—include *Rukat v. Rukat* [1975] Fam. 63, *Banik v. Banik* [1973] 1 W.L.R. 860 and *Balraj v. Balraj* [1981] 11 Fam. 110. Despite the lack of success (though we do not know how often it was successfully invoked, as in *Parker v. Parker* and *Le Marchant v. Le Marchant*, as a bargaining counter), the Law Commission recommended its retention and its extension to divorce generally (see para. 5.76). The government White Paper, *Looking To The Future*, accepted this view (see para. 4.47). It said it did not intend to change the statutory wording (though this has now happened) "or the way in which the law in this area is now applied" (perhaps it has forgotten that the courts, not governments, apply the law!). In effect it accepted that the hardship defence was likely to be invoked rarely. There must be a suspicion that, initially at least, it will be invoked more often than was the case with the previous legislation.
    The order preventing divorce on hardship grounds is the only bar on divorce in the Act. Attempts were made to introduce others, including a ban on all divorces where there was a child of the family under 16 years (see *Hansard*, H.L. Vol. 568, cols. 803–827). There was also an attempt to introduce a "statement of conscientious objection", under which parties to a marriage might, at the time of their marriage or at any time thereafter, declare by deed that neither would apply for a divorce order (see *Hansard*, H.C. Vol. 279, cols. 561–581).
    Section 10 provides that an order preventing divorce may be made on application by the other party when the court is satisfied that dissolution would result in substantial financial or other hardship to that party or a child of the family and that it would be wrong in all the circumstances for the marriage to be dissolved. Hardship is defined to include the loss of a chance to obtain a future benefit, as well as the loss of an existing benefit.

Subs. (1)
    Divorce order. The hardship ground does not apply to applications for a separation order.
    The court may. It has discretion, to some extent circumscribed by subs. (2).
    On the application of the other party. I.e., not of its own motion. Nor may a child of the family apply (see *per* Lord Chancellor *Hansard*, H.L. Vol. 570, col. 26).
    Is not dissolved. Although the court may have to make extensive enquiries, there does not appear to be any provision allowing it to postpone the decision on whether it makes an order preventing divorce. It seems it either makes the divorce order or orders that the marriage is not to be dissolved.

Subs. (2)

This provides the ground upon which an order preventing divorce may be made. Dissolution must result in substantial hardship *and* it must be wrong for the marriage to be dissolved.

An order. It may include conditions (see s.10(5)).

Only if the court is satisfied. I.e., on a balance of probabilities.

Dissolution. In most cases it is breakdown or separation that constitutes the substantial hardship. The court must be satisfied that it is the *dissolution* of the marriage which will cause the hardship in question.

Substantial. The original Family Law Bill used the word "grave" as in s.5 of the Matrimonial Causes Act 1973. The amendment was made at Report stage in the House of Lords (see *Hansard*, H.L. Vol. 570, cols. 25–33). The Lord Chancellor, after referring to the rarity with which s.5 was invoked, said he wished the new provision to be "meaningful" (col. 25). "Substantial", he said, "is a less strict test" (col. 26). He explained that he had put this word in because he believed it would be understood by "ordinary people" (col. 30). He also explained that what was in issue was "objective" hardship (*idem*). He referred to the facts in the case of *Lee v. Lee* (see above). "Lowering" the standard of hardship from "grave" to "substantial" is "as low as it can go" advised the Lord Chancellor, in response to Lords who saw no need for any qualification at all (see col. 32). "Substantial" adds little to "hardship": if the hardship is not substantial the law, on *de minimis* principles, would take little notice of it anyway.

Financial hardship. This concept was used in the Matrimonial Causes Act 1973 and has a corpus of jurisprudence attached to it. Most case law has focused on the loss of pension rights (and see s.10(6)). There must be a real likelihood of the pension accruing to the other party: accordingly the chances of a young wife being able to establish the defence are remote (*Mathias v. Mathias* [1972] Fam. 287). If in some form the pension can be made up from other sources, such as supplementary benefit (now Income Support), there is unlikely to be financial hardship (*Reiterbund v. Reiterbund* [1974] 1 W.L.R. 788, affirmed [1975] Fam. 99). There is no shame to be attached to the receipt of state benefits (*per* Finer J. in *Reiterbund*). Where the loss of pension (in this case, a police occupational pension) could not be compensated from the husband's other resources and there was a substantial monetary gap between the financial provision that the husband could provide and the financial benefits which the wife would receive if she remained married, the defence was made out (see *Julian v. Julian* [1972] 116 S J 763). The more valuable the rights, the more likely it is that their loss will be considered a source of financial hardship (see *Le Marchant v. Le Marchant* [1977] 1 W.L.R. 559). In reading existing case law, two things should be borne in mind: first, the lower standard ("substantial" as opposed to "grave") which will now have to be met; secondly, the greater facility in this Act to distribute pension assets more equitably (see the pension-splitting provisions in ss.16 and 17 for Scotland).

Other hardship. There is no definition in the statute or the previous legislation or in the case law of what might count as other hardship. There is no case in which the defence has been successfully raised. All the reported cases have sought to rely on the social stigma attached to divorce in religious communities or foreign countries of which the respondent/other party is a member or inhabitant. Whilst the strength of the respondent's views and feelings have been noted, the courts have held that the question is ultimately determined according to an objective standard of reasonableness. See *Banik v. Banik* [1973] 1 W.L.R. 860 where Ormrod J. had "pooh-poohed" Mrs Banik's claim that she would be a social outcast in the society (in Bombay) in which she lived. Divorce, she had said, was anathema to her on religious, moral and social grounds. The Court of Appeal said that this was a possible defence and that the court should enquire into it. It might then come to the conclusion that her degree of shame or disgrace amounted to "grave hardship". This was a matter of "fact and degree". On rehearing, Hollings J. held that the divorce would only cause inconvenience (see *Banik v. Banik (No. 2)* [1973] 3 Fam. Law 174).

In *Parghi v. Parghi* [1973] 117 S.J. 582, the court said that if the wife did not believe in divorce—as she claimed—then the decree need not affect her belief and she would remain married to her husband according to her religion, though not in the eyes of the civil law. In *Rukat v. Rukat* [1975] Fam. 63, where the pretence of a subsisting marriage had been kept up by a Sicilian woman for 25 years, her belief was judged "sincere" but inadequate to substantiate the defence. Again, it should be stressed that the standard of "other" hardship has now been lowered to "substantial" from "grave". "Substantial" qualifies "hardship", as "grave" did (see *Rukat v. Rukat*). In the light of a pronounced shift towards "family values", in the light of the end of the "fault" facts, it is possible that there will be successful invocations of the revamped defence. To succeed in persuading a court to make an order preventing divorce it will be necessary to demonstrate objectively real hardship and this might be easier to show where the other party belongs to a minority community which takes a negative and stigmatising attitude to divorce. But the courts will need to be convinced that the other hardship stems from dissolution of the marital ties rather than from separation or breakdown.

Or to a child of the family. This was not in the previous legislation. It was not recommended by the Law Commission and was neither in the Government's Proposals nor in the Family Law Bill as originally presented. It was moved by the Lord Chancellor at Report stage in the House of Lords in response to demands made when the Bill was in Committee (see *Hansard*, H.L. Vol. 570, col. 26 and see the debates at *Hansard*, H.L. Vol. 568, cols. 1007–1015). Whether dissolution will result in substantial hardship to a child of the family depends on a number of matters but pre-eminent amongst these must be whether such a child will suffer, in the sense that there will be a poorer outcome for the child, as a result of the dissolution of his/her parent's marriage. If, as the Exeter study for example suggests, parental conflict, rather than divorce, is the primary source of difficulties experienced by children, and if it is the case that high levels of conflict are closely associated with poorer outcomes for children, then divorce may benefit many children rather than causing them hardship or detriment. This is, of course, a general research finding and may not be apposite to the particular child.

The child him or herself cannot raise the hardship defence. It clearly cannot be raised by the court of its motion. Therefore, it will necessarily be raised by the other party. It would be, said the Lord Chancellor (*Hansard*, H.L. Vol. 570, col. 26) "an intolerable burden on children to provide that they themselves might be involved in making such an application." He thought they could "easily be put under pressure by [a] parent to apply for such an order" (*idem*). He was of the opinion that: "We cannot have a situation in which we pitch child against parent in a battle about whether the marriage should be legally dissolved." (*idem*). He also took the view, perhaps optimistically, that "hardship to the children will be pretty easy to recognise once it is brought to the court's attention" (*Hansard*, H.L. Vol. 570, col. 673).

It would be wrong. In deciding whether it would be wrong to dissolve the marriage, the court is to look at all circumstances, including the parties' conduct and the interests of any child of the family. Under the 1973 legislation, the interests of the parties and of any children (not just children of the family or those under 18 years: see *Allen v. Allen* [1974] 4 Fam. Law 83 noting children meant "offspring") and of other persons, for example a new partner were to be considered. Although these considerations are not specifically included, there is no reason why a court should not consider these interests when determining whether dissolution of a marriage would be "wrong". "Wrong" has been said to mean "unjust", "not right" (see Davies L.J. in *Brickell v. Brickell* [1973] 3 W.L.R. 602). In *Reiterbund v. Reiterbund* it was said that the court must exclude from its consideration the fact that the petition was brought by a "guilty" husband against a non-consenting wife, because this would be tantamount to striking out the five-year fact: *a fortiori* this reasoning must apply where fault is totally removed from divorce, as is the intention of the 1996 scheme. It has been said that "conduct" is not confined to "misconduct", that is to a matrimonial offence in the old sense (see *Brickell v. Brickell* [1973] 2 W.L.R. 602). Said Davies L.J.: "If very gross conduct were shown, or if misconduct were shown, then it is one of the matters to which the court must have regard in deciding whether or not it was wrong to dissolve the marriage." But in *Dorrell v. Dorrell* [1972] 1 W.L.R. 1087, it was said "conduct" does not mean conduct in the sense of the old matrimonial offence. It is submitted that "conduct" in the new provision must be broadly interpreted and not confined to the old matrimonial offences. For example, financial mismanagement (see, in another context *Martin v. Martin* [1976] Fam. 335) could well be "conduct" which a court might consider. In considering whether dissolution of the marriage would be "wrong", other matters which may be considered are the length of the marriage, the age of the parties (in *Mathias v. Mathias* [1972] Fam. 287 the respondent was 32, a young able-bodied wife with experience at a variety of jobs) and the "broader aspect" *viz.*, "whether a marriage which has so hopelessly broken down for so long should be preserved or whether it is not right in the public interest to put an end to it" *per* Karminski L.J. in *Mathias v. Mathias*. It was said in this case to be "ridiculous to keep alive this shell of a marriage." *per* Davies L.J. There will be situations where there is going to be grave financial hardship but for *Mathias*-type considerations it would not be wrong to dissolve the marriage: since both paras. (a) and (b) must be satisfied, there should be no order preventing divorce.

Subs. (3)

This provides that, on an application by one or both of the parties, the court is to cancel the order preventing divorce unless it is still satisfied that the circumstances in s.10(2)(a) and (b) are met. There is no reason why the same considerations should apply: for example, there may be other reasons than those previously identified to conclude that it would be wrong to dissolve the marriage. It must be assumed that the acquisition of an order preventing divorce will operate as a bargaining counter: cancellations on the initiative of both parties or even just the "other party" may be sought when a better deal has been secured. This is reminiscent of the way in which s.5 of the 1973 Act was used (see *Parker v. Parker* [1972] 2 W.L.R. 21, *Le Marchant v. Le Marchant* [1977] 1 W.L.R. 559).

Subs. (4)

Where the court cancels an order preventing divorce, it may make a divorce order only if there is an application under ss.3 or 4(3).

Cancelled. I.e., under s.10(3).

Subs. (5)

An order preventing divorce may include conditions (for example, taking out a second mortgage or buying a deferred annuity) and these must be satisfied before an application to cancel the order may be made.

Subs. (6)

This subsection defines "hardship". It includes the loss of any existing benefit (perhaps obviously, but omitted from s.5 of the 1973 Act), as well as the loss of a chance of acquiring a future benefit.

Future benefit. Most obviously pension rights, including occupational pension rights, but also the surrender value of an insurance policy (*Bennett v. Bennett* [1978] 9 Fam. Law 19), the value of a retirement lump sum (*Richardson v. Richardson* [1978] 9 Fam. Law 86) and money obtained from the sale of a family business (*Trippas v. Trippas* [1973] 2 W.L.R. 585).

Welfare of children

Welfare of children

11.—(1) In any proceedings for a divorce order or a separation order, the court shall consider—

(a) whether there are any children of the family to whom this section applies; and

(b) where there are any such children, whether (in the light of the arrangements which have been, or are proposed to be, made for their upbringing and welfare) it should exercise any of its powers under the Children Act 1989 with respect to any of them.

(2) Where, in any case to which this section applies, it appears to the court that—

(a) the circumstances of the case require it, or are likely to require it, to exercise any of its powers under the Children Act 1989 with respect to any such child,

(b) it is not in a position to exercise the power, or (as the case may be) those powers, without giving further consideration to the case, and

(c) there are exceptional circumstances which make it desirable in the interests of the child that the court should give a direction under this section,

it may direct that the divorce order or separation order is not to be made until the court orders otherwise.

(3) In deciding whether the circumstances are as mentioned in subsection (2)(a), the court shall treat the welfare of the child as paramount.

(4) In making that decision, the court shall also have particular regard, on the evidence before it, to—

(a) the wishes and feelings of the child considered in the light of his age and understanding and the circumstances in which those wishes were expressed;

(b) the conduct of the parties in relation to the upbringing of the child;

(c) the general principle that, in the absence of evidence to the contrary, the welfare of the child will be best served by—

(i) his having regular contact with those who have parental responsibility for him and with other members of his family; and

(ii) the maintenance of as good a continuing relationship with his parents as is possible; and

(d) any risk to the child attributable to—

(i) where the person with whom the child will reside is living or proposes to live;

      (ii) any person with whom that person is living or with whom he proposes to live; or

      (iii) any other arrangements for his care and upbringing.

(5) This section applies to—

(a) any child of the family who has not reached the age of sixteen at the date when the court considers the case in accordance with the requirements of this section; and

(b) any child of the family who has reached that age at that date and in relation to whom the court directs that this section shall apply.

DEFINITIONS

"children of the family": s.24(1).
"divorce order": s.2(1)(a).
"separation order": s.2(1)(b).

GENERAL NOTE

This section amends s.41 of the Matrimonial Causes Act 1973. The amendments were originally tucked away in a Schedule (Sched. 8, para. 23) but, as a result of pressure from children's organisations, it was decided to place the full text of the procedure on the face of the Act. Essentially, however, the function of the court under this procedure remains as it has been under the existing law.

The list of factors which a court should take into account when deciding whether the circumstances are such as to require it to exercise its powers under the Children Act are extended, and now include a requirement to have regard to the wishes and feelings of the child in the light of his age and understanding and the circumstances in which those wishes were expressed; a requirement to have regard to the conduct of the parties in relation to the upbringing of the child; the principle that, in the absence of evidence to the contrary, the welfare of the child will be best served by the child having regular contact with those who have parental responsibility for him and with other members of his family; and a requirement for the court to have regard to any risk to the child which may be attributable to actual or proposed arrangements for the child's future.

Since the function of the court remains the same as under the existing law, the court has no jurisdiction to make a residence order or a contact order under s.11. Such orders, if they are to be made (and note the presumption against making orders in s.1(5) of the Children Act 1989) must continue to be made under s.8 of the Children Act. In exercising its jurisdiction under that Act, the court will apply the paramountcy principle in s.1(1) and the welfare checklist in s.1(3).

The court retains the power in exceptional circumstances to refuse to make a divorce or separation order. There are no published statistics of the current incidence of the use of s.41 M.C.A. 1973 (to delay divorce), nor is there any real expectation that things will change as a result of the amendments contained in this section. In reality, divorcing parents are given an autonomy which other categories of parents are denied. Even within divorce, the law appears to have the capacity to be either abstentionist or heavy-handed. Théry's comment that the Children Act 1989 "polarises ... two categories of divorcing spouses: those for whom the law rubber stamps their autonomous decisions; and those upon whom control and regulation are to be imposed" (in C. Smart and S. SevenLuijsen (eds), *Child Custody and the Politics of Gender* (Routledge 1989) p.94) seems absolutely right.

Subs. (1)

The court is to consider whether there are any children of the family in respect of whom it should exercise its powers.

The court shall consider. The message conveyed by the word "consider" is one of minimal intervention. The contrast with adoption could not be greater.

Children of the family ... this section applies. See s.11(5) (children under 16 years) and s.11(6) (older children where the court has directed this section applies).

It should exercise any of its powers. Principally, to make a residence or contact order under s.8 of the Children Act 1989, but also to make other "section 8 orders" (specific issue and prohibited steps orders) and family assistance orders (see s.16 of the Children Act). The court also has the power to direct the local authority to investigate the child's circumstances where it appears to the court that it may be appropriate for a care or supervision order to be made with respect of the child (see s.37 of the Children Act 1989). For an example of the use of s.37 see *Re H (a minor) (Section 37 Direction)* [1993] 2 F.L.R. 541 (where the court was concerned about the ability of lesbians to care in the long-term). The court can exercise all of these powers of its own motion.

Subs. (2)

The court has the power, where it needs to exercise its powers, cannot do so without further consideration and there are exceptional circumstances, to direct that a divorce order or separation order is not made until it directs otherwise.

Circumstances ... require. The welfare of the child is now the only consideration (see s.11(3)).

In any case to which this section applies. See s.11(5), (6).

Any of its powers under the Children Act. I.e., under ss.8, 16 or 37 (see the General Note to this section).

Any such child. That is a child of the family (see s.11(1)).

Exceptional circumstances. This is an indication of how non-interventionist this provision is intended to be.

Subs. (3)

The paramountcy test governs for the first time the exercise of this discretion.

Paramount. Where the child's welfare is paramount "it rules upon or determines the course to be followed" *per* Lord MacDermott in *J v. C* [1970] A.C. 668, 710. The child's welfare is the sole consideration: other factors are only relevant insofar as they assist the court in ascertaining what is best for the child.

Subs. (4)

The provision now incorporates a framework for decision-making. The list of factors in this subsection offers both guidance and constraint. It could have the effect of turning a rubber-stamping process into one with some judicial input. Particularly important is the reference to the wishes and feelings of the child: that this is placed first (and not on lexical principles) is of symbolic importance too. The emphasis on the assessment of risk is also significant.

On the evidence before it. This immediately cuts down the value of the provision. It is not likely that in most cases evidence of the wishes and feelings of the child will be before the court, despite the exhortation in s.12(2)(a)(iii). *Cf* the Children Act 1989 where the welfare checklist refers to "the ascertainable" wishes and feelings of the child.

Wishes and feelings of the child. The importance of this in the light of our obligation to comply with the UN Convention on the Rights of the Child (Art. 12) cannot be underestimated. Although the child's wishes and feelings are placed first in the list, there is no intention that these wishes and feelings are to be determinative (and see *Re W (minors) (residence order)* [1992] 2 F.C.R. 461; *Re W (a minor) (residence order)* [1993] 2 F.L.R. 625).

Age and understanding. The older the child, the greater the weight attached to the child's views. See *Re P (minors) (wardship)* [1992] 2 F.C.R. 681, 687 *per* Butler-Sloss L.J. But even an older child's wishes can be so contrary to his/her long-term welfare that a court may feel justified in overriding them (see *Re R (a minor) (wardship: medical treatment)* [1992] Fam. 11 and *Re W (a minor) (medical treatment: courts jurisdiction)* [1993] Fam. 64).

Conduct of the parties ... child. It should be stressed that it is their conduct in relation to the child that is in issue, not conduct in relation to each other. Matrimonial misconduct is not an issue, or, indeed, relevant. See *S (BD) v. S (BJ) (Infants: Care and Consent)* [1977] 1 All E.R. 656 and *Re K (Wardship: Care and Control)* [1977] 1 All E.R. 647.

Regular contact. Contact has been described as the right of the child (see *M v. M* (Child: Access) [1973] 2 All E.R. 81; *Re H (minors)* (Access) [1992] 1 F.L.R. 148).

Parental responsibility. Both parents have parental responsibility and retain it after divorce. Nor do they cease to have it because some other person (even a local authority with a care order) subsequently acquires it (see Children Act 1989, s.2(1), (6)). Parental responsibility can be acquired by obtaining a residence order (see Children Act 1989, s.12(2)).

Other members of his family. Family is not defined. "Other members of his family" is wider than the more usually used expression "relative" (defined in s.105 of the Children Act 1989). A cousin is a member of his family, not a relative.

Maintenance of ... continuing relationship. On which, see J. Wallerstein and J. Kelly, *Surviving The Breakup,* (Free Press, 1980) and the corrective offered by Amato and Keith (1991) 110(1) Psychological Bulletin 26. See further the General Note on s.1 above.

Any risk ... attributable to. "Attributable to" is wider than "caused by". A good parent without a settled environment may not "cause" any risk, but risk may be "attributable" to the parent's way of life, whether this lifestyle is desired or not. The situation of "travellers" may be instructive.

Subs. (5)

This section extends to children of the family under 16 years and older children where the court makes a direction.

Child of the family. For the meaning of which, see s.105 of the Children Act 1989 (step-children "treated" by both parties as a child of their family are included).

To whom the court directs. Such as mentally or physically disabled children of the family who are over 16 years, even over 18.

Supplementary

Lord Chancellor's rules

12.—(1) The Lord Chancellor may make rules—
(a) as to the form in which a statement is to be made and what information must accompany it;
(b) requiring the person making the statement to state whether or not, since satisfying the requirements of section 8, he has made any attempt at reconciliation;
(c) as to the way in which a statement is to be given to the court;
(d) requiring a copy of a statement made by one party to be served by the court on the other party;
(e) as to circumstances in which such service may be dispensed with or may be effected otherwise than by delivery to the party;
(f) requiring a party who has made a statement to provide the court with information about the arrangements that need to be made in consequence of the breakdown;
(g) as to the time, manner and (where attendance in person is required) place at which such information is to be given;
(h) where a statement has been made, requiring either or both of the parties—
    (i) to prepare and produce such other documents, and
    (ii) to attend in person at such places and for such purposes,
as may be specified;
(i) as to the information and assistance which is to be given to the parties and the way in which it is to be given;
(j) requiring the parties to be given, in such manner as may be specified, copies of such statements and other documents as may be specified.

(2) The Lord Chancellor may make rules requiring a person who is the legal representative of a party to a marriage with respect to which a statement has been, or is proposed to be, made—
 (a) to inform that party, at such time or times as may be specified—
    (i) about the availability to the parties of marriage support services;
    (ii) about the availability to them of mediation; and
    (iii) where there are children of the family, that in relation to the arrangements to be made for any child the parties should consider the child's welfare, wishes and feelings;
(b) to give that party, at such time or times as may be specified, names and addresses of persons qualified to help—
    (i) to effect a reconciliation; or
    (ii) in connection with mediation; and
(c) to certify, at such time or times as may be specified—
    (i) whether he has complied with the provision made in the rules by virtue of paragraphs (a) and (b);
    (ii) whether he has discussed with that party any of the matters mentioned in paragraph (a) or the possibility of reconciliation; and
    (iii) which, if any, of those matters they have discussed.

(3) In subsections (1) and (2) "specified" means determined under or described in the rules.

(4) This section does not affect any power to make rules of court for the purposes of this Act.

DEFINITIONS
"children of the family": s.24(1).
"party": s.24(1).
"statement": s.24(1).

GENERAL NOTE
This section gives the Lord Chancellor power to make procedural rules.

Subs. (1)
A statement. That is, of marital breakdown.
Requirements of s.8. On attending an information meeting.
Arrangements ... in consequences of the breakdown. See s.9.
As may be specified. That is determined under or described in the rules (see s.12(3)).

Subs. (2)
Child's welfare, wishes and feelings. See also s.11(4)(a).
Certify whether. Note the word "whether". The provision does not say "certify that". The legal representative may accordingly certify that s/he has not informed the party of the availability of marriage support services, of mediation and that they should consider their child's welfare, wishes and feelings. This is reminiscent of s.6(1) of the Matrimonial Causes Act 1973, which was a "dead letter" from its earliest days.

Resolution of disputes

Directions with respect to mediation

13.—(1) After the court has received a statement, it may give a direction requiring each party to attend a meeting arranged in accordance with the direction for the purpose—
  (a) of enabling an explanation to be given of the facilities available to the parties for mediation in relation to disputes between them; and
  (b) of providing an opportunity for each party to agree to take advantage of those facilities.
(2) A direction may be given at any time, including in the course of proceedings connected with the breakdown of the marriage (as to which see section 25).
(3) A direction may be given on the application of either of the parties or on the initiative of the court.
(4) The parties are to be required to attend the same meeting unless—
  (a) one of them asks, or both of them ask, for separate meetings; or
  (b) the court considers separate meetings to be more appropriate.
(5) A direction shall—
  (a) specify a person chosen by the court (with that person's agreement) to arrange and conduct the meeting or meetings; and
  (b) require such person as may be specified in the direction to produce to the court, at such time as the court may direct, a report stating—
      (i) whether the parties have complied with the direction; and
      (ii) if they have, whether they have agreed to take part in any mediation.

DEFINITION
"child of the family": s.24(1).

GENERAL NOTE
This section enables the court, after it has received a statement of marital breakdown, to direct that the parties attend a meeting explaining mediation and providing the parties with an opportunity to make use of mediation. The parties are to attend the same meeting unless one or both ask for separate meetings, or the court considers separate meetings to be more appropriate.
Mediation is central to the reformed process of divorce. It was recommended by the Law Commission (*The Ground for Divorce* (1992) Law Com. No. 192, paras. 5.30–5.39), although it concluded that there were dangers in relying "too heavily upon ... mediation instead of more traditional methods of negotiation and adjudication" (para. 5.34). It listed these as:

"Exploitation of the weaker partner by the stronger, which requires considerable skill and professionalism for the conciliator to counteract while remaining true to the neutral role required; considerable potential for delay, which is damaging both to the children and often to the interests of one of the adults involved; and the temptation for the court to postpone deciding some very difficult and painful cases which ought to be decided quickly." (para. 5.34).

The Government reached the view that "a greater use of mediation as part of the divorce process will help it achieve the objectives of a good divorce system" (*Looking To The Future*, para. 5.21). It concluded that it should not be made compulsory, although there should be "a definite encouragement to couples to use family mediation" (*idem*). It accepted that through the mediation process:

" * marriages which are capable of being saved are more likely to be identified than through the legal process; referral to marriage guidance can occur at any time and the door to reconciliation is always kept open, as spouses do not have to take up opposing stances from the outset;

* spouses are enabled to take responsibility for the breakdown of their marriage, can acknowledge responsibility for the ending of their marriage and deal with matters of fault, blame, anger and hurt with the minimum of bitterness and hostility;

* couples are encouraged to look to their responsibilities—the responsibilities of marriage and parenthood—and to co-operate in making arrangements for the future rather than focusing on the past and engaging in recrimination." (para. 5.21).

Considerable concern has been expressed about the move to mediation (see, for example, John Eekelaar (1995) 48 Current Legal Problems 195 and, in the context of domestic violence, Trina Grillo (1991) 100 Yale Law Journal 1545, K. Fischer *et al* (1993) 46 SMU Law Review 2117 and F. Kaganas and C. Piper (1994) Journal of Social Welfare and Family Law 265). The Government is aware of concerns in the domestic violence context (see paras. 5.29–5.30). Concern has also been expressed about the impact on children (see Christine Piper (1994) 6 Journal of Child Law 98, Martin Richards (1995) 7 Child and Family Quarterly 223, and Michael Freeman (1996) 9 Representing Children 42). See also generally Stephen Cretney's Joseph Jackson Memorial Lecture (1996) 146 New Law Journal 91. The Government's response is that "mediation services ... are very conscious of children's needs" (para. 5.32). It thought it "likely that within the not too distant future mediators will be specifically trained to deal appropriately with the interests of children during mediation, and will receive guidance on when and what circumstances it is appropriate to involve children in mediation" (para. 5.33).

Subs. (1)
The power to adjourn includes the power to adjourn to enable parties to comply with a s.13 direction and to resolve disputes amicably. The maximum period for adjournments will be provided by rules (see s.14(3)).

Includes. The court retains its power to adjourn for other reasons.

Direction under s.13. I.e., a direction to attend a mediation meeting or meetings.

Disputes to be resolved amicably. Including through mediation, but also by means of negotiation and counselling. The parties will have to report on mediation (see s.14(4)).

Subs. (2)
In considering adjournments, the court is directed to have regard in particular the need to protect interests of children of the family.

Subs. (3)
Rules will prescribe the maximum period of an adjournment.

Subs. (4)
Where the purpose of the adjournment is for enabling disputes to be settled amicably, a report is to be ordered about mediation efforts and the prognosis of success of further mediation.

The court shall order. There is no discretion.

Adjournments

14.—(1) The court's power to adjourn any proceedings connected with the breakdown of a marriage includes power to adjourn—

(a) for the purpose of allowing the parties to comply with a direction under section 13; or

(b) for the purpose of enabling disputes to be resolved amicably.

(2) In determining whether to adjourn for either purpose, the court shall have regard in particular to the need to protect the interests of any child of the family.

(3) If the court adjourns any proceedings connected with the breakdown of a marriage for either purpose, the period of the adjournment must not exceed the maximum period prescribed by rules of court.

(4) Unless the only purpose of the adjournment is to allow the parties to comply with a direction under section 13, the court shall order one or both of them to produce to the court a report as to—

(a) whether they have taken part in mediation during the adjournment;
(b) whether, as a result, any agreement has been reached between them;
(c) the extent to which any dispute between them has been resolved as a result of any such agreement;
(d) the need for further mediation; and
(e) how likely it is that further mediation will be successful.

DEFINITION
"child of the family": s.24(1).

GENERAL NOTE
This section deals with the powers of the court to adjourn proceedings connected with the breakdown of a marriage, with a view to attending a mediation meeting or for the purposes of enabling disputes to be resolved amicably. The need to protect the interests of children is stressed.

Subs. (1)
The power to adjourn includes the power to adjourn to enable parties to comply with a s.13 direction and to resolve disputes amicably. The maximum period for adjournments will be prescribed by rules (see s.14(3)).
Includes: the court retains its power to adjourn for other reasons.
Directions under s.13: to attend a mediation meeting or meetings.
Disputes to be resolved amicably: including through mediation, but also by means of negotiation and counselling. The parties will have to report on mediation (see s.14(4)).

Subs. (2)
In considering adjournments the court is directed to have regard in particular to the need to protect the interests of children of the family.

Subs. (3)
Rules will prescribe the maximum period of an adjournment.

Subs. (4)
Where the purpose of the adjournment is for enabling disputes to be settled amicably, a report is to be ordered about mediation efforts and the prognosis for success of further mediation.
The court shall order: there is no discretion.

Financial provision

Financial arrangements

15.—(1) Schedule 2 amends the 1973 Act.
(2) The main object of Schedule 2 is—
(a) to provide that, in the case of divorce or separation, an order about financial provision may be made under that Act before a divorce order or separation order is made; but
(b) to retain (with minor changes) the position under that Act where marriages are annulled.

(3) Schedule 2 also makes minor and consequential amendments of the 1973 Act connected with the changes mentioned in subsection (1).

GENERAL NOTE
This section sets out the object of Sched. 2, which is to provide that financial provision under the Matrimonial Causes Act 1973 may be made before a divorce order or separation order is made. It provides that the position set out in the 1973 Act is retained in the case of annulment of marriages. See, further, the commentary on Sched. 2.

Division of pension rights: England and Wales

16.—(1) The Matrimonial Causes Act 1973 is amended as follows.

(2) In section 25B (benefits under a pension scheme on divorce, etc.), in subsection (2), after paragraph (b), insert—

"(c) in particular, where the court determines to make such an order, whether the order should provide for the accrued rights of the party with pension rights ("the pension rights") to be divided between that party and the other party in such a way as to reduce the pension rights of the party with those rights and to create pension rights for the other party.".

(3) After subsection (7) of that section, add—

"(8) If a pensions adjustment order under subsection (2)(c) above is made, the pension rights shall be reduced and pension rights of the other party shall be created in the prescribed manner with benefits payable on prescribed conditions, except that the court shall not have the power—

(a) to require the trustees or managers of the scheme to provide benefits under their own scheme if they are able and willing to create the rights for the other party by making a transfer payment to another scheme and the trustees and managers of that other scheme are able and willing to accept such a payment and to create those rights; or

(b) to require the trustees or managers of the scheme to make a transfer to another scheme—

(i) if the scheme is an unfunded scheme (unless the trustees or managers are able and willing to make such a transfer payment); or

(ii) in prescribed circumstances.

(9) No pensions adjustment order may be made under subsection (2)(c) above—

(a) if the scheme is a scheme of a prescribed type, or

(b) in prescribed circumstances, or

(c) insofar as it would affect benefits of a prescribed type."

(4) In section 25D (pensions: supplementary), insert—

(a) in subsection (2)—

(i) at the end of paragraph (a), the words "or prescribe the rights of the other party under the pension scheme,"; and

(ii) after paragraph (a), the following paragraph—

"(aa) make such consequential modifications of any enactment or subordinate legislation as appear to the Lord Chancellor necessary or expedient to give effect to the provisions of section 25B; and an order under this paragraph may make provision applying generally in relation to enactments and subordinate legislation of a description specified in the order,";

(b) in subsection (4), in the appropriate place in alphabetical order, the following entries—

" 'funded scheme' means a scheme under which the benefits are provided for by setting aside resources related to the value of the members' rights as they accrue (and 'unfunded scheme' shall be construed accordingly);

'subordinate legislation' has the same meaning as in the Interpretation Act 1978;"; and

(c) after subsection (4), the following subsection—

"(4A) Other expressions used in section 25B above shall be construed in accordance with section 124 (interpretation of Part I) of the Pensions Act 1995."

DEFINITIONS
    "accrued rights": Pensions Act 1995, s.124(2).
    "managers": Pensions Act 1995, s.124(1).
    "trustees": Pensions Act 1995, s.124(1).

GENERAL NOTE
    This section provides for the Matrimonial Causes Act 1973 to be amended to allow for pension-splitting on divorce. It was not in the original Bill although such a provision has been advocated for some time, including in the debates which led to the Pensions Act 1995.
    The need for this provision can best be understood against the background of work patterns of women. Martin and Roberts' study (*Women and Employment: A Lifetime Perspective* (DOE/OPCS, 1984)) showed that women were economically active for only 65 per cent of their working lives. That this limited participation relates to marriage is clear from Gregory and Foster's study *The Consequences of Divorce* (OPCS, 1990). They found that, whereas 98 per cent of husbands were economically active at separation, only 62 per cent of wives were. And only 21 per cent of wives had worked full-time continually throughout marriage, compared to 70 per cent of husbands. Twenty five per cent of divorcing women had not worked during marriage and full-time work declined with family size, so that 54 per cent of those with three or more dependent children had not worked full-time during marriage. Part-time work was common amongst divorcing women: a third had never worked full-time, but only a minority of those with children under five years or with more than three dependent children worked outside the home. The effect of spending periods outside the labour market continues after divorce: only 21 per cent of those who never worked during marriage were economically active three months after divorce and, of these, four per cent were unemployed.
    These patterns have a marked effect on women's pensions. The state pension schemes take account of periods of caring for children or invalids by providing Home Responsibilities Credits, which reduce the number of years for which contributions must be made, but these pensions are very low. More valuable occupational pensions usually require contributions throughout a working life of 40 years for a full pension. 10.7 million workers (48 per cent of the working population) are members of occupational pensions schemes, but only 37 per cent of women workers are scheme members (Government Actuary's Department, *Ninth Survey of Occupational Pension Schemes* 1991 (HMSO, 1994), Table 2.3). Women are less likely to be scheme members because of the types of work (e.g. part-time) they do, and because many of them work part-time (only 16 per cent of part-time workers belong to pension schemes; many schemes are not open to part-time workers). Women scheme members have lower pensions because their broken employment histories reduce their final salaries and the length of their scheme membership. Those without access to occupational pensions may take out private pensions, but women's lower earnings mean they can contribute relatively little to a private pension.
    As a result, twice as many women as men—about two-thirds of the female population—will have an income below poverty level for their retirement.
    Where couples remain married, the wife is protected by partial dependence on the husband's pension, and in the event of his death she will normally receive income in the form of a widow's pension (usually half the retirement pension). If the couple divorces, she may obtain an order which can be paid from the husband's earnings or pension, but the emphasis on the "clean break" means that few women do: if she does not, she may have no access to the benefits derived from contributions made during the marriage. Nor will she become her husband's widow, although she may be able to claim under the Inheritance (Provision for Family and Dependants) Act 1975 (c. 63).
    The Matrimonial Causes Act 1973 (s.25(2)(h)) allowed consideration of loss of pension when a court assessed financial provision or the reallocation of property. The House of Lords in *Brooks v. Brooks* [1995] 3 All E.R. 257 came to the assistance of some divorced women when it held that a husband's pension trust could be interpreted as a post-nuptial settlement and was therefore variable under the Matrimonial Causes Act 1973, s.24(1)(c). But this was only possible because the wife was an employee of the company, the scheme was in surplus and the Inland Revenue was willing to allow payment to her as if she had belonged to the scheme. As Masson notes, "the decision to treat the scheme, rather than the husband's rights as a scheme member, as a post-nuptial settlement was purely pragmatic and without principle" (in "Right To Divorce and Pension Rights" in M. Freeman (ed.), *Divorce: Where Next?* (Dartmouth, 1996), p.107, 114).
    The Pensions Act 1995 contains provisions for earmarking, so that courts can make deferred orders for maintenance or a lump sum and pension scheme managers or trustees can be required to make payments from a member's pension to a former spouse (s.166, adding ss.25B, 25C and 25D to the Matrimonial Causes Act). Regulations will provide for spouses to have information about a scheme member's rights and for the valuation of pensions (see the Matrimonial Causes Act 1973, s.25D(2)). Under this legislation, the size of the payment is likely to remain until the date of retirement and orders even for lump sums will be variable. Pensions against which orders have been made will need to be traced to ensure that the order is modified and applicable to any

arrangement which accepts a transfer of the pension (see the Matrimonial Causes Act 1973, s.25D). The Government was unclear how this could be arranged at the time the provisions were debated (see *Hansard*, Standing Committee D on Pensions Bill, col. 807). Under the 1995 reforms, payments will only be made whilst the scheme member receives a pension. The former spouse's retirement income is thus linked to the date of the member's retirement. If a scheme member dies, the former spouse will not be entitled to a share of the widow's/widower's pension (Matrimonial Causes Act 1973, s.25B(4)). Payments will be treated for all purposes as payments by the scheme member and so will be taxed as his income (Matrimonial Causes Act 1973, s.25B(6)). Those divorced before these provisions are implemented will not be able to benefit from them (see the Pensions Act 1995, s.166(6)). Masson has commented that: "These provisions do not provide a simple and comprehensive arrangement which can ensure fair compensation in all cases but create a complex and costly mechanism which will leave the majority of wives without security in retirement" (*op cit* at p.123).

When the Pensions Bill was before Parliament there was intense lobbying for the introduction of pension-splitting. The Government maintained it was too difficult and too expensive (in terms of lost revenue and payments from the unfunded public sector schemes). In *Brooks v. Brooks* [1995] 3 All E.R. 257, 267, Lord Nicholls acknowledged that legislation was still required to make pension-splitting generally available.

The Government resisted pension-splitting this time too. This section is the result of a Government defeat in the House of Lords (for the debate see *Hansard*, H.L. Vol. 569, cols. 1610–1635).

This section provides that when a court is considering financial provision under s.23 of the Matrimonial Causes Act 1973 it shall consider whether the order should provide for the accrued rights of the party with pension rights to be divided between that party and the other party so as to reduce the pension rights of the party with those rights and create pension rights for the other party. However, no such order may be made if the scheme is of a prescribed type. These exemptions await rules by the Lord Chancellor and could potentially railroad this provision.

The section also provides that the court shall not have the power to require trustees or managers of the scheme to provide benefits under their scheme if they are able and willing to create the rights for the other party by making a transfer payment to another scheme, and the trustees and managers of that other scheme are able and willing to accept such a payment and to create those rights; or the power to require the trustees or managers of the scheme to make a transfer to another scheme if the scheme is an unfunded one, unless the trustees or managers are able and willing to make such a transfer payment.

Subs. (2)

This provides that, in any proceedings for a financial provision order under s.23 of the Matrimonial Causes Act 1973, where a party to the marriage has, or is likely to have, any benefit under a pension scheme, the court shall consider whether the order it makes should provide for pension-splitting.

Pension-splitting requires a court order (as was recommended by the Pensions Management Institute report, *Pensions and Divorce* (PMI, 1993), para. 20.2). Presumably this includes a consent order. Even so, this will increase the burden on the court and runs counter to the shift towards private ordering which, of course, this Act encourages.

The order may provide for periodical payments in addition to a lump sum. If it takes the form of periodical payments it may be variable. Lump sums cannot be varied.

It is not clear whether the provision is retrospective. The presumption against retrospection is strong, but may result in wives holding back on divorce until this provision comes into operation. But there is a power in s.23(1) of the Matrimonial Causes Act 1973 to make orders at the time of divorce "or at any time thereafter", and this has been held to allow a petition to be varied so that the court could grant a lump sum or property adjustment order even though there was no power to do so when the divorce was granted (see *Chaterjee v. Chaterjee* [1976] 1 All E.R. 719). It might be possible to employ this strategy in the context of pension-splitting too.

Such an order. That is, an order under s.23 of the Matrimonial Causes Act 1973. It cannot be done under s.24, even (presumably) by consent.

To be divided. In what percentages is up to the court. The assumption of a 50-50 split is not mandated by the legislation.

Subs. (3)

This provides that courts will not be able to order trustees or managers to provide benefits under their own scheme if they are able and willing to create rights for the other party by making a transfer payment to another scheme, and the trustees and managers of that other scheme are able and willing to accept such a payment and to create those rights. Nor will the courts have the power to require trustees or managers to make a transfer to another scheme if the scheme is an unfunded one, unless the trustees or managers are able and willing to make such a transfer payment. Pension adjustment orders are also excluded in circumstances to be prescribed.

Division of pension assets: Scotland

17. Section 10 of the Family Law (Scotland) Act 1985 (sharing of value of matrimonial property), is amended as follows—
  (a) in subsection (5) at the end of paragraph (b), insert ", and
       (c) in the assets in respect of which either party has accrued rights to
            benefits under a pension scheme"; and
  (b) after subsection (5) insert—
            "(5A) In the case of an unfunded pension scheme, the court may
            not make an order which would allow assets to be removed from
            the scheme earlier than would otherwise have been the case.".

GENERAL NOTE
This section provides for pension-splitting in Scotland.

Grounds for financial provision orders in magistrates' courts

18.—(1) In section 1 of the Domestic Proceedings and Magistrates' Courts Act 1978, omit paragraphs (c) and (d) (which provide for behaviour and desertion to be grounds on which an application for a financial provision order may be made).

(2) In section 7(1) of that Act (powers of magistrates' court where spouses are living apart by agreement), omit "neither party having deserted the other".

GENERAL NOTE
This section amends the Domestic Proceedings and Magistrates' Courts Act 1978 so as to omit remaining fault grounds (behaviour and desertion) as bases on which an application for a financial provision order may be made. It also amends s.7(1) of that Act where there is a reference to desertion, which is now to be omitted. These amendments extirpate all reference to matrimonial offences left in family legislation.

Jurisdiction and commencement of proceedings

Jurisdiction in relation to divorce and separation

19.—(1) In this section "the court's jurisdiction" means—
  (a) the jurisdiction of the court under this Part to entertain marital pro-
       ceedings; and
  (b) any other jurisdiction conferred on the court under this Part, or any
       other enactment, in consequence of the making of a statement.
(2) The court's jurisdiction is exercisable only if—
  (a) at least one of the parties was domiciled in England and Wales on the
       statement date;
  (b) at least one of the parties was habitually resident in England and
       Wales throughout the period of one year ending with the statement
       date; or
  (c) nullity proceedings are pending in relation to the marriage when the
       marital proceedings commence.
(3) Subsection (4) applies if—
  (a) a separation order is in force; or
  (b) an order preventing divorce has been cancelled.
(4) The court—
  (a) continues to have jurisdiction to entertain an application made by ref-
       erence to the order referred to in subsection (3); and
  (b) may exercise any other jurisdiction which is conferred on it in conse-
       quence of such an application.
(5) Schedule 3 amends Schedule 1 to the Domicile and Matrimonial Proceedings Act 1973 (orders to stay proceedings where there are proceedings in
other jurisdictions).
(6) The court's jurisdiction is exercisable subject to any order for a stay
under Schedule 1 to that Act.

(7) In this section—
"nullity proceedings" means proceedings in respect of which the court has jurisdiction under section 5(3) of the Domicile and Matrimonial Proceedings Act 1973; and
"statement date" means the date on which the relevant statement was received by the court.

DEFINITIONS
"marital proceedings": s.20.
"order preventing divorce": s.10(2).
"separation order": s.2(1)(b).
"statement": s.24(1).

GENERAL NOTE
This, in combination with Sched. 3, deals with the circumstances in which courts in England and Wales have jurisdiction to make a divorce order or separation order.

The principal novelty of this provision is contained in subs. (4). Where a separation order is obtained, or there was an application for a divorce order, though this was not granted on hardship grounds (see s.10), so that an order preventing divorce was made instead which order has now been cancelled, the court's jurisdiction continues, so that it will be able to make a divorce order even though none of the jurisdictional grounds in s.19(2) is satisfied now. Accordingly, courts will be able to dissolve marriages where neither party is domiciled or habitually resident in England and Wales. Whether such orders will be universally recognised is dubious: the result is that some "limping marriages" will be created by this provision.

Subs. (1)
This defines "the courts' jurisdiction".

Subs. (2)
Jurisdiction depends on one of the parties being domiciled in England and Wales, or habitually resident for one year in England and Wales or on nullity proceedings being pending when marital proceedings (that is divorce or separation proceedings) commence.

At least one. It is not necessary for both parties to satisfy the jurisdictional criteria. It matters not which party does, whether it be the applicant or the other party. It should be remembered that one spouse can acquire a domicile separate from that of the other.

Domiciled. For the meaning of this, standard private international law books should be consulted.

On the statement date. See s.19(7). The rule is, as it was at common law, "once competent, always competent" (see *Leon v. Leon* [1967] P. 275, 284). If the rule were otherwise, the other party domiciled in England could frustrate a statement made by an applicant, who is domiciled and resident abroad, by changing his/her domicile between the statement being received by the court and the hearing of the application.

Habitually resident ... one year. "Habitual" is not easy to define. It has been said that there is no difference between "ordinary" and "habitual" residence (see *Barnet London Borough Council v. Shah* [1983] 2 A.C. 309, *Kapur v. Kapur* [1984] F.L.R. 920). In the latter Bush J. said "habitually" means "settled practice or usually" (p.926). The concept of habitual residence is less demanding in terms of intention than domicile. A respondent has been held to be habitually resident in England for the purposes of divorce jurisdiction even though she spent one-third of the relevant year either on holiday in Spain or visiting her children in the USA and Canada (see *Oundjian v. Oundjian* [1979] 1 F.L.R. 198). It is possible to have more than one habitual residence (see *Re V (Abduction: Habitual Residence)* [1995] 2 F.L.R. 992). This was decided in the context of child abduction legislation: its extension to divorce is supported by Cheshire and North, *Private International Law* (12th edition, 1992, p.632).

It should be stressed again that it is possible for an English court to make a divorce order where the other party has no connection with England whatsoever. How this fits with information meetings, etc., does not seem to have been thought through by Parliament. However, the court may stay the application (see s.19(6)).

Nullity proceedings are pending. See s.19(7). So, if, for example, a husband petitions for nullity but before the petition is heard he abandons his English residence, the wife, who is domiciled and resident abroad, could bring marital proceedings in this country. Our jurisdictional rules seem unnecessarily generous and could cause recognition problems. It is difficult to see how the requirements of the Act will be satisfied in such a case, but, as said in the previous note, consideration has not been given to these problems. Jurisdiction is, however, exercisable subject to any order for a stay (see s.19(6)).

Subs. (2)

This creates new and additional jurisdictional grounds. If there is a separation order, the court will continue to have jurisdiction to entertain a divorce application even though the jurisdictional criteria are no longer satisfied. In effect, if a wife obtains a separation order the husband can have this converted into a divorce order even though neither of them is domiciled in England and neither lives in England. The provision also applies where there is an order preventing divorce and this is cancelled. In effect, if a husband seeks a divorce on the jurisdictional ground of the wife's habitual residence in England, but she (on hardship grounds) persuades the court to make an order preventing divorce, he can ask for the order to be cancelled and a divorce order made, even though she no longer lives in England, and he has no connection with England at all. This assumes the court has jurisdiction to cancel an order preventing divorce: there seems to be a lacuna in the Act because there are no stated jurisdictional criteria for an application for a cancellation of such an order.

Subs. (5)

This amends Sched. 1 of the Domicile and Matrimonial Proceedings Act 1973, dealing with stays of proceedings. The details are in Sched. 3. See the Note to that Schedule.

Subs. (6)

The jurisdictional criteria are very liberal. But if satisfied, the court has no general discretion to refuse jurisdiction (see *per* Bush J. in *Kapur v. Kapur* [1984] F.L.R. 920, 922: "If the court has jurisdiction ... there is no way in which the court could decline jurisdiction on the ground of hardship, apparent unfairness or any other ground"). The width of the jurisdictional rules is such that there is a risk of other proceedings being pursued in another jurisdiction (or jurisdictions) simultaneously.

Where it appears to the court, on an application of a party to the marriage for divorce, that proceedings for divorce or nullity are continuing elsewhere in the British Isles, that the parties to the marriage have resided together after its celebration, that the place where they resided together when those proceedings began is that other jurisdiction in the British Isles, and that either of the parties was habitually resident there for a year ending with the date on which they last resided there together, the English court *must*, on the application of one of the spouses (*i.e.* not by acting of its own motion), order the English proceedings to be stayed. The object of this elaborate scheme is to ensure that the proceedings are heard in the appropriate forum.

Where it appears to the court that any proceedings are pending in another jurisdiction in respect of, or capable of affecting, the validity or subsistence of the marriage in question, then the English court *has a discretion* to stay its own proceedings. The basis for the exercise of the courts' discretion is the balance of fairness and convenience between the parties, having regard to all relevant factors, including the convenience of witnesses and delay or expense likely to result from a decision whether or not to stay the proceedings. On the balance see *Shemshadfard v. Shemshadfard* [1981] 1 All E.R. 726; *Gadd v. Gadd* [1984] 1 W.L.R. 1435; *Thyssen-Bornemisza v. Thyssen-Bornemisza* [1985] F.L.R. 670, affirmed [1986] Fam. 1; *K v. K* [1986] 2 F.L.R. 411; *De Dampierre v. De Dampierre* [1988] A.C. 92; *T v. T* [1995] 2 F.L.R. 660. It is now clear that discretion ought to be exercised using principles of the doctrine of *forum non conveniens*, which have developed in the late 1970s and the 1980s in the context of commercial cases (see *Spiliada Maritime Corporation v. Cansulex Ltd* [1987] A.C. 460). This means that the discretion ought to be exercised to grant a stay if the defendant (other party) can point to another forum which is the appropriate one for trial of the proceedings, provided that the applicant does not show that justice cannot be done there (see further R. Schuz (1989) 38 I.C.L.Q. 946).

Time when proceedings for divorce or separation begin

20.—(1) The receipt by the court of a statement is to be treated as the commencement of proceedings.

(2) The proceedings are to be known as marital proceedings.

(3) Marital proceedings are also—

(a) separation proceedings, if an application for a separation order has been made under section 3 by reference to the statement and not withdrawn;

(b) divorce proceedings, if an application for a divorce order has been made under section 3 by reference to the statement and not withdrawn.

(4) Marital proceedings are to be treated as being both divorce proceedings and separation proceedings at any time when no application by reference to the statement, either for a divorce order or for a separation order, is outstanding.

(5) Proceedings which are commenced by the making of an application under section 4(3) are also marital proceedings and divorce proceedings.

(6) Marital proceedings come to an end—

(a) on the making of a separation order;

(b) on the making of a divorce order;

(c) on the withdrawal of the statement by a notice in accordance with section 5(3)(a);

(d) at the end of the specified period mentioned in section 5(3)(b), if no application under section 3 by reference to the statement is outstanding;

(e) on the withdrawal of all such applications which are outstanding at the end of that period;

(f) on the withdrawal of an application under section 4(3).

DEFINITIONS

"divorce order": s.2(1)(a).
"separation order": s.2(1)(b).
"statement": s.24(1).
"withdrawal": s.24(2), (3).

GENERAL NOTE

This section provides that the date on which the court receives a statement of marital breakdown is, as a general rule, to be treated as the date when marital proceedings commence. It also provides for when marital proceedings come to an end.

Intestacy

Intestacy: effect of separation

21. Where—

(a) a separation order is in force, and

(b) while the parties to the marriage remain separated, one of them dies intestate as respects any real or personal property,

that property devolves as if the other had died before the intestacy occurred.

DEFINITION

"separation order": s.2(1)(b).

GENERAL NOTE

This section provides that when a separation order is in force and one of the parties dies intestate, property devolves as if the surviving party had died before the intestacy occurred.

Marriage support services

Funding for marriage support services

22.—(1) The Lord Chancellor may, with the approval of the Treasury, make grants in connection with—

(a) the provision of marriage support services;

(b) research into the causes of marital breakdown;

(c) research into ways of preventing marital breakdown.

(2) Any grant under this section may be made subject to such conditions as the Lord Chancellor considers appropriate.

(3) In exercising his power to make grants in connection with the provision of marriage support services, the Lord Chancellor is to have regard, in particular, to the desirability of services of that kind being available when they are first needed.

GENERAL NOTE

This section gives the Lord Chancellor power to make grants in connection with the provision of marriage support services and to fund research into the causes of marital breakdown and into ways of preventing this happening. The Lord Chancellor stressed that it was support of marriage, not "alternative lifestyles" that would be funded (see *Hansard*, H.L. Vol. 573, col. 1063).

Provision of marriage counselling

23.—(1) The Lord Chancellor or a person appointed by him may secure the provision, in accordance with regulations made by the Lord Chancellor, of marriage counselling.

(2) Marriage counselling may only be provided under this section at a time when a period for reflection and consideration—
(a) is running in relation to the marriage; or
(b) is interrupted under section 7(8) (but not for a continuous period of more than 18 months).

(3) Marriage counselling may only be provided under this section for persons who would not be required to make any contribution towards the cost of mediation provided for them under Part IIIA of the Legal Aid Act 1988.

(4) Persons for whom marriage counselling is provided under this section are not to be required to make any contribution towards the cost of the counselling.

(5) Marriage counselling is only to be provided under this section if it appears to the marriage counsellor to be suitable in all the circumstances.

(6) Regulations under subsection (1) may—
(a) make provision about the way in which marriage counselling is to be provided; and
(b) prescribe circumstances in which the provision of marriage counselling is to be subject to the approval of the Lord Chancellor.

(7) A contract entered into for the purposes of subsection (1) by a person appointed under that subsection must include such provision as the Lord Chancellor may direct.

(8) If the person appointed under subsection (1) is the Legal Aid Board, the powers conferred on the Board by or under the Legal Aid Act 1988 shall be exercisable for the purposes of this section as they are exercisable for the purposes of that Act.

(9) In section 15 of the Legal Aid Act 1988 (availability of, and payment for, representation under Part IV of the Act), after subsection (3H) insert—
"(3I) A person may be refused representation for the purposes of any proceedings if—
(a) the proceedings are marital proceedings within the meaning of Part II of the Family Law Act 1996; and
(b) he is being provided with marriage counselling under section 23 of that Act in relation to the marriage."

DEFINITION
"period for reflection and consideration": s.7.

GENERAL NOTE
This section enables the Lord Chancellor to fund marriage counselling for those who would not be required to contribute towards the cost of mediation. The effect is to create "a level playing field between marriage counselling and mediation" (*per* Lord Irvine of Lairg, *Hansard*, H.L. Vol. 573, col. 1061). The section is about marriage counselling: "there is no question . . . of authorising counselling in relation to alternative lifestyles" (*per* Lord Chancellor, *Hansard*, H.L. Vol. 573, col. 1063).

Interpretation

Interpretation of Part II etc.

24.—(1) In this Part—
"the 1973 Act" means the Matrimonial Causes Act 1973;
"child of the family" and "the court" have the same meaning as in the 1973 Act;
"divorce order" has the meaning given in section 2(1)(a);
"divorce proceedings" is to be read with section 20;
"marital proceedings" has the meaning given in section 20;
"non-molestation order" has the meaning given by section 42(1);
"occupation order" has the meaning given by section 39;

"order preventing divorce" has the meaning given in section 10(2);
"party", in relation to a marriage, means one of the parties to the marriage;
"period for reflection and consideration" has the meaning given in section 7;
"separation order" has the meaning given in section 2(1)(b);
"separation proceedings" is to be read with section 20;
"statement" means a statement of marital breakdown;
"statement of marital breakdown" has the meaning given in section 6(1).

(2) For the purposes of this Part, references to the withdrawal of an application are references, in relation to an application made jointly by both parties, to its withdrawal by a notice given, in accordance with rules of court—
  (a) jointly by both parties; or
  (b) separately by each of them.

(3) Where only one party gives such a notice of withdrawal, in relation to a joint application, the application shall be treated as if it had been made by the other party alone.

GENERAL NOTE
This is the interpretation section of this Part of the Act. There is also interpretative provision in subss. (2) and (3) on the meaning of withdrawal of applications.

Connected proceedings

25.—(1) For the purposes of this Part, proceedings are connected with the breakdown of a marriage if they fall within subsection (2) and, at the time of the proceedings—
  (a) a statement has been received by the court with respect to the marriage and it is or may become possible for an application for a divorce order or separation order to be made by reference to that statement;
  (b) such an application in relation to the marriage has been made and not withdrawn; or
  (c) a divorce order has been made, or a separation order is in force, in relation to the marriage.

(2) The proceedings are any under Parts I to V of the Children Act 1989 with respect to a child of the family or any proceedings resulting from an application—
  (a) for, or for the cancellation of, an order preventing divorce in relation to the marriage;
  (b) by either party to the marriage for an order under Part IV;
  (c) for the exercise, in relation to a party to the marriage or child of the family, of any of the court's powers under Part II of the 1973 Act;
  (d) made otherwise to the court with respect to, or in connection with, any proceedings connected with the breakdown of the marriage.

DEFINITIONS
"divorce order": s.2(1)(a).
"order preventing divorce": s.10(2).
"separation order": s.2(1)(b).
"statement": s.24(1).
"withdrawn": s.24(2), (3).

GENERAL NOTE
This section sets out the proceedings which will be proceedings connected with the breakdown of a marriage. The definition only embraces the proceedings listed in subs. (2) if there has been a statement of marital breakdown which has not lapsed, has not been withdrawn or a divorce has taken place or a separation order is in force. Proceedings which may be connected are listed in subs. (2) and are broadly defined.

PART III

LEGAL AID FOR MEDIATION IN FAMILY MATTERS

Legal aid for mediation in family matters

26.—(1) In the Legal Aid Act 1988 insert, after section 13—

"PART IIIA

MEDIATION

Scope of this Part

13A.—(1) This Part applies to mediation in disputes relating to family matters.

(2) "Family matters" means matters which are governed by English law and in relation to which any question has arisen, or may arise—

    (a) under any provision of—
        (i) the 1973 Act;
        (ii) the Domestic Proceedings and Magistrates' Courts Act 1978;
        (iii) Parts I to V of the Children Act 1989;
        (iv) Parts II and IV of the Family Law Act 1996; or
        (v) any other enactment prescribed;
    (b) under any prescribed jurisdiction of a prescribed court or tribunal; or
    (c) under any prescribed rule of law.

(3) Regulations may restrict this Part to mediation in disputes of any prescribed description.

(4) The power to—
    (a) make regulations under subsection (2), or
    (b) revoke any regulations made under subsection (3),
is exercisable only with the consent of the Treasury."

(2) In section 2 of the 1988 Act, after subsection (3), insert—

"(3A) "Mediation" means mediation to which Part IIIA of this Act applies; and includes steps taken by a mediator in any case—
    (a) in determining whether to embark on mediation;
    (b) in preparing for mediation; and
    (c) in making any assessment under that Part."

(3) In section 43 of the 1988 Act, after the definition of "legal representative" insert—

" "mediator" means a person with whom the Board contracts for the provision of mediation by any person."

GENERAL NOTE

This section amends the Legal Aid Act 1988 by, *inter alia*, inserting a new s.13A into that Act. It provides definitions of "family matters", "mediation" and "mediator".

Subs. (1)

Legal Aid for mediation is confined to family matters governed by English law. Since English law has always applied the *lex fori* to choice of law questions relating to divorce and judicial separation, in effect holding that once the court has jurisdiction questions of choice of law do not arise, divorce and separation questions will always be governed by English law. The domicile or nationality of the parties is irrelevant, so long as the court has jurisdiction, which it can assume on the ground of a year's habitual residence (see s.19(2)(b)). However, if a question about the validity of the marriage arises in the course of divorce or separation and reference needs to be made to a foreign *lex loci celebrationis* (because a matter was celebrated abroad) or to a foreign *lex* (or *leges*) *domicilii*, where a question of capacity to marry arises, the matter will not be governed by English law—unless for the purposes of this section English law is taken to include its conflict of laws rules, which view does not commend itself.

Provision and availability of mediation

27. After section 13A of the 1988 Act, insert—

"**Provision and availability of mediation**
13B.—(1) The Board may secure the provision of mediation under this Part.

(2) If mediation is provided under this Part, it is to be available to any person whose financial resources are such as, under regulations, make him eligible for mediation.

(3) A person is not to be granted mediation in relation to any dispute unless mediation appears to the mediator suitable to the dispute and the parties and all the circumstances.

(4) A grant of mediation under this Part may be amended, withdrawn or revoked.

(5) The power conferred by subsection (1) shall be exercised in accordance with any directions given by the Lord Chancellor.

(6) Any contract entered into by the Board for the provision of mediation under this Part must require the mediator to comply with a code of practice.

(7) The code must require the mediator to have arrangements designed to ensure—

    (a) that parties participate in mediation only if willing and not influenced by fear of violence or other harm;

    (b) that cases where either party may be influenced by fear of violence or other harm are identified as soon as possible;

    (c) that the possibility of reconciliation is kept under review throughout mediation; and

    (d) that each party is informed about the availability of independent legal advice.

(8) Where there are one or more children of the family, the code must also require the mediator to have arrangements designed to ensure that the parties are encouraged to consider—

    (a) the welfare, wishes and feelings of each child; and

    (b) whether and to what extent each child should be given the opportunity to express his or her wishes and feelings in the mediation.

(9) A contract entered into by the Board for the provision of mediation under this Part must also include such other provision as the Lord Chancellor may direct the Board to include.

(10) Directions under this section may apply generally to contracts, or to contracts of any description, entered into by the Board, but shall not be made with respect to any particular contract."

DEFINITIONS
    "mediation": s.26(2).
    "mediator": s.26(3).

GENERAL NOTE
    This section amends the Legal Aid Act 1988 by inserting a new s.13B. This allows the Legal Aid Board to secure the provision of mediation to persons whose financial resources make them eligible for mediation under regulations. It also provides that mediation should be granted only if it appears to a mediator that mediation is suitable. There is to be a code of practice and mediators will be required to have arrangements designed to ensure that participation in mediation is genuinely voluntary (but see s.29). In addition it will require mediators to keep under review the possibility of reconciliation throughout mediation. Mediators are also to be required to ensure that parties are encouraged to consider the welfare, wishes and feelings of children and whether children should be given the opportunity to express wishes and feelings in the mediation.

Payment for mediation

28.—(1) After section 13B of the 1988 Act, insert—

"**Payment for mediation under this Part**
    13C.—(1) Except as provided by this section, the legally assisted person is not to be required to pay for mediation provided under this Part.
    (2) Subsection (3) applies if the financial resources of a legally assisted person are such as, under regulations, make him liable to make a contribution.
    (3) The legally assisted person is to pay to the Board in respect of the costs of providing the mediation, a contribution of such amount as is determined or fixed by or under the regulations.
    (4) If the total contribution made by a person in respect of any mediation exceeds the Board's liability on his account, the excess shall be repaid to him.
    (5) Regulations may provide that, where—
    (a) mediation under this Part is made available to a legally assisted person, and
    (b) property is recovered or preserved for the legally assisted person as a result of the mediation,
a sum equal to the Board's liability on the legally assisted person's account is, except so far as the regulations otherwise provide, to be a first charge on the property in favour of the Board.
    (6) Regulations under subsection (5) may, in particular, make provision—
    (a) as to circumstances in which property is to be taken to have been, or not to have been, recovered or preserved; and
    (b) as to circumstances in which the recovery or preservation of property is to be taken to be, or not to be, the result of any mediation.
    (7) For the purposes of subsection (5), the nature of the property and where it is situated is immaterial.
    (8) The power to make regulations under section 34(2)(f) and (8) is exercisable in relation to any charge created under subsection (5) as it is exercisable in relation to the charge created by section 16.
    (9) For the purposes of subsections (4) and (5), the Board's liability on any person's account in relation to any mediation is the aggregate amount of—
    (a) the sums paid or payable by the Board on his account for the mediation, determined in accordance with subsection (10);
    (b) any sums paid or payable in respect of its net liability on his account, determined in accordance with subsection (11) and the regulations–
            (i) in respect of any proceedings, and
            (ii) for any advice or assistance under Part III in connection with the proceedings or any matter to which the proceedings relate,
        so far as the proceedings relate to any matter to which the mediation relates; and
    (c) any sums paid or payable in respect of its net liability on his account, determined in accordance with the regulations, for any other advice or assistance under Part III in connection with the mediation or any matter to which the mediation relates.
    (10) For the purposes of subsection (9)(a), the sums paid or payable by the Board on any person's account for any mediation are—
    (a) sums determined under the contract between the Board and the mediator as payable by the Board on that person's account for the mediation; or

(b) if the contract does not differentiate between such sums and sums payable on any other person's account or for any other mediation, such part of the remuneration payable under the contract as may be specified in writing by the Board.

(11) For the purposes of subsection (9)(b), the Board's net liability on any person's account in relation to any proceedings is its net liability on his account under section 16(9)(a) and (b) in relation to the proceedings."

(2) In section 16(9), after paragraph (b) insert "and

"(c) if and to the extent that regulations so provide, any sums paid or payable in respect of the Board's liability on the legally assisted person's account in relation to any mediation in connection with any matter to which those proceedings relate."

(3) At the end of section 16, insert—

"(11) For the purposes of subsection (9)(c) above, the Board's liability on any person's account in relation to any mediation is its liability on his account under section 13C(9)(a) and (c) above in relation to the mediation."

DEFINITIONS
"mediation": s.26(2).

GENERAL NOTE
This amends the Legal Aid Act 1988 by inserting a new s.13C. It provides that, under regulations, contributions will be payable to the mediator in respect of mediation. It further provides that regulations may be made giving the Legal Aid Board a first charge on property recovered or preserved as a result of mediation. It also amends s.16 of the 1988 Act, so that regulations may provide that the costs of mediation are included in the charge created by that section in favour of the Legal Aid Board.

Mediation and civil legal aid

29. In section 15 of the 1988 Act, after subsection (3E) insert—

"(3F) A person shall not be granted representation for the purposes of proceedings relating to family matters, unless he has attended a meeting with a mediator—

(a) to determine—

(i) whether mediation appears suitable to the dispute and the parties and all the circumstances, and

(ii) in particular, whether mediation could take place without either party being influenced by fear of violence or other harm; and

(b) if mediation does appear suitable, to help the person applying for representation to decide whether instead to apply for mediation.

(3G) Subsection (3F) does not apply—

(a) in relation to proceedings under—

(i) Part IV of the Family Law Act 1996;

(ii) section 37 of the Matrimonial Causes Act 1973;

(iii) Part IV or V of the Children Act 1989;

(b) in relation to proceedings of any other description that may be prescribed; or

(c) in such circumstances as may be prescribed.

(3H) So far as proceedings relate to family matters, the Board, in determining under subsection (3)(a) whether, in relation to the proceedings, it is reasonable that a person should be granted representation under this Part—

(a) must have regard to whether and to what extent recourse to mediation would be a suitable alternative to taking the proceedings; and

(b) must for that purpose have regard to the outcome of the meeting held under subsection (3F) and to any assessment made for the purposes of section 13B(3)."

DEFINITIONS
"family matters": s.26(1).
"mediator": s.26(3).
"mediation": s.26(2).

GENERAL NOTE
This section amends s.15 of the Legal Aid Act 1988 by inserting new subss. (3F), (3G) and (3H), to provide that, for the purposes of determining whether to grant representation for the purposes of proceedings relating to family matters—with exceptions that are specified—there must first be a meeting with a mediator to determine whether mediation appears suitable and, if it does, to help the person applying for representation to decide whether instead to apply for mediation. The requirement to attend a meeting with a mediator before receiving legally aided representation is said to put parties in a better position to make an "informed choice" (*per* Lord Chancellor, *Hansard*, H.L. Vol. 573, col. 1104). This presumption in favour of mediation does not apply to proceedings under Pt. IV of the Act, the Parts of the Children Act dealing with the protection of children, or to s.37 of the Matrimonial Causes Act 1973.

PART IV

INTRODUCTION TO PT IV
The core of this Part of the Act was originally presented as the Family Homes and Domestic Violence Bill in 1995 as one further legislative response to what Sir George Baker P. called "domestic hooliganism" (see *Davis v. Johnson* [1978] 1 All E.R. 841, 860). There are, however, a number of major changes. The earliest legislation on domestic violence dates from 1878 (the invention of the "separation order"). The social problem was then discretely veiled until its rediscovery in the early 1970s. Erin Pizzey's *Scream Quietly or The Neighbours Will Hear* (Penguin, 1974) drew attention to the phenomenon of battered women in a dramatic way. There followed legislation in 1976 (the Domestic Violence and Matrimonial Proceedings Act) and in 1978 (the Domestic Proceedings and Magistrates' Courts Act, ss.16–18). There were landmark judicial decisions as well: *Davis v. Johnson* [1979] A.C. 264, establishing that ouster orders could be made for the benefit of non-entitled cohabitants; and *Richards v. Richards* [1984] A.C. 174, that the criteria governing the exercise of the judicial discretion to oust a spouse were found in s.1(3) of the Matrimonial Homes Act 1983, despite the fact that the original version of this Act had been enacted in 1967 to protect deserted wives rather than battered ones and it antedated the rediscovery of domestic violence by several years. Nor should the rejection of the marital rape immunity by the House of Lords in *R v. R* [1992] 1 A.C. 599 (confirmed in the Criminal Justice and Public Order Act 1994 (c. 33), s.142) be underestimated for there is a clear relationship between wife assault and marital rape (Irene Frieze (1983) 8 Signs 532).

Despite the legislation, and despite a shift in police attitudes from non-interventionist to pro-arrest (on the ambivalence of which, see Rebecca Morley and Audrey Mullender (1992) 6 International Journal of Law and the Family 265), violence against women in the domestic setting shows no sign of abating. Betsy Stanko recently called it the "most significant problem damaging the health and safety of women" and blamed "husbands, boyfriends, former spouses and intimate companions", a list which is particularly interesting in the light of the new Act (see (1993) 33 British Journal of Criminology 449). In 1990 there were 226 female homicide victims: of these 43 per cent were killed by their partners and 19 per cent by another member of the family. By contrast, of 381 male homicide victims, 9 per cent were killed by their partners (the statistics do not distinguish offensive from defensive killings) and 17 per cent by another member of the family. (See Home Office, *Gender and the Criminal Justice System*, HMSO, 1992). Wife-beating is perhaps the most under-reported crime. It will not be conquered by civil legislation. It is not a "breakdown in the social order", but rather "an affirmation of a particular sort of social order". It is "not dysfunctional: quite the reverse, it appears functional". It has to be "considered in a particular cultural context" (see M.D.A. Freeman, *State, Law and the Family: Critical Perspectives* (1984), Tavistock, at p.51). And its effects impact upon the children of the family too, so much so that wife-battering could be, and is now coming to be regarded as a form of child abuse.

This Part of this Act will no more remove domestic violence from our midst than previous legislation has done. Nevertheless, it contains measures which must be welcomed, even if the welcome can only be a qualified one.

The Background to this part of the Act

The Act is largely based on the recommendations of the Law Commission (*Domestic Violence and the Occupation of the Family Home* (1992) Law Com. No. 207) and reproduces to a large extent the Bill appended to that report. (For good critiques of the report and the Working Paper which preceded it see M. Hayes (1990) 53 M.L.R. 222 and M. Hayes and C. Williams (1992) 22 Fam Law 497.) Most of the Law Commission's recommendations were endorsed by the House of Commons Home Affairs Committee's report *Domestic Violence* (H.C. 245-I, 1993). The Committee rejected the Law Commission proposal to give the police the power to apply for orders (paras. 5.18–5.23 and draft clause 17) as "laudable but fundamentally misguided" (para. 118). The Act adopts the Law Commission view rather than that of the Home Affairs Committee. But it does not expressly give the police these powers: rather it allows for Rules of Court to be made for a "prescribed person" to be known as a "representative" to act on behalf of another in relation to Pt. IV proceedings (see s.60).

Of the existing law, the Law Commission said that the civil remedies provided were "complex, confusing and lack integration" (para. 1.2). They quote with approval Lord Scarman's remarks in *Richards v. Richards* [1984] A.C. 174, 206–207 that the statutory provisions were "a hotchpot of enactments of limited scope passed into law to meet specific situations or to strengthen the powers of specified courts. The sooner the range, scope and effect of these powers are rationalised into a coherent and comprehensive body of statute law, the better". The Law Commission accordingly saw its aims as (i) "to remove the gaps, anomalies and inconsistencies in the existing remedies, with a view to synthesising them, so far as possible, into a clear, simple and comprehensive code"; (ii) to retain the "level of protection" available under the existing law; and (iii) "to seek to avoid exacerbating hostilities between the adults involved, so far as this is compatible with providing proper and effective protection both for adults and for children" (this third goal being compatible with the Children Act 1989 and with its proposals for divorce which are now largely embodied in Pt. II of this Act) (para. 1.2).

The existing law has been the subject of considerable criticism both from academics and researchers and from the judiciary. As examples of the former may be cited J. Barron, *Not Worth the Paper ...?* (1990); S. Edwards and A. Halpern (1988) J.S.W.L. 110; and M. Wright (1980) N.L.J. 127. Much of the judicial criticism emphasised the limited jurisdiction of the 1976 Act, in particular the failure to address violence after parties have split up. As an example, see Lord Donaldson M.R. in *Duo v. Osborne (Formerly Duo)* [1992] 2 F.L.R. 425, who observed most appositely that "very often the need for a non-molestation injunction buttressed by a power of arrest is greater when the parties have recently split up or the marriage has recently ended than it was during the earlier stages in the relationship" (at pp.434–435). The law in relation to injunctions after marriages have broken up and after the end of cohabitations and relationships has been complex and confusing. Thorpe J. in *Pearson v. Franklin* attempted a "rational reconciliation" of a series of some nine reported cases since *Richards v. Richards*. He argued that all depended upon whether the parties were spouses, former spouses, cohabitants or former cohabitants (see [1994] 1 F.L.R. 246, 250), but such categorisation does scant justice to the mental gymnastics indulged in by the judges in these cases. That litigants in *Pearson v. Franklin* were encouraged to take advantage of a provision in the Children Act 1989 (s.15 and Sched. 1, para. 1(2)(e)(i)) which had not only not been designed to tackle this problem but, not surprisingly, contained no criteria governing the ouster discretion (which fact escaped the attention of the Court of Appeal) is worthy testimony to the failure of the legislation. Had the twins in *Pearson v. Franklin* not been the children of both parties, the Children Act provision would not have worked as the expedient it did (the couple not being married, the children could not have been "children of the family").

Where there should have been a code, there was a patchwork quilt, the pieces of which had not been sewn together very well. The new Act is an attempt to create a code. It provides for a single consistent set of remedies (non-molestation orders and occupation orders) which will be available in all courts having jurisdiction in family matters.

This part of the Act also makes important amendments to the Children Act 1989. In particular, it tackles the problem detected by the courts in *Nottinghamshire C.C. v. P* [1994] Fam 18, namely the restrictions upon local authorities using a prohibited steps order to exclude a sexually abusive father from the family home (although inherent jurisdiction has since been successfully invoked in *Re S* [1994] 1 F.L.R. 623 and in *Devon C.C. v. S* [1994] Fam. 169). There is now power to include an exclusion requirement in both an interim care order (see new s.38A of the Children Act 1989) and in an emergency protection order (see new s.44A of the Children Act 1989 (see Sched. 6)).

A Summary of this part of the Act's Provisions

The new orders in this part of the Act are designed to protect a designated list of persons set out in s.62 and classified as "associated persons". The Act thus rejects, as the Law Commission recommended it should (paras. 3.8–3.26), the precedents of New South Wales, South Australia, Western Australia and Tasmania, where the range of applicants is unlimited. To the Law Commission "to remove all restrictions would involve the creation of something approaching a new tort of harassment or molestation" (para. 3.8). But since the Law Commission Report the courts, moving away from *Patel v. Patel* [1988] 2 F.L.R. 179, have developed both the torts of trespass (see *Burnett v. George* [1992] 1 F.L.R. 525; *Pidduck v. Molloy* [1992] 2 F.L.R. 202) and that of nuisance (see *Khorasandjian v. Bush* [1993] Q.B. 727 and *Burris v. Azadani* [1996] 1 F.L.R. 266) and in so doing have undercut the Law Commission's reasoning. The scope of neither tortious action is entirely clear (see S. Cretney (1993) All E.R. Annual Review 231; A. Mullis (1993) All E.R. Annual Review; E. Cooke (1994) 57 M.L.R. 289; J. Ford (1994) 53 C.L.J. 14; J. Bridgeman and M.A. Jones (1994) 14 Legal Studies 180), and an opportunity for clarification has thus been missed. As a result of the Act those who have lived in the same household (see s.62(3)(c)) will be able to invoke the statutory remedies: those who have not, even if they have had a sexual relationship, will have to resort to the inchoate tort of "unreasonable harassment". It is clear that gay relationships are included within the scope of the Act, provided they come within s.62(3)(c).

The Act incorporates within its protective umbrella those children who come within the concept of "relevant child" (see s.62(2)). This widens the existing law, in particular by giving the court complete discretion to include any children whose interests the court considers relevant (see s.62(2)(c)).

Section 30 reproduces, with minor modifications, those subsections of s.1 of the Matrimonial Homes Act 1983 which are not separately found in other sections of this Act. (Thus subs. (2) is now s.33 of the 1996 Act; subsection (3) is now incorporated into s.33(6), (7) of the 1996 Act; and subs. (4) is now incorporated into s.33(10) of the 1996 Act). The new concept "matrimonial home rights" to describe statutory rights of occupation in the home granted under this Act replaces the term "rights of occupation", which was used in the 1983 Act. Section 30, subject to the provisions of the Act, gives protection against eviction to a spouse who is not entitled to occupy the dwelling-house to a spouse who is neither so entitled nor in occupation.

Section 31 largely reproduces s.2 of the Matrimonial Homes Act 1983. It provides that the matrimonial home rights given to a spouse by s.30 shall be a charge on the other spouse's estate or interest in the dwelling-house. What was s.2(5) of the 1983 Act is incorporated in s.30(3) of the 1996 Act.

Section 32 and Sched. 4 reproduce, with consequential amendments, the sections of the Matrimonial Homes Act 1983 relating to the conveyancing aspects of matrimonial home rights. Sections 3–6 of the 1983 Act are now found in Sched. 4, paras. 3–6 of the 1996 Act.

Section 33 is based on the Matrimonial Homes Act 1983, s.1(2). It deals with the court's power to make occupation orders where the applicant is entitled to occupy the dwelling-house either by virtue of matrimonial home rights under s.30, or by virtue of the general law. Under this section, an applicant entitled to occupy the dwelling-house may apply for an order against any one with whom she is associated, provided that the dwelling-house in question is or was intended by the other party to be their common home. The regulatory orders which may be made by the court are listed in s.33(3) and the factors to which the court is to have regard in making such orders are set out in s.33(6). These factors are subject to a balance of harm test which imposes an overriding requirement for the court to make an order if it appears that the applicant or child is likely to suffer significant harm if an order is *not* made which is greater than the harm the respondent or a child is likely to suffer if the order *is* made. "Harm" is defined in s.63.

The section also makes provision for declaratory orders (s.33(4)), and for matrimonial home rights to continue after the death of the other spouse or the termination of the marriage where it considers this appropriate (s.33(5)). Where an agreement to marry is terminated, an application can only be made within three years of the termination of the agreement (s.33(2)). An order under this section may be made for a specified period, until the occurrence of a specified event or until further order (s.33(10)).

Section 34 is taken from s.2(5) of the Matrimonial Homes Act 1983. It deals with the effect of an order under s.33 where one spouse's matrimonial home rights are a charge on the estate or interest of the other spouse or of the trustees for the other spouse, and a person has derived title under the other spouse or under the trustees.

Section 35 deals with the power of the court to make occupation orders when the applicant is not entitled to occupy the dwelling-house, but the respondent is so entitled. These applications may only be made between former spouses. The section confers certain occupation rights upon the applicant for the duration of the order, and it sets out the criteria to be applied by the court (s.35(6)). The section provides that orders under this section may contain certain regulatory provisions set out in subs. (5). It requires the court, in exercising its power to grant occupation rights under this section, to consider certain factors which are set out in s.35(6). These include conduct of the parties in relation to each other and otherwise, how recently they parted, the length of time since the marriage was dissolved or annulled, and the existence of any pending proceedings between them for financial provision or relating to the legal or beneficial ownership of the dwelling-house (s.35(6)). In addition, the section provides that an order under it cannot be made or continue to have effect after the death of either party and must be of limited duration (s.35(9), (10)).

Section 36 addresses the power of the court to make occupation orders when the applicant is a cohabitant or former cohabitant who is not entitled to occupy the dwelling house and the respondent is a cohabitant or former cohabitant who is so entitled. In addition to the factors which the court has to consider for former spouses under s.35, it must also consider certain additional factors including the nature of the parties' relationship (s.36(6)(e)), and whether there are any children (s.36(6)(g)). The maximum duration of orders is six months: they may be extended once only and only for up to six months (s.36(10)).

Section 37 allows occupation orders in favour of spouses and former spouses to be made where neither party is entitled to occupy the dwelling house. Orders must be limited so as to have effect for a specified period not exceeding six months, but may be extended on one or more occasions, but not by more than six months at a time. The court may make such of the regulatory orders listed in s.37(3) as might be relevant between two non-entitled parties (*viz.* to regulate the occupation of the dwelling-house; to require the respondent to leave the dwelling-house or part thereof; to require the respondent to allow the applicant to enter and remain in the dwelling-house; and to exclude the respondent from a defined area around the dwelling-house). The same criteria are to apply as under s.33(6) and (7).

Section 38 allows occupation orders in favour of cohabitants and former cohabitants to be made where neither party is entitled to occupy the dwelling-house. It also reproduces the effect of the Domestic Violence and Matrimonial Proceedings Act 1976 in this respect. It includes criteria for the exercise of jurisdiction, in part based on s.1(3) of the Matrimonial Homes Act 1983 (see s.38(4), (5)). Orders have a maximum duration of six months: they may be renewed for up to six months, but only once.

Section 39 defines an occupation order as an order under ss.33, 35, 36, 37 and 38, and regulates the circumstances in which they can be made. It provides that, if an application for an order is made under any of these sections and the court believes it does not have the power to make such an order, it may make an order under one of the other four sections (s.39(3)). Section 39(4) ensures that neither an application nor an order under any of the relevant sections will prevent either party from subsequently claiming an interest in the property unless the court has adjudicated upon the issue.

Section 40 provides for the court, when granting an occupation order under ss.33, 35 or 36 (or at any time thereafter) to make ancillary orders imposing certain obligations on either party or granting either party the possession or use of furniture or other contents contained in the dwelling-house. These obligations may relate to the repair and maintenance of the dwelling-house, the discharge of outgoings such as rent and mortgage, the payment of rent to the party who has been ousted, the taking of reasonable care of the furniture or other contents of the dwelling-house or the taking of reasonable steps to keep the dwelling-house and any contents secure.

Section 41 provides that, whenever the court is considering making an occupation order in favour of a cohabitant or former cohabitant, it must take into account the fact that the parties have not given each other the commitment involved in marriage.

Section 42 gives the court power to make non-molestation orders. "Molestation" is not defined in the Act. Although violence is a form of molestation, it is clear that molestation may take place without the threat or use of violence. The cases establish that any conduct which is a sufficient harassment of the victim as to call for intervention by the court can be the subject of a non-molestation order (see *Horner v. Horner* [1982] Fam. 90 (hanging of scurrilous notices on school railings); *Spencer v. Camacho* (1984) 4 F.L.R. 662 (rifling through handbag); *George v. George* [1986] 2 F.L.R. 347 (abusive letters and shouting obscenities); *Vaughan v. Vaughan* [1973] 1 W.L.R. 1159 (following applicant around and making "perfect nuisance" of oneself)). It was suggested in *Johnson v. Walton* [1990] 1 F.L.R. 350 that the respondent must intend to cause distress or harm, but this seems an unnecessary restriction.

The section extends the range of applicants who are eligible for protection by such an order to include, for example, former spouses, former cohabitants, relatives, parents of a child and parties to the same family proceedings. Where an agreement to marry is terminated, an application can only be made within three years of the termination of the agreement.

The criteria for a non-molestation order are set out in s.42(5). These include the requirement to have regard to the need to secure the health, safety and well-being of the applicant and of any relevant child.

Section 43 (which was not amongst the Law Commission's recommendations) provides that a child under the age of 16 years may only apply for an order with leave of the court and that the court may grant leave only if it is satisfied that the child has sufficient understanding to make the application. This follows precedents in the Children Act 1989. The implications of a child applying to exclude a parent are bound to be deemed controversial when the issue is confronted in practice, in rather the same way as the so-called cases of children "divorcing" their parents were so regarded in 1992 and 1993 (on this see M. Freeman in M. Freeman (ed.), *Divorce: Where Next?* (Dartmouth, 1996), p.159).

Section 44 sets out the evidence required to establish the existence of an agreement to marry (and takes account of betrothal and other similar ceremonies amongst religions and cultural minorities).

Section 45 deals with the power of the court to make *ex parte* orders, and sets out the matters the court must take into account when making such orders. In part the section adopts guidance laid down by Ormrod L.J. in the early case of *Ansah v. Ansah* [1977] Fam. 138, 142, 143 (which was quoted with approval by Lord Donaldson M.R. in *G v. G* [1990] 4 F.L.R. 395, 398, but which has been treated more specifically by Russell L.J. in *Jones v. Jones* [1993] 2 F.L.R. 377, 381 (Ormrod L.J.'s observations said to have little general principle)).

Section 46 enables the court to accept undertakings from any party to the proceedings. This was not in the Law Commission's recommendations and puts into statutory form long-standing practice. The section provides that an undertaking is enforceable in the same way as a court order, except that no power of arrest may be attached to an undertaking and the court may not accept an undertaking in circumstances where a power of arrest is appropriate.

Section 47 (and Sched. 5) provide for the court's powers to arrest for breach of, and to attach a power of arrest to, an occupation or non-molestation order. They extend and bring into line in all courts the enforcement procedures formerly found in s.18 of the Domestic Proceedings and Magistrates' Courts Act 1978 and s.2 of the Domestic Violence and Matrimonial Proceedings Act 1976. They give the High Court and the county court power to remand and power to issue arrest warrants and provide for bail requirements to be attached to a remand where necessary to ensure that there is no interference with witnesses, or to prevent other obstruction with the course of justice.

Section 48 gives the court new powers to remand the respondent for medical examination and reports. The need for this was drawn to the attention of the Law Commission by the Council of Her Majesty's Circuit Judges (see para. 5.17).

Section 49 provides for the variation and discharge of occupation orders and non-molestation orders.

Section 50 gives a magistrates' court power to suspend execution of a committal order relating to breach of certain requirements. The High Court and the county court already have this power.

Section 51 gives magistrates' courts the power to make a hospital order or guardianship order under s.37 of the Mental Health Act 1983 (c. 20) or an interim hospital order under s.38 of that Act for breach of an order or exclusion requirement, instead of a committal to custody. This is in line with their powers in other proceedings, and gives magistrates' courts similar powers to those of the higher courts in this respect.

Section 52 (together with Sched. 6) amends the Children Act 1989, plugging gaps that Parliament declined to fill during the passage of the Children Bill and which have caused problems in practice (as the case of *Nottinghamshire C.C. v. P* [1994] Fam 18 amply illustrates). It will now be possible for the court to make an ouster order for the protection of children when making an emergency protection order or when making an interim care order. This will permit the removal of a suspected abuser from the home and obviate the need to remove the child from an abusive environment.

Section 53 gives effect to Sched. 7. It is derived from the power to transfer tenancies in the Matrimonial Homes Act 1983, and extends the power to cohabitants. Schedule 7 enables the court to require the transferee to make a payment to the transferor. It also enables the court to defer the making of such a payment in certain circumstances.

Sections 54–56 are derived from s.8 of the Matrimonial Homes Act 1983, which is substantially reproduced. These provisions deal principally with the effect of matrimonial home rights and occupation rights orders on mortgages and the registration of charges.

Section 57, following the Children Act model, generally provides for a unified jurisdiction between the High Court, county courts and magistrates' courts. The Lord Chancellor is given the power to specify by order proceedings which may be commenced only in particular courts (s.57(3)–(5)) and for transfer of proceedings. An order may also be made for the principal registry of the Family Division of the High Court to be treated as if it were a county court (s.57(9)).

Section 58 provides for the powers of the court in relation to contempt of court to be exercised by the "relevant judicial authority" (this is defined in s.63(1)).

Section 59 provides for the powers of magistrates' courts under the Act. It stipulates that magistrates' courts do not have the power to determine property disputes. Magistrates may decline jurisdiction in any proceedings under the Act if they consider the case can more conveniently be dealt with by another court (s.59(2)).

Section 60 enables rules of court to be made authorising representatives to act on behalf of another in domestic violence proceedings. The section is "purely permissive and drawn widely" (*per* The Lord Chancellor, *Hansard*, H.L. Vol. 573, col. 1108). It could authorise the police (or probation or social services or other welfare organisations) to seek occupation orders or non-molestation orders on behalf of those entitled to do so themselves. The section is the result of a late initiative in the House of Commons.

Section 61 deals with the jurisdiction of courts to hear appeals.

Section 62 provides definitions, for this Part of the Act, of "cohabitants", "relevant child" and "associated persons". This is the first legislation to use these concepts, which are discussed in detail in the General Note to s.62. It should, though, be noted here that the Act uses the term "cohabitant", and not "cohabitee". It is to be hoped, and expected, that "cohabitant" will replace the more colloquial (but grammatically incorrect and arguably sexist) expression "cohabitee".

FAMILY HOMES AND DOMESTIC VIOLENCE

Rights to occupy matrimonial home

Rights concerning matrimonial home where one spouse has no estate, etc.

30.—(1) This section applies if—
  (a) one spouse is entitled to occupy a dwelling-house by virtue of
      (i) a beneficial estate or interest or contract; or
      (ii) any enactment giving that spouse the right to remain in occupation; and
  (b) the other spouse is not so entitled.
  (2) Subject to the provisions of this Part, the spouse not so entitled has the following rights ("matrimonial home rights")—
  (a) if in occupation, a right not to be evicted or excluded from the dwelling-house or any part of it by the other spouse except with the leave of the court given by an order under section 33;
  (b) if not in occupation, a right with the leave of the court so given to enter into and occupy the dwelling-house.
  (3) If a spouse is entitled under this section to occupy a dwelling-house or any part of a dwelling-house, any payment or tender made or other thing done by that spouse in or towards satisfaction of any liability of the other spouse in respect of rent, mortgage payments or other outgoings affecting the dwelling-house is, whether or not it is made or done in pursuance of an order under section 40, as good as if made or done by the other spouse.
  (4) A spouse's occupation by virtue of this section—
  (a) is to be treated, for the purposes of the Rent (Agriculture) Act 1976 and the Rent Act 1977 (other than Part V and sections 103 to 106 of that Act), as occupation by the other spouse as the other spouse's residence, and
  (b) if the spouse occupies the dwelling-house as that spouse's only or principal home, is to be treated, for the purposes of the Housing Act 1985 and Part I of the Housing Act 1988, as occupation by the other spouse as the other spouse's only or principal home.
  (5) If a spouse ("the first spouse")—
  (a) is entitled under this section to occupy a dwelling-house or any part of a dwelling-house, and
  (b) makes any payment in or towards satisfaction of any liability of the other spouse ("the second spouse") in respect of mortgage payments affecting the dwelling-house,
the person to whom the payment is made may treat it as having been made by the second spouse, but the fact that that person has treated any such payment as having been so made does not affect any claim of the first spouse against

the second spouse to an interest in the dwelling-house by virtue of the payment.

(6) If a spouse is entitled under this section to occupy a dwelling-house or part of a dwelling-house by reason of an interest of the other spouse under a trust, all the provisions of subsections (3) to (5) apply in relation to the trustees as they apply in relation to the other spouse.

(7) This section does not apply to a dwelling-house which has at no time been, and which was at no time intended by the spouses to be, a matrimonial home of theirs.

(8) A spouse's matrimonial home rights continue—

(a) only so long as the marriage subsists, except to the extent that an order under section 33(5) otherwise provides; and

(b) only so long as the other spouse is entitled as mentioned in subsection (1) to occupy the dwelling-house, except where provision is made by section 31 for those rights to be a charge on an estate or interest in the dwelling-house.

(9) It is hereby declared that a spouse—

(a) who has an equitable interest in a dwelling-house or in its proceeds of sale, but

(b) is not a spouse in whom there is vested (whether solely or as joint tenant) a legal estate in fee simple or a legal term of years absolute in the dwelling-house,

is to be treated, only for the purpose of determining whether he has matrimonial home rights, as not being entitled to occupy the dwelling-house by virtue of that interest.

DEFINITIONS

"dwelling-house": s.63(1) and (4).
"mortgage payments": s.63(1).

GENERAL NOTE

This section reproduces with some minor modifications part of s.1 of the Matrimonial Homes Act 1983. Other parts of this section are in ss.31, 32 and 34 of this Act. The new concept "matrimonial home rights"—to describe statutory rights of occupation in the home granted under this Act—replaces the term "rights of occupation", first used in the 1967 Matrimonial Homes Act and subsequently in the 1983 Act. The section, subject to the provisions of the Act, gives protection against eviction to a spouse who is not entitled to occupy the dwelling-house but who is in occupation, and gives the right, with the leave of the court, to occupy the dwelling-house to the spouse who is neither so entitled nor in occupation. The major innovation of this section (see s.30(7)) extends the rights under this section to a dwelling-house intended as a matrimonial home but never occupied as such (and see para. 4.4 of the Law Commission Report).

Subss. (1) and (2)

These subsections are derived from s.1(1) of the 1983 Act. They define the nature and extent of "matrimonial home rights".

One spouse. Rights to occupy the matrimonial home apply only to spouses.

Dwelling house. Note the breadth of the meaning of this (see s.63(1)).

Beneficial estate. With certain exceptions, ordinary rules of property law are applied to determine ownership of the matrimonial home: see *Pettitt v. Pettitt* [1970] A.C. 777 and *Gissing v. Gissing* [1971] A.C. 886.

Interest. Where documents are silent as regards beneficial interests, they are not necessarily conclusive as regards that interest: an implied, resulting or constructive trust may have been created.

Contract. On which, see *Balfour v. Balfour* [1919] 2 K.B. 571 and *Gould v. Gould* [1969] 3 All E.R. 728.

By virtue of any enactment. For example, a statutory tenant under the Rent Act or a secure tenant under the Housing Act 1985.

Not so entitled. This includes a spouse with an equitable interest: see s.30(9). This provision was not in the original Matrimonial Homes Act and was inserted by s.38 of the Matrimonial Proceedings and Property Act 1970. This was necessary since an equitable interest in unregistered land cannot be protected and could be defeated by a sale or mortgage by the other spouse.

Under s.30. The criteria for which are in s.33(6) and (7).

Not in occupation. A non-entitled spouse out of occupation has a conditional right of occupation which is capable of being protected in the manner prescribed by the Act. But it cannot be enforced until leave is obtained (see *Watts v. Waller* [1973] 1 Q.B. 153). So her charge may be registered even though she has not yet been given leave by the court to enter and occupy. If she then were to make an unsuccessful application for leave, the registration would be cancelled.

Subs. (3)

This subsection, which is derived from s.1(5) of the 1983 Act, ensures that a spouse having matrimonial home rights may pay rent, mortgage payments or other outgoings affecting the dwelling-house, and that this shall have the same effect as if done by the other spouse.

Any payment. The stumbling block is that the mortgagee is not bound to give the non-entitled spouse notice of the entitled spouse's default. See the facts of *Hastings and Thanet Building Society v. Goddard* [1970] 1 W.L.R. 1544, where the Court of Appeal rejected suggestions that a mortgagor's spouse in occupation should be given notice of the proceedings or that he or she should be informed that the mortgagor had fallen into arrears (see p.1548). Further, even if the non-entitled spouse becomes aware of the position and is made a party to re-possession proceedings at the outset, the court has only limited power to afford time for payment (see the Administration of Justice Act 1970, s.36). See also, s.40(1)(b).

Subs. (4)

This subsection is derived from s.1(6) of the 1983 Act. It ensures that occupation by a spouse with matrimonial home rights is treated as occupation by the other spouse for the purpose of certain enactments dealing with security of tenure. The wording of s.1(6) has been amended slightly in both paragraphs. In (a), the original s.1(6) had provided that a spouse's occupation be treated as "possession" for the purposes of the Rent (Agriculture) Act 1976 (c. 80) and the Rent Act 1977 (c. 42). But, the protection of these enactments is dependent on the occupation rather than possession of the tenant. In (b), the original s.1(6) had stated that a spouse's occupation by virtue of this section be treated as occupation by the other spouse for the purpose of the Housing Acts. But to obtain protection as a secure tenant or an assured tenant under the Housing Acts, the tenant must occupy the dwelling-house "as his only or principal home".

Subs. (5)

This subsection reproduces s.1(7) of the 1983 Act without substantive change. It provides that a mortgagee may treat the payment of mortgage instalments by a spouse with matrimonial home rights as having been made by the other spouse. Such payments do not affect the right of the paying spouse to claim the acquisition of an interest in the property by virtue of such payment.

Subs. (6)

This subsection reproduces s.1(8) of the 1983 Act without substantive change. It provides that where a spouse has matrimonial home rights by reason of the other spouse being a beneficiary under a trust, then subss. (3) to (5) apply in relation to the trustees.

Subs. (7)

This subsection is largely derived from s.1(10) of the 1983 Act, but the scope of this is extended so that the new subsection now applies to a dwelling-house which has been or was intended by both spouses to be a matrimonial home (implementing the recommendation in para. 4.4 of the Law Commission report).

Been ... a matrimonial home. The section thus does not apply to a dwelling-house where a couple have lived together only before marriage, unless both of them intended this to be their matrimonial home after they married. Nor does it apply to property acquired in the name of one spouse after a separation. *Syed v. Syed* (1980) 1 F.L.R. 129 would still pose the same problems (no implied licence to occupy).

Subs. (8)

This subsection provides that matrimonial home rights subsist for the duration of the marriage only, unless an order is made extending them beyond divorce or death (under s.33(5)). It also provides that they subsist only so long as the other spouse is entitled to occupy the matrimonial home, except where provision is made (see s.31) for those rights to be a charge on an estate or interest in the home.

Subs. (9)

This subsection, which reproduces s.1(11) of the 1983 Act, provides that a spouse who has an equitable as opposed to a legal interest in the home, or in its proceeds of sale, has the same matrimonial home rights as has a spouse who has no interest in the home at all.

Equitable interest. It is important for a spouse who believes she has an equitable interest to register her matrimonial home rights under s.31 because there is always the danger that a court may subsequently decide she does not have an equitable interest. This is of particular import- ance in the case of unregistered land because an equitable interest is not registerable as a land charge under the Land Charges Act 1972 (c. 61). In such circumstances she is afforded protec- tion if she remains on the premises by the doctrine of constructive notice even when her husband is also in occupation (see *Hodgson v. Marks* [1971] Ch. 892, 934–935; *Williams and Glyn's Bank Ltd v. Boland* [1981] A.C. 487, 505–506, 511; and *Kingsnorth Finance Ltd v. Tizard* [1986] 2 All E.R. 54; but *cf Caunce v. Caunce* [1969] 1 All E.R. 722. But if she leaves, then her equitable interest—and the right of occupation which flows from that interest—may well be defeated by a purchaser for value without notice of it.

Effect of matrimonial home rights as charge on dwelling-house

31.—(1) Subsections (2) and (3) apply if, at any time during a marriage, one spouse is entitled to occupy a dwelling-house by virtue of a beneficial estate or interest.

(2) The other spouse's matrimonial home rights are a charge on the estate or interest.

(3) The charge created by subsection (2) has the same priority as if it were an equitable interest created at whichever is the latest of the following dates—

(a) the date on which the spouse so entitled acquires the estate or interest;
(b) the date of the marriage; and
(c) 1st January 1968 (the commencement date of the Matrimonial Homes Act 1967).

(4) Subsections (5) and (6) apply if, at any time when a spouse's matri- monial home rights are a charge on an interest of the other spouse under a trust, there are, apart from either of the spouses, no persons, living or unborn, who are or could become beneficiaries under the trust.

(5) The rights are a charge also on the estate or interest of the trustees for the other spouse.

(6) The charge created by subsection (5) has the same priority as if it were an equitable interest created (under powers overriding the trusts) on the date when it arises.

(7) In determining for the purposes of subsection (4) whether there are any persons who are not, but could become, beneficiaries under the trust, there is to be disregarded any potential exercise of a general power of appointment exercisable by either or both of the spouses alone (whether or not the exer- cise of it requires the consent of another person).

(8) Even though a spouse's matrimonial home rights are a charge on an estate or interest in the dwelling-house, those rights are brought to an end by—

(a) the death of the other spouse, or
(b) the termination (otherwise than by death) of the marriage,
unless the court directs otherwise by an order made under section 33(5).

(9) If—

(a) a spouse's matrimonial home rights are a charge on an estate or inter- est in the dwelling-house, and
(b) that estate or interest is surrendered to merge in some other estate or interest expectant on it in such circumstances that, but for the merger, the person taking the estate or interest would be bound by the charge,

the surrender has effect subject to the charge and the persons thereafter entitled to the other estate or interest are, for so long as the estate or interest surrendered would have endured if not so surrendered, to be treated for all purposes of this Part as deriving title to the other estate or interest under the other spouse or, as the case may be, under the trustees for the other spouse, by virtue of the surrender.

(10) If the title to the legal estate by virtue of which a spouse is entitled to occupy a dwelling-house (including any legal estate held by trustees for that spouse) is registered under the Land Registration Act 1925 or any enactment replaced by that Act—

    (a) registration of a land charge affecting the dwelling-house by virtue of this Part is to be effected by registering a notice under that Act; and

    (b) a spouse's matrimonial home rights are not an overriding interest within the meaning of that Act affecting the dwelling-house even though the spouse is in actual occupation of the dwelling-house.

(11) A spouse's matrimonial home rights (whether or not constituting a charge) do not entitle that spouse to lodge a caution under section 54 of the Land Registration Act 1925.

(12) If—

    (a) a spouse's matrimonial home rights are a charge on the estate of the other spouse or of trustees of the other spouse, and

    (b) that estate is the subject of a mortgage,

then if, after the date of the creation of the mortgage ("the first mortgage"), the charge is registered under section 2 of the Land Charges Act 1972, the charge is, for the purposes of section 94 of the Law of Property Act 1925 (which regulates the rights of mortgagees to make further advances ranking in priority to subsequent mortgages), to be deemed to be a mortgage subsequent in date to the first mortgage.

(13) It is hereby declared that a charge under subsection (2) or (5) is not registrable under subsection (10) or under section 2 of the Land Charges Act 1972 unless it is a charge on a legal estate.

DEFINITIONS
    "dwelling-house": s.63(1), (4).
    "matrimonial home rights": s.30(2).
    "mortgage": s.63(1).
    "mortgagee": s.63(1).

GENERAL NOTE
    This section reproduces s.2 of the 1983 Act with some minor changes. References in the 1983 Act to "rights of occupation" are changed to "matrimonial home rights". What was s.2(5) of the 1983 Act will now be found in s.30(3).

Subss. (1) to (3)
    These subsections provide that, where at any time during the subsistence of the marriage, one spouse is entitled to occupy a dwelling-house by virtue of a beneficial estate or interest, the other spouse's rights of occupation shall be a charge on that estate or interest, having the like priority as if it were an equitable interest created at whichever is the latest of the following dates: (i) the date when the spouse so entitled acquires the estate or interest; (ii) the date of the marriage; (iii) January 1, 1968. It has been said that advisers of a spouse with a right of occupation should consider a precautionary registration when the state of the marriage offers any risk to the occupying spouse (*Miles v. Bull* [1969] 1 Q.B. 258, 260).
    Priority. As to the priority of a Class F charge, see *Hastings and Thanet Building Society v. Goddard* [1970] 1 W.L.R. 1242, overruled [1970] 1 W.L.R. 1544; see also *Perez-Adamson v. Perez-Rivas* [1987] Fam. 89 and *Whittingham v. Whittingham* [1979] Fam. 9. As to the improper use of such a charge (and its setting aside) see *Barnett v. Hassett* [1982] 1 W.L.R. 1385. For the rights of tenants in common in actual possession see *City of London Building Society v. Flegg* [1988] A.C. 54 (distinguishing *Williams and Glyn's Bank v. Boland* [1981] A.C. 487). As to the relevant date for ascertaining whether an interest in registered land was protected by actual occupation as an overriding interest, and as to what constitutes actual occupation at the relevant time, see *Lloyds Bank plc v. Rosset* [1991] 1 A.C. 107.
    Dwelling-house. Note that the wider meaning of this does not apply in this context.
    Estate. See note on s.30.
    Interest. See note on s.30.

Subss. (4) to (6)
    This subsection provides that if, at any time when a spouse's rights of occupation are a charge on an interest of the other spouse under a trust, and there are, the spouses apart, no persons,

living or unborn, who are or could become beneficiaries under the trust, those rights shall be a charge also on the estate or interest of the trustees for the other spouse, having the like priority as if it were an equitable interest created, under powers overriding the trusts on the date when it arises.

Subs. (7)
This subsection provides that in determining for the purposes of the previous subsection whether there are any persons who could become beneficiaries under the trust, there is to be disregarded any potential exercise of a general power of appointment exercisable by either or both of the spouses alone (whether or not such exercise requires the consent of another person).

Subs. (8)
This subsection provides that, notwithstanding that a spouse's rights of occupation are a charge on an estate or interest, those rights shall be brought to an end by the death of the other spouse or by divorce or nullity, unless during the marriage the court has ordered that this shall not be so (it may do so under s.33(5) and in circumstances without restriction: previously it could only do so in the event of a matrimonial dispute or estrangement).

Subs. (9)
This subsection provides that where a spouse's rights of occupation are a charge on an estate or interest, and that estate or interest is surrendered so as to merge in some other estate or interest expectant thereon in such circumstances that, but for the merger, the person taking the estate or interest surrendered would be bound by the charge, the surrender shall have effect subject to the charge, and the persons thereafter entitled to the other estate or interest shall, for so long as the estate or interest surrendered would have endured, if not so surrendered, be treated for all purposes of this Act as deriving title to the other estate or interest under the other spouse or, as the case may be, under the trustees for the other spouse by virtue of the surrender.

Subs. (10)
This subsection provides that where the title to the legal estate by virtue of which a spouse is entitled to occupy a dwelling-house is registered, registration of a land charge affecting it is effected by registering a notice under the Land Registration Act 1925 (c. 21). This applies also where the legal estate is held by trustees for that spouse. The subsection also provides that a spouse's rights of occupation shall not be an overriding interest within the meaning of the 1925 Act, notwithstanding that the spouse is in actual occupation of the dwelling-house.
Notice. See also the Matrimonial Homes and Property Act 1981 (c. 24), s.4(1), which provides for amendment of the Land Registration Act 1925, s.64, so as to obviate the need to produce a land certificate when application is made for registration of a notice.

Subs. (11)
This subsection provides that a spouse's rights of occupation do not entitle that spouse to lodge a caution under the Land Registration Act.

Subs. (12)
This subsection provides that where a spouse's rights of occupation are a charge on the estate of the other spouse (or trustees for the other spouse), and the estate is the subject of a mortgage, then if, after the creation of the mortgage, the charge is registered, the charge shall for the purposes of s.94 of the Law of Property Act 1925 be deemed to be a mortgage subsequent in date to the first-mentioned mortgage (which will accordingly take priority).

Subs. (13)
This subsection provides that a charge under s.5(1) or (2) of this Act is not registrable by notice under s.2 of the Land Charges Act 1972 or s.5(6) of this Act, unless it is a charge on a legal estate.

Further provisions relating to matrimonial home rights

32. Schedule 4 re-enacts with consequential amendments and minor modifications provisions of the Matrimonial Homes Act 1983.

GENERAL NOTE
This section, with Sched. 1, reproduces with consequential amendments, the sections of the 1983 Act relating to the conveyancing aspects of matrimonial home rights. See further the General Note to Sched. 4, below.

Occupation orders

Occupation orders where applicant has estate or interest etc. or has matrimonial home rights

  33.—(1) If—

(a) a person ("the person entitled")—

    (i) is entitled to occupy a dwelling-house by virtue of a beneficial estate or interest or contract or by virtue of any enactment giving him the right to remain in occupation, or

    (ii) has matrimonial home rights in relation to a dwelling-house, and

(b) the dwelling-house—

    (i) is or at any time has been the home of the person entitled and of another person with whom he is associated, or

    (ii) was at any time intended by the person entitled and any such other person to be their home,

the person entitled may apply to the court for an order containing any of the provisions specified in subsections (3), (4) and (5).

  (2) If an agreement to marry is terminated, no application under this section may be made by virtue of section 62(3)(e) by reference to that agreement after the end of the period of three years beginning with the day on which it is terminated.

  (3) An order under this section may—

(a) enforce the applicant's entitlement to remain in occupation as against the other person ("the respondent");

(b) require the respondent to permit the applicant to enter and remain in the dwelling-house or part of the dwelling-house;

(c) regulate the occupation of the dwelling-house by either or both parties;

(d) if the respondent is entitled as mentioned in subsection (1)(a)(i), prohibit, suspend or restrict the exercise by him of his right to occupy the dwelling-house;

(e) if the respondent has matrimonial home rights in relation to the dwelling-house and the applicant is the other spouse, restrict or terminate those rights;

(f) require the respondent to leave the dwelling-house or part of the dwelling-house; or

(g) exclude the respondent from a defined area in which the dwelling-house is included.

  (4) An order under this section may declare that the applicant is entitled as mentioned in subsection (1)(a)(i) or has matrimonial home rights.

  (5) If the applicant has matrimonial home rights and the respondent is the other spouse, an order under this section made during the marriage may provide that those rights are not brought to an end by—

(a) the death of the other spouse; or

(b) the termination (otherwise than by death) of the marriage.

  (6) In deciding whether to exercise its powers under subsection (3) and (if so) in what manner, the court shall have regard to all the circumstances including—

(a) the housing needs and housing resources of each of the parties and of any relevant child;

(b) the financial resources of each of the parties;

(c) the likely effect of any order, or of any decision by the court not to exercise its powers under subsection (3), on the health, safety or well-being of the parties and of any relevant child; and

(d) the conduct of the parties in relation to each other and otherwise.

(7) If it appears to the court that the applicant or any relevant child is likely to suffer significant harm attributable to conduct of the respondent if an order under this section containing one or more of the provisions mentioned in subsection (3) is not made, the court shall make the order unless it appears to it that—

   (a) the respondent or any relevant child is likely to suffer significant harm if the order is made; and

   (b) the harm likely to be suffered by the respondent or child in that event is as great as, or greater than, the harm attributable to conduct of the respondent which is likely to be suffered by the applicant or child if the order is not made.

(8) The court may exercise its powers under subsection (5) in any case where it considers that in all the circumstances it is just and reasonable to do so.

(9) An order under this section—

   (a) may not be made after the death of either of the parties mentioned in subsection (1); and

   (b) except in the case of an order made by virtue of subsection (5)(a), ceases to have effect on the death of either party.

(10) An order under this section may, in so far as it has continuing effect, be made for a specified period, until the occurrence of a specified event or until further order.

DEFINITIONS

   "associated": s.62(3).
   "court; the": s.57.
   "dwelling-house": s.63(1) and (4).
   "harm": s.63(1), (3).
   "health": s.63(1).
   "matrimonial home rights": s.30.
   "relevant child": s.62(2).

GENERAL NOTE

This section deals with the court's power to make occupation orders where the applicant is entitled to occupy the dwelling-house either by virtue of the general law or by virtue of matrimonial home rights under s.30. Under this section, an applicant entitled to occupy the dwelling-house may apply for an order against anyone with whom he is associated, provided that the dwelling-house in question is, or was, intended by both parties to be their common home.

The section lists the regulatory orders which may be made by the court and sets out the factors to which the court is to have regard in making such orders. These factors are subject to a balance of harm test which imposes an overriding requirement for the court to make an order if it appears that the applicant or child is likely to suffer significant harm if an order is not made which is greater than the harm that the respondent or a child is likely to suffer if the order is made. Provision is also made for declaratory orders and for matrimonial home rights to continue after the death of the other spouse or the termination of the marriage where it considers it appropriate. Where an agreement to marry is terminated, an application can only be made within three years of the termination of the agreement.

An order under this section may be for a specified period, until the occurrence of a specified event, or until further order. See also s.39: the court may make an order under ss.35 and 37 where it has no power to make an order under s.33 (s.39(3)). See also the additional provisions that can be included in an occupation order (s.40).

Subs. (1)

This subsection provides that any person so entitled may apply for an occupation order against anyone with whom s/he is associated (as defined in s.62(3)), provided that the dwelling-house in question is, was or was intended by both parties to be their common home.

Estate … interest … contract … enactment. See the General Note to s.30, above.

Subs. (2)

This subsection provides that where an agreement to marriage is terminated, an application may only be made within three years of the termination.

Agreement to marry. On the evidence for which, see s.44.

Terminated. The date of a termination may not always be clear. The Act requires no evidence as such of termination. Disputes may well hinge upon what constitutes termination of an engagement. Is an agreement to marry terminated by a demand for the return of an engagement ring or only when it is returned? Is the unrequested return of a ring a termination of the agreement to marry or is it necessary that he accepts its return?

Subs. (3)

This subsection lists the "regulatory" orders which may be included in an order made under this section. The factors to which the court is to have regard in making regulatory orders are set out in s.33(6), but these are subject to the "balance of harm" test in s.33(7). This imposes an overriding requirement for the court to make an order if it appears that the applicant or a child is likely to suffer significant harm if an order is not made which is greater than the harm that the respondent or a child is likely to suffer if the order is made.

(*a*) *Remain.* To be used to prevent eviction. See also s.33(4) (it may be coupled with a declaratory order).

(*b*) *Enter and remain.* This order may only have value if used in conjunction with the order in paragraph (f) (and see *Davis v. Johnson* [1979] A.C. 264, 342 *per* Lord Salmon). It was also said by Lord Salmon *obiter* (*ibid*) that an order of this nature (he was referring to a similar one in the DVMPA 1976) should not be made unless the court was satisfied that the applicant was driven from the home by serious molestation or locked out without reasonable justification. It is submitted that these qualifications were both unnecessary and unjustified and that the dictum should not be followed. It should be noted that there is no power to require the respondent to permit a *relevant child* to enter and remain. This omission—also in earlier legislation—is strange but should not cause difficulties in practice. A respondent who will not allow a child to re-enter could himself be required to leave.

Part of the dwelling-house. This can be used by applicants excluded from the whole dwelling-house and by those already in the dwelling-house but excluded from a part of it.

(*c*) *Regulate the occupation.* This language is extraordinarily wide. In practice such an order is likely to find its readiest use where contact arrangements envisage the non-residential parent spending time with the children in the former matrimonial home.

(*d*) *Prohibit.* See s.33(10) on duration.

(*e*) *Restrict.* See s.33(10) on duration.

(*f*) *Part.* Such as a bedroom.

(*g*) *Defined area.* The meaning of "area" has not been classified by the courts. Examples of orders are that the respondent should not enter "that area of King's Lynn in which lies the matrimonial home" (see *Tuck v. Nicholls* [1989] 1 F.L.R. 283) and an order in *Vaughan v. Vaughan* [1973] 3 All E.R. 449 not to go within 50 miles of the wife—this part of the order was widely reported in newspapers but is not in the law report). It was said by Hale J., giving evidence to the Special Public Committee, that courts have "got to be very careful not to use the power oppressively" (*Minutes*, para. 39). In *Burris v. Azadani* [1996] 1 F.L.R. 266 the Court of Appeal accepted the concept of an "exclusion zone" order. Neither statute nor authority precluded the making of such an order.

Subs. (4)

This subsection gives the court power to declare that the applicant is entitled to occupy a dwelling house or has matrimonial home rights. The criteria in s.33(6) do not apply. An order under this subsection does not need criteria "as in principle these rights exist automatically and independently of the merits of enforcing or retaining them" (Law Com. para. 4.3).

Subs. (5)

This subsection (together with s.33(8)) enables the court to provide for matrimonial home rights to continue after the death of the other spouse or the termination of the marriage where it considers that in all the circumstances it is just and reasonable to do so.

Brought to an end. But note that the order may be for a specified period, until the occurrence of a specified event or until further order (see s.7(10)). The Law Commission cites as an example: "the spouse might be permitted to occupy the dwelling house for a certain length of time or until a certain event occurred, such as the conclusion of a claim under the Inheritance (Provision for Family and Dependants) Act 1975 (c. 63).

Termination. I.e., by divorce and, presumably, by annulment. Under the Matrimonial Causes Act 1973 a marriage is terminated by a decree absolute (see *Hennie v. Hennie* [1993] 2 F.L.R. 351). When Pt. II of this Act comes into operation it will be terminated ("dissolved") by an order which comes into force on being made (s.2(2)).

Subs. (6)

This subsection sets out the criteria to be used by the courts in making regulatory orders. These are subject to a "balance of harm" test in s.33(7). There is no attempt to prioritise the welfare of any relevant child. The Law Commission clearly rejected suggestions that regulatory orders should be governed by a welfare paramountcy test (see paras. 4.29–4. 31 and *Minutes* paras. 17–18). The 1995 Bill did not refer to conduct: the 1996 Act specifically includes this.

All the circumstances. And not, therefore, only those listed. The Law Commission in its Working Paper No. 113, *Domestic Violence and Occupation of the Family Home* (1989) thought it difficult to know what matters might be thought relevant under this head (see p.27). The fact that the house is owned and/or lived in by other persons could be a relevant circumstance: see *Chaudhry v. Chaudhry* [1987] 1 F.L.R. 347 (wife sought order to re-enter home of which father-in-law was joint owner with husband and house was partly occupied by the husband's relatives). Disapproved as considerations are (i) to allow the dust to settle (*Summers v. Summers* [1986] 1 F.L.R. 343) and (ii) to bring a man to his senses (*Burke v. Burke* [1987] 2 F.L.R. 71). As far as orders which oust are concerned (and (d), (e), (f) and (g) may come into this category), courts have insisted that, since such orders are "Draconian" they require strong justification (*Summers v. Summers* [1986] 1 F.L.R. 343; *Wiseman v. Simpson* [1988] 1 W.L.R. 35; *Shipp v. Shipp* [1988] 1 F.L.R. 345; *Blackstock v. Blackstock* [1991] 2 F.L.R. 308). It is to be assumed that courts will continue to see ousting in whatever shape as a last resort: the "Draconian" rhetoric is unlikely to be lost. The "balance of harm" test in s.33(7) may ultimately diminish the force of this sentiment, but the two principles are reconcilable: the order, it may be argued, is not Draconian where the likelihood of the applicant or a relevant child suffering significant harm is greater than that which the respondent or a relevant child might suffer in the event of an order being made.

Housing needs ... resources of the parties. Note the remarks of Purchas L.J. in *G v. J (Ouster Order)* [1993] 1 F.L.R. 1008 ("The court has no power to decide such a case simply as a matter of housing policy"). Where the respondent has a source of alternative accommodation, courts have been more willing to exclude (see *Baggott v. Baggott* [1986] 1 F.L.R. 377; *Scott v. Scott* [1992] 1 F.L.R. 529). But even where there is an alternative source, it does not follow that the court will exclude the respondent (see *Shipp v. Shipp* [1988] 1 F.L.R. 345, where it was said by the Court of Appeal that the possible practical impact of a temporary ouster order "might make it practically impossible for the husband to reverse the arrangements which he would be bound to make in the intervening period and go back to live in the matrimonial home, if it was held at the adjourned hearing that he should be allowed to do so" *per* Nourse L.J. at p.347). It has been held that the prospect of the parties being rehoused by a local authority is a relevant factor, so that an application by a wife may be refused if the housing authority has a statutory obligation under the Housing Act 1985 to rehouse her but not her husband (see *Wooton v. Wooton* [1984] F.L.R. 871; *Thurley v. Smith* [1984] F.L.R. 875). "Courts are in effect being used (by housing authorities) to provide a lever which enables the authority to take certain decisions which it is reluctant to take without a court order" (*per* D. Pearl in M. Freeman (ed.), *Essays in Family Law* (1985), p.20, 21). Thornton's warning should also be noted: "if the authorities concerned continue to insist upon exclusion orders as a prerequisite to housing, they will risk trapping battered women in a "Catch 22" position, unable to secure rehousing without an order, and unable to obtain an order because of the housing duties owed to them" ((1989) JSWL 67, 73).

There will be cases where housing needs can be satisfied without excluding the respondent (by, for example, regulating occupation or by restricting rights or by requiring the respondent to leave part of the house). Indeed, he may be agreeable to one of these solutions, and she may be better off with such an order than no order at all. (It is worth examining *G v. J* [1993] 1 F.L.R. 1008, where he offered to live separately from her under the same roof and eventually she failed to have him ousted, despite allegations of violence). An instance where the Court of Appeal approved such an arrangement is *E v. E (Ouster Order)* [1995] 1 F.L.R. 224, and it did so despite accepting evidence that the husband had twice tried to rape his wife. Although where allegations of rape or attempted rape are substantiated "one would normally expect an ouster order to follow" (*per* Balcombe L.J. at p.225), the court was impressed (perhaps over-impressed) by the wife's evidence "Separate rooms would help, yes. I don't necessarily want him to go. I want my safety and peace. I don't want any more aggravation". It is doubtful whether under this legislation *E v. E* would be decided similarly: note s.33(6)(c)—did the court give sufficient consideration to the wife's "safety"?

Housing needs ... of any relevant child. In *Richards v. Richards* [1984] A.C. 174, the House of Lords rejected the notion that occupancy of the matrimonial home should be governed by the paramountcy principle. The Court of Appeal has said (see *Gibson v. Austin* [1992] 2 F.L.R. 437 and *R v. M* [1994] 1 F.L.R. 760) that *Richards v. Richards* has not been overruled by s.1(1) of the Children Act 1989, though its rejection of the argument is far from convincing—where the father lives surely relates to the "upbringing" of the child). The cases examining housing needs of the children need to be scrutinised in the light of the "balance of harm" test in this Act and the new criterion in s.33(6) ("health, safety or well-being"). In *Re T (A Minor); T v. T (Ouster Order)* [1987] 1 F.L.R. 181 it has been held that normally the court should first decide who is to be the parent with whom the children are to have their home, and then go on to decide whether or not to oust the other parent. An application for an occupation order may be made upon an application for a residence order (see s.39(2)), and this should be done where the issue of occupation of the home arises at the same time as an application for a residence order under s.8 of the Children Act 1989. (For problems where this was not done see *Re M (Minors) (Disclosure of Evidence)* [1994] 1 F.L.R. 760.)

In *Lee v. Lee* [1984] F.L.R. 243 the Court of Appeal accorded considerable weight to "the needs of children to re-establish a family unit in the family home". But note that the child was in care and a return to the home hinged on the mother's accommodation being improved. But *cf Tuck v. Nicholls* [1989] 1 F.L.R. 283 ("nobody would wish to leave a baby in circumstances where that child might be at risk". Nevertheless the possibility was countenanced of leaving the child in the same house as a child sex abuser); and *G v. J (Ouster Order)* [1993] 1 F.L.R. 1008 (where the Court of Appeal was unwilling to give decisive weight to the interests of the child where the merits of the case were evenly divided between the adult parties); and see also *Wiseman v. Simpson* [1988] 1 W.L.R. 35 and *Blackstock v. Blackstock* [1991] 2 F.L.R. 308. The case of *G v. J (Ouster Order)* is particularly instructive for understanding the new law. The county court judge had ousted the father because "the combination of needs of [the mother] and [the 6-month-old child] indicates that the balance is in favour of them residing in the house" (p.1012). What tipped the balance was the "primacy" of the baby's interest (he stressed "primacy", not "paramountcy"). The Court of Appeal ruled that this "tipping of the balance" approach was not the correct test and was short of what was required to justify, what they reiterated was, a Draconian order. It is submitted that the county court judge's reasoning anticipated the language of this Act and that under the "balance of harm" test the father would be ousted. The allegations in *G v. J*, if satisfactorily proved, offer clear evidence that the baby was at risk of significant harm immeasurably greater than the inconvenience the father would suffer by being forced to leave his home. Another case which, it is submitted, would now be decided differently is *Hopper v. Hopper* (note) [1978] 1 W.L.R. 1342.

Financial resources. See, as an example of where this influenced the court, *Baggott v. Baggott* [1986] 1 F.L.R. 377 (the husband obviously had financial resources because he had offered to raise £20,000 to provide a fund to enable either himself or his wife to live elsewhere).

Likely effect of any order. The importance of producing the necessary evidence cannot be stressed too much. See *Wiseman v. Simpson* [1988] 1 W.L.R. 35 (mother claimed that arguing between parents was retarding the development of 18-month-old child but no evidence brought to support this allegation: the Court of Appeal accepted that expert evidence not essential but concluded assertions too uncertain a basis for a finding that child's development was being retarded and, if so, for any causative link between home tensions and this). In view of the importance of producing professional evidence (and this includes social work and police evidence as well as medical and psychiatric assessments), the impact of recent case law developments should be noted. For example, should the ruling in *Oxfordshire County Council v. M* [1994] 1 F.L.R. 175 (that legal professional privilege has to yield to the overriding principle in the Children Act and in wardship jurisdiction, that the interests of children are paramount) extend by analogy to questions of occupation orders? The reluctance of the Court of Appeal, even after the Children Act, to apply children principles to ouster applications suggests not; but is it not unduly frustrating a court's quest to assess the effect or not of an order on a child's health or well-being, if it is denied access to information within the keeping of a local authority? See also *Cleveland County Council v. F* [1995] 1 F.L.R. 797 (note Hale J.'s *per curiam* remark at p.802 that children need to be protected, not only against the risk of harm from their parents, but also against the risk of an unjustified separation from their parents). The question must also be raised as to whether decisions such as *Re B* [1993] 1 F.L.R. 191 ought to have precedential force in this area. In *Re B* the Court of Appeal acknowledged that a court has power in a children case (extending *Official Solicitor v. K* [1965] A.C. 201) to act upon evidence adduced by one party, or given by a welfare officer, which is not disclosed to the other party. It held that this power should only be exercised in the most exceptional circumstances, and only where the court is satisfied that the disclosure of evidence would be so detrimental to the welfare of the child as to outweigh the requirements for a fair trial. It must be stressed that to do this would be to fly in the face of existing law and practice in the area of ouster. But such a development may be necessary if courts are to assess probabilities in the way envisaged by s.33(6) and (7).

Health. Including mental health (s.63(1)).

Relevant child. See s.62(2).

Conduct of the parties. This may be taken into account even if the party concerned is not morally culpable: see for example *J (H.D.) v. J (A.M.)* [1980] 1 All E.R. 156 (where the respondent was a chronic schizophrenic).

Subs. (7)

This subsection ("the balance of harm" test) imposes an overriding requirement for the court to make an order if it appears that the applicant or a child is likely to suffer significant harm if an order is not made which is greater than that the respondent or a child is likely to suffer if the order is made.

The Law Commission argues (para. 4.34) that "by placing an emphasis on the need for a remedy rather than on the conduct which gave rise to that need, the criteria will not actually put a premium on allegations of violence and thus may avoid the problems which would be generated by a scheme which focuses upon it". In practice it is unlikely that the focus will be deflected from allegations of violence. The Law Commission offers a pious aspiration rather than an accurate prediction of likely practice. It also stresses (*ibid.*) that the new test "will avoid giving rise to a situation in which the court is put in the undesirable position of having to choose between the interests of a child and those of an adult, as, in cases where there is a risk of significant harm to a child, the duty to make the order will come into operation and the child's welfare will effectively become the paramount consideration". This also seems an optimistic assessment: the reluctance of the Court of Appeal to deviate from the *Richards v. Richards* [1984] A.C. 174 line even after the Children Act, with its clear paramountcy language, does not lead one to expect that courts will interpret the more convoluted language of this section as to arrive at a paramountcy conclusion.

Any relevant child. See s.62(2) for the meaning of this.

Is likely to suffer significant harm. On the meaning of "harm" see s.63(1), (3). The concept of "significant harm" is drawn from s.31 of the Children Act 1989. "Significant" has been held to mean either "considerable, or noteworthy or important" (see Booth J. in *Humberside County Council v. B* [1993] 1 F.L.R. 257). It has been held that "likely to suffer" should not be equated with a balance of probabilities (*Newham London Borough v. AG* [1993] 1 F.L.R. 281). The court should rather, it was held, evaluate the chance. Given the "real significant likelihood" of the child suffering significant harm if a care order was not made, it was held in *Newham* that the threshold test in s.31(2) was met. In *Re H and R (Child Sexual Abuse: Standard of Proof)* [1996] 1 F.L.R. 80 'likely' was interpreted (in the context of s.31(2)) to connote a real possibility, one that could not be sensibly ignored. In *Re H (A Minor) (Section 37 Direction)* [1993] 2 F.L.R. 541, Scott Baker J. expressed the opinion that, in looking to the future, one was not limited to the immediate future. Whilst that must be correct in the context of the Children Act, such a statement can have less force when dealing with occupation orders. And certainly Scott Baker J.'s view that the time frame could include "years hence" cannot be of any authority within the context of this Act.

It should be noted that the harm has to be "significant": *cf* the balance of "harm" only to the respondent or a child (as opposed to "any relevant child").

Subs. (8)

This subsection circumscribes s.33(5) and gives the court power to continue matrimonial home rights after the death of the other spouse or termination of the marriage where it considers it is just and reasonable to do so. For the sort of problems that may occur see *Hennie v. Hennie* [1993] 2 F.L.R. 351.

Subs. (9)

This subsection re-iterates that an order under this section cannot be made, nor can it continue to have effect, after the death of either party.

By virtue of subsection 5(a). The court may by order extend rights beyond death. And see also s.33(8).

Subs. (10)

This subsection deals with the duration of an order under this section.

Specified period. It is to be anticipated that many orders will continue, as previously, to have a limited duration.

Until further order. It may be varied or revoked.

Effect of order under s.33 where rights are charge on dwelling-house

34.—(1) If a spouse's matrimonial home rights are a charge on the estate or interest of the other spouse or of trustees for the other spouse—

(a) an order under section 33 against the other spouse has, except so far as a contrary intention appears, the same effect against persons deriving

title under the other spouse or under the trustees and affected by the charge, and
(b) sections 33(1), (3), (4) and (10) and 30(3) to (6) apply in relation to any person deriving title under the other spouse or under the trustees and affected by the charge as they apply in relation to the other spouse.
(2) The court may make an order under section 33 by virtue of subsection (1)(b) if it considers that in all the circumstances it is just and reasonable to do so.

DEFINITION
"matrimonial home rights": s.30.

GENERAL NOTE
This section is derived from s.2(5) of the 1983 Act. It deals with the effect of an order under s.33 where one spouse's matrimonial home rights are a charge on the estate or interest of the other spouse, or of the trustees for the other spouse, and a person has derived title under the other spouse or under the trustees.

Subs. (1)
Paragraph (a) provides that such persons are affected by the charge as it applies in relation to the other spouse; para. (b) applies s.33(1), (3), (4) and (10) and s.30(3) to (6) to such persons.

Subs. 2
This subsection lays down a broad criterion ("just and reasonable") for making an order under this section.

One former spouse with no existing right to occupy

35.—(1) This section applies if—
(a) one former spouse is entitled to occupy a dwelling-house by virtue of a beneficial estate or interest or contract, or by virtue of any enactment giving him the right to remain in occupation;
(b) the other former spouse is not so entitled; and
(c) the dwelling-house was at any time their matrimonial home or was at any time intended by them to be their matrimonial home.
(2) The former spouse not so entitled may apply to the court for an order under this section against the other former spouse ("the respondent").
(3) If the applicant is in occupation, an order under this section must contain provision—
(a) giving the applicant the right not to be evicted or excluded from the dwelling-house or any part of it by the respondent for the period specified in the order; and
(b) prohibiting the respondent from evicting or excluding the applicant during that period.
(4) If the applicant is not in occupation, an order under this section must contain provision—
(a) giving the applicant the right to enter into and occupy the dwelling-house for the period specified in the order; and
(b) requiring the respondent to permit the exercise of that right.
(5) An order under this section may also—
(a) regulate the occupation of the dwelling-house by either or both of the parties;
(b) prohibit, suspend or restrict the exercise by the respondent of his right to occupy the dwelling-house;
(c) require the respondent to leave the dwelling-house or part of the dwelling-house; or
(d) exclude the respondent from a defined area in which the dwelling-house is included.
(6) In deciding whether to make an order under this section containing provision of the kind mentioned in subsection (3) or (4) and (if so) in what manner, the court shall have regard to all the circumstances including—

(a) the housing needs and housing resources of each of the parties and of any relevant child;

(b) the financial resources of each of the parties;

(c) the likely effect of any order, or of any decision by the court not to exercise its powers under subsection (3) or (4), on the health, safety or well-being of the parties and of any relevant child;

(d) the conduct of the parties in relation to each other and otherwise;

(e) the length of time that has elapsed since the parties ceased to live together;

(f) the length of time that has elapsed since the marriage was dissolved or annulled; and

(g) the existence of any pending proceedings between the parties—

(i) for an order under section 23A or 24 of the Matrimonial Causes Act 1973 (property adjustment orders in connection with divorce proceedings etc.);

(ii) for an order under paragraph 1(2)(d) or (e) of Schedule 1 to the Children Act 1989 (orders for financial relief against parents); or

(iii) relating to the legal or beneficial ownership of the dwelling-house.

(7) In deciding whether to exercise its power to include one or more of the provisions referred to in subsection (5) ("a subsection (5) provision") and (if so) in what manner, the court shall have regard to all the circumstances including the matters mentioned in subsection (6)(a) to (e).

(8) If the court decides to make an order under this section and it appears to it that, if the order does not include a subsection (5) provision, the applicant or any relevant child is likely to suffer significant harm attributable to conduct of the respondent, the court shall include the subsection (5) provision in the order unless it appears to the court that—

(a) the respondent or any relevant child is likely to suffer significant harm if the provision is included in the order; and

(b) the harm likely to be suffered by the respondent or child in that event is as great as or greater than the harm attributable to conduct of the respondent which is likely to be suffered by the applicant or child if the provision is not included.

(9) An order under this section—

(a) may not be made after the death of either of the former spouses; and

(b) ceases to have effect on the death of either of them.

(10) An order under this section must be limited so as to have effect for a specified period not exceeding six months, but may be extended on one or more occasions for a further specified period not exceeding six months.

(11) A former spouse who has an equitable interest in the dwelling-house or in the proceeds of sale of the dwelling-house but in whom there is not vested (whether solely or as joint tenant) a legal estate in fee simple or a legal term of years absolute in the dwelling-house is to be treated (but only for the purpose of determining whether he is eligible to apply under this section) as not being entitled to occupy the dwelling-house by virtue of that interest.

(12) Subsection (11) does not prejudice any right of such a former spouse to apply for an order under section 33.

(13) So long as an order under this section remains in force, subsections (3) to (6) of section 30 apply in relation to the applicant—

(a) as if he were the spouse entitled to occupy the dwelling-house by virtue of that section; and

(b) as if the respondent were the other spouse.

DEFINITIONS
"court; the": s.57.
"dwelling-house": s.63(1), (4).

"harm": s.63(1), (3).
"relevant child": s.62(2).

GENERAL NOTE

This section deals with the power of the court to make occupation orders when the applicant former spouse is not entitled to occupy the dwelling-house but the respondent former spouse is so entitled. There are more restrictive criteria and effects (for example, an order may last initially only for six months (see s.35(10)), and occupation rights granted to non-entitled applicants are personal only and are not therefore capable of registration as a charge against the property or valid against a purchaser).

Subs. (1)

This subsection provides that a former spouse may apply for an order under this section in relation to a dwelling-house which was at any time the matrimonial home, or was intended by both to be their matrimonial home.

Former spouse. Including a polygamously-married spouse (see s.63(5)). The guilty party in a bigamous marriage cannot apply (and see *Whiston v. Whiston* [1995] 2 F.L.R. 268).

Entitled. See s.30 (giving "matrimonial home rights").

Beneficial estate, interest, contact, enactment. See the General Note to s.30.

Not so entitled. See s.30.

Subs. (2)

This provides that a former spouse with no existing right to occupy may apply against the other former spouse for an order.

An order.

For what this *must* contain if *not* in occupation see s.35(4) (occupation rights).

For what it *must* contain if *in* occupation see s.35(3).

For what it *may* additionally contain see s.35(5) (regulatory orders).

For criteria for occupation rights see s.35(6).

For criteria for the grant of regulatory orders see s.35(7) and (8).

For duration see s.35(10).

Subs. (3)

This subsection provides that every order made under s.35 confers certain occupation rights on applicants already in occupation for the duration of the order. This is in effect the first stage of the process. Having decided in favour of the applicant, the court may then decide on the merits whether a regulatory order ought to be made. In practice, as the Law Commission acknowledges, the two stages will usually be "telescoped" (para. 4.18). The importance of keeping the two stages conceptually distinct is pinpointed by the Law Commission in the context of cohabitation, where its example is more obviously apposite: "there may ... be cases in which the applicant's case for an occupation rights order is not particularly strong (perhaps because she has lived with the respondent only for a matter of weeks) but in which her need is so great that it would nevertheless be just for her application to be granted (perhaps because she is ill, has the respondent's baby to care for and nowhere else to go)" (para. 4.18).

Is in occupation. See s.35(4) for provision where s/he is not.

Subs. (4)

This subsection provides that every order made under this section for applicants *not* already in occupation must give them the right to enter and occupy the house and must require the respondent to permit the exercise of those rights.

Not in occupation. See s.35(3) for provision where the applicant is already *in* occupation.

Subs. (5)

This subsection provides that, in addition to granting an occupation rights order under s.35(2), an order made under this section may contain any of the regulatory provisions listed in this subsection. In certain circumstances (on which, see s.35(8)) the court must include one of these provisions in the order.

Subs. (6)

This subsection lays down the criteria to which the court is to have regard in exercising its power to grant occupation rights under s.39(3) or (4). It requires the court to consider the criteria prescribed, which include housing needs, financial resources, conduct and the length of time which has passed since the parties lived together and since the divorce or annulment.

Shall have regard. Note the obligation; it is not a discretion.

All the circumstances including. And, therefore, not just those listed.

Housing needs ... resources. See the General Note to s.33(6), above.

Financial resources. See the General Note to s.33(6), above.

Likely resources. See the General Note to s.33(6), above.

Conduct of parties. See the General Note to s.33(6), above.

Length of time . . . ceased to live together. Although no guidance can be offered on length as such, it must follow that the longer the efflux of time since the parties lived together, the less likely it will be that the court will make an order. But factors such as children, disability and ill-health may tilt the balance back even after a lengthy period of time.

Length of time . . . marriage dissolved or annulled. Similar considerations to those expounded in the previous note apply.

Existence of any pending proceedings. Which might have the effect of regulating occupation.

Subs. (7)

This provides that courts are to have regard to all circumstances, including housing needs and resources, financial resources, the likely effect of an order, conduct and length of time since the parties ceased to live together, in deciding whether to include one or more of the regulatory powers listed in subs. (5).

Shall have regard. It is mandatory to do so.

All the circumstances including. The list in s.35(6)(a)–(e) is not exclusive of other considerations.

Subs. (8)

Where the court makes an order under this section it must contain a regulatory provision listed in subs. (5) if the result of not making one is that an applicant or relevant child is likely to suffer significant harm attributable to the respondent's conduct, unless the respondent or any relevant child is likely to suffer significant harm as great or greater than that which it can be anticipated the applicant or relevant child will suffer if the provision in question is not included. The court is thus required to undertake a balancing exercise.

If the order does not include. Section 35(5) does not mandate one of these provisions (see "may").

Likely to suffer significant harm. In the context of s.31(2)(a) of the Children Act 1989, where the phrasing is identical, the House of Lords has held ([1996] 1 F.L.R. 80) that "likely" refers to "a real possibility, a possibility that cannot be ignored having regard to the nature and gravity of the feared harm in the particular case" (*Re H and R (Child Sexual Abuse: Standard of Proof)* [1996] 1 F.L.R. 80, *per* Lord Nicholls at p.95).

Attributable to the conduct of the respondent. Note that the section does not say "caused by". It is submitted that "attributable to" is capable of bearing a wider meaning.

Shall include . . . unless. It is only to include a regulatory provision if the balance of harm test so requires.

Subs. (9)

This provides that a s.35 order may not be made after the death of either of the former spouses and that, once made, it ceases to have effect on the death of either of them.

Subs. (10)

Orders are for up to six months, but may be extended on more than one occasion for periods not exceeding six months.

Limited . . . . So long as the order is in force, s.30(3) to (6) applies to the applicant as if s/he were the spouse entitled to occupy the house by virtue of that section and as if the respondent were the other spouse (see s.35(13)).

Subs. (11)

This provides that a former spouse, with an equitable interest in the dwelling-house or in the proceeds of sale of such, has the same matrimonial home rights as a former spouse who has no interest in the home at all. See also the General Note to s.30(9), above.

A former spouse. Who may apply for an occupation order under s.33 (see s.35(12)).

Subs. (12)

The right of a former spouse to apply for a s.33 occupation order is preserved.

Subs. (13)

This provides that, whilst s.35 orders are in force, applicants may make mortgage payments, pay rent and make other disbursements and that occupation by them is to be treated as occupation by the other former spouse for the purpose of certain enactments dealing with security of tenure (see s.30(4)).

One cohabitant or former cohabitant with no existing right to occupy

36.—(1) This section applies if—
  (a) one cohabitant or former cohabitant is entitled to occupy a dwelling-house by virtue of a beneficial estate or interest or contract or by virtue of any enactment giving him the right to remain in occupation;
  (b) the other cohabitant or former cohabitant is not so entitled; and
  (c) that dwelling-house is the home in which they live together as husband and wife or a home in which they at any time so lived together or intended so to live together.

(2) The cohabitant or former cohabitant not so entitled may apply to the court for an order under this section against the other cohabitant or former cohabitant ("the respondent").

(3) If the applicant is in occupation, an order under this section must contain provision—
  (a) giving the applicant the right not to be evicted or excluded from the dwelling-house or any part of it by the respondent for the period specified in the order; and
  (b) prohibiting the respondent from evicting or excluding the applicant during that period.

(4) If the applicant is not in occupation, an order under this section must contain provision—
  (a) giving the applicant the right to enter into and occupy the dwelling-house for the period specified in the order; and
  (b) requiring the respondent to permit the exercise of that right.

(5) An order under this section may also—
  (a) regulate the occupation of the dwelling-house by either or both of the parties;
  (b) prohibit, suspend or restrict the exercise by the respondent of his right to occupy the dwelling-house;
  (c) require the respondent to leave the dwelling-house or part of the dwelling-house; or
  (d) exclude the respondent from a defined area in which the dwelling-house is included.

(6) In deciding whether to make an order under this section containing provision of the kind mentioned in subsection (3) or (4) and (if so) in what manner, the court shall have regard to all the circumstances including—
  (a) the housing needs and housing resources of each of the parties and of any relevant child;
  (b) the financial resources of each of the parties;
  (c) the likely effect of any order, or of any decision by the court not to exercise its powers under subsection (3) or (4), on the health, safety or well-being of the parties and of any relevant child;
  (d) the conduct of the parties in relation to each other and otherwise;
  (e) the nature of the parties' relationship;
  (f) the length of time during which they have lived together as husband and wife;
  (g) whether there are or have been any children who are children of both parties or for whom both parties have or have had parental responsibility;
  (h) the length of time that has elapsed since the parties ceased to live together; and
  (i) the existence of any pending proceedings between the parties—
      (i) for an order under paragraph 1(2)(d) or (e) of Schedule 1 to the Children Act 1989 (orders for financial relief against parents); or

(ii) relating to the legal or beneficial ownership of the dwelling-house.

(7) In deciding whether to exercise its powers to include one or more of the provisions referred to in subsection (5) ("a subsection (5) provision") and (if so) in what manner, the court shall have regard to all the circumstances including—

(a) the matters mentioned in subsection (6)(a) to (d); and

(b) the questions mentioned in subsection (8).

(8) The questions are—

(a) whether the applicant or any relevant child is likely to suffer significant harm attributable to conduct of the respondent if the subsection (5) provision is not included in the order; and

(b) whether the harm likely to be suffered by the respondent or child if the provision is included is as great as or greater than the harm attributable to conduct of the respondent which is likely to be suffered by the applicant or child if the provision is not included.

(9) An order under this section—

(a) may not be made after the death of either of the parties; and

(b) ceases to have effect on the death of either of them.

(10) An order under this section must be limited so as to have effect for a specified period not exceeding six months, but may be extended on one occasion for a further specified period not exceeding six months.

(11) A person who has an equitable interest in the dwelling-house or in the proceeds of sale of the dwelling-house but in whom there is not vested (whether solely or as joint tenant) a legal estate in fee simple or a legal term of years absolute in the dwelling-house is to be treated (but only for the purpose of determining whether he is eligible to apply under this section) as not being entitled to occupy the dwelling-house by virtue of that interest.

(12) Subsection (11) does not prejudice any right of such a person to apply for an order under section 33.

(13) So long as the order remains in force, subsections (3) to (6) of section 30 apply in relation to the applicant—

(a) as if he were a spouse entitled to occupy the dwelling-house by virtue of that section; and

(b) as if the respondent were the other spouse.

DEFINITIONS

"child": s.63(1), (3).
"cohabit": s.62(1)(a).
"court; the": s.57.
"dwelling-house": s.63(1), (4).
"former cohabitant": s.62(1)(b).
"harm": s.63(1).
"relevant child": s.62(2).

GENERAL NOTE

This section provides for the situation where the applicant is a cohabitant or former cohabitant who is not entitled to occupy the dwelling-house and the respondent is a cohabitant or former cohabitant who is so entitled. Provision is made for courts to make occupation orders in favour of such applicants against such respondents. In addition to the factors which the court had to consider for former spouses (see s.35), the court must also consider certain additional factors including the nature of the parties' relationship. Under this section (contrast s.35), the balance of harm test does not impose a duty on the court to make an order containing certain specified provisions.

Parental responsibility. See s.63(1) (and see Children Act 1989, s.2).

Subs. (1)

For this section to apply there must be an "entitled" cohabitant or former cohabitant, a "non-entitled" cohabitant or former cohabitant, and the dwelling-house in question must be the home in which they live or lived together as husband and wife or intended to do so.

Cohabitant. See the General Note to s.62, below.

Former cohabitant. Note that this does not include cohabitants who have subsequently married each other.

Estate ... interest ... contract ... enactment. See the General Note to s.30, above.

Not so entitled. Where that person has an equitable interest, see s.36(11).

Live together as husband and wife. See the General Note to s.62, below.

Subs. (2)

The non-entitled cohabitant (or former cohabitant) may apply for an occupation order against the other cohabitant (or former cohabitant).

An order.

For what this *must* contain if *not* in occupation, see s.36(4).

For what this *must* contain if *in* occupation, see s.36(3).

For what it *may* additionally contain, see s.36(5).

For criteria for occupation rights, see s.36(6).

For criteria for the grant of regulatory orders, see s.36(7), (8).

For duration, see s.36(10).

Subs. (3)

Every order must confer certain occupation rights on applicants already in occupation. See further the General Note to s.35(3), above.

Is in occupation. Where not, see s.36(4).

Specified in the order. The period must not exceed six months but may be extended *once only* for a further specified period not exceeding six months (see s.36(10)).

Subs. (4)

Every order must confer certain occupation rights on applicants not in occupation.

Not in occupation. Where in occupation, see s.36(3).

Specified in the order. See the General Note to s.36(3), above.

Subs. (5)

In addition to granting an occupation rights order under s.36(2), an order made under this section may contain any of the regulatory provisions listed.

Subs. (6)

This subsection lays down the criteria to which the court is to have regard in exercising its power to grant occupation rights under s.36(3) or (4). The criteria are similar to those in s.35(6) (governing former spouses) but there are three additions: the nature of the parties' relationship, the length of the cohabitation, and whether the couple have had children or have or have had parental responsibility for children.

Housing needs ... resources. See notes on s.33(6), above.

Financial resources. See notes on s.33(6), above.

Likely effect of any order. See note on s.33(6), above.

Conduct of the parties. See note on s.33(6), above.

Nature of the parties' relationship. In issue will be such questions as their commitment to each other, financial arrangements, whether there are children of the relationship and whether they hold themselves out to the world as living in a quasi-marital relationship. In particular, the court is to have regard to the "fact that they have not given up each other the commitment involved in marriage" (see s.41). See further the discussion on "living together as husband and wife" in the General Note to s.62, and the General Note to s.41.

Length of time ... as husband and wife. It is submitted that the real question is one of quality rather than quantity and relates to factors just referred to in the note on "nature of the parties' relationship". See also, further, the discussion on "living together as husband and wife" in the General Note to s.62.

Children of both parties. Only the mother will have parental responsibility for such children (see the Children Act 1989, s.2(2)(a)), unless the father acquires it by agreement with the mother (the Children Act 1989, s.4(1)(b)) or by court order (parental responsibility order (see the Children Act 1989, s.4(1)(a)) or residence order (see the Children Act 1989, s.12(2))). But, in determining whether to make an order, the question is whether they had children together, not whether he obtained parental responsibility. It is his commitment to her that is in issue: not any commitment to children he fathers by her.

Parental responsibility. They could both have parental responsibility even though neither is a parent (they may have had vested in them both a residence order). They also might both have parental responsibility where the child is a legitimate child of his by marriage (to another woman) and the female cohabitant has a residence order in her favour. As an unmarried man, the male cohabitant can acquire parental responsibility in five ways:

  (i) by agreement with the mother;

  (ii) by court order (parental responsibility order);

 (iii) by being appointed a guardian by the court;
 (iv) by being appointed a guardian by the mother or another guardian but he can only do this after the mother's death; or
 (v) by acquiring a residence order.
Length of time ... ceased to live together. See the note to s.33(6), above.
Existence of any pending proceedings. See the note on s.33(6), above.

Subs. (7)
 This provides that courts are to have regard to all the circumstances, including housing needs and resources, financial resources, the likely effect of an order and conduct, as well as addressing the balance of harm equation in deciding whether to include one or more of the regulatory powers listed in subs. (5). The matters to be addressed are not the same as where the parties are former spouses.

Subs. (8)
 This subsection states the balance of harm equation.
 Likely to suffer significant harm. There must be a real possibility, one that cannot sensibly be ignored. See *Re H and R (Child Sexual Abuse: Standard of Proof)* [1996] 1 F.L.R. 80, 95.
 Attributable to the conduct of the respondent. Not caused by. See the note to s.35(8), above.

Subs. (9)
 This provides that a s.36 order may not be made after the death of either of the parties, and that, once made, it ceases to have effect on the death of either of them.

Subs. (10)
 Orders are for up to six months, but may be extended once only for a further period not exceeding six months. No order can accordingly last for longer than one year: contrast the position in the case of former spouses (s.35(10)).
 Limited. So long as the order is in force, s.30(3) to (6) applies in relation to the applicant as if s/he were an entitled spouse and as if the respondent were the other spouse (see s.36(13)).

Subs. (11)
 This provides that a person with an equitable interest in the dwelling-house or in the proceeds of the sale of it is to be treated as not being entitled to occupy the dwelling-house by virtue of that interest for the purpose of determining whether s/he is eligible to apply under s.36 for an order.

Subs. (12)
 The right of a person with an equitable interest to apply for an occupation order under s.33 is preserved.

Subs. (13)
 This provides that, whilst s.36 orders are in force, applicants may make mortgage payments, pay rent out and make other disbursements. It also provides that occupation by them is to be treated as occupation by the other person for the purpose of certain enactments dealing with security of tenure.

Neither spouse entitled to occupy

 37.—(1) This section applies if—
 (a) one spouse or former spouse and the other spouse or former spouse occupy a dwelling-house which is or was the matrimonial home; but
 (b) neither of them is entitled to remain in occupation—
  (i) by virtue of a beneficial estate or interest or contract; or
  (ii) by virtue of any enactment giving him the right to remain in occupation.
 (2) Either of the parties may apply to the court for an order against the other under this section.
 (3) An order under this section may—
 (a) require the respondent to permit the applicant to enter and remain in the dwelling-house or part of the dwelling-house;
 (b) regulate the occupation of the dwelling-house by either or both of the spouses;
 (c) require the respondent to leave the dwelling-house or part of the dwelling-house; or

(d) exclude the respondent from a defined area in which the dwelling-house is included.

(4) Subsections (6) and (7) of section 33 apply to the exercise by the court of its powers under this section as they apply to the exercise by the court of its powers under subsection (3) of that section.

(5) An order under this section must be limited so as to have effect for a specified period not exceeding six months, but may be extended on one or more occasions for a further specified period not exceeding six months.

DEFINITIONS
"court; the": s.57.
"dwelling-house": s.63(1), (4).

GENERAL NOTE
This section allows occupation orders in favour of spouses and former spouses to be made where neither party is entitled to occupy the dwelling-house. It essentially reproduces the Domestic Violence and Matrimonial Proceedings Act 1976 in this respect. Orders are of defined duration but may be renewed more than once (see s.37(5)).

Subs. (1)
This subsection gives the court the power to make occupation orders between spouses and former spouses, where neither party is entitled to occupy the dwelling-house. This might be used, for example, where neither party wished to assert a right to occupy, or where they could not prove one.
Estate ... interest ... contract ... enactment. See the General Note to s.30, above.

Subs. (2)
Both parties have the capacity to apply against the other for an order.
An order. See s.37(3) for the types of order.

Subs. (3)
This subsection enables the court to make such of the regulatory orders listed in s.33(3) as might be relevant between two non-entitled parties: *viz.*, to regulate the occupation of the dwelling-house; to require the respondent to allow the applicant to enter and remain in the dwelling-house; to require the respondent to leave the dwelling-house or part of it; and/or to exclude the respondent from a defined area around the dwelling-house.
Enter and remain. This may only have value if used in conjunction with the order in para. (c).
Part of the dwelling-house. Given the width of dwelling-house, this could include a garage or a garden.
Regulate the occupation. This is expressed very widely and could be useful in assisting contact arrangements with a non-residential parent spending time with children in a former matrimonial home.
Defined area. The meaning of "area" has not been categorised by the courts. However, in a recent case (*Burris v. Azadani* [1996] 1 F.L.R. 266) the Court of Appeal accepted the concept of an "exclusion zone" order. The court was alert to the civil liberties implications of excluding a man from an area.

Subs. (4)
This subsection provides that, in making orders under this section, the court shall apply the same criteria that it applies when exercising its powers to make regulatory orders under s.33(6) and (7).

Subs. (5)
This subsection impresses upon s.37 *occupation* orders a period of defined duration. They are limited to six months, but are subject to limitless extensions each not exceeding six months.

Neither cohabitant nor former cohabitant entitled to occupy

38.—(1) This section applies if—
(a) one cohabitant or former cohabitant and the other cohabitant or former cohabitant occupy a dwelling-house which is the home in which they live or lived together as husband and wife; but
(b) neither of them is entitled to remain in occupation—

(i) by virtue of a beneficial estate or interest or contract; or

(ii) by virtue of any enactment giving him the right to remain in occupation.

(2) Either of the parties may apply to the court for an order against the other under this section.

(3) An order under this section may—

(a) require the respondent to permit the applicant to enter and remain in the dwelling-house or part of the dwelling-house;

(b) regulate the occupation of the dwelling-house by either or both of the parties;

(c) require the respondent to leave the dwelling-house or part of the dwelling-house; or

(d) exclude the respondent from a defined area in which the dwelling-house is included.

(4) In deciding whether to exercise its powers to include one or more of the provisions referred to in subsection (3) ("a subsection (3) provision") and (if so) in what manner, the court shall have regard to all the circumstances including—

(a) the housing needs and housing resources of each of the parties and of any relevant child;

(b) the financial resources of each of the parties;

(c) the likely effect of any order, or of any decision by the court not to exercise its powers under subsection (3), on the health, safety or well-being of the parties and of any relevant child;

(d) the conduct of the parties in relation to each other and otherwise; and

(e) the questions mentioned in subsection (5).

(5) The questions are—

(a) whether the applicant or any relevant child is likely to suffer significant harm attributable to conduct of the respondent if the subsection (3) provision is not included in the order; and

(b) whether the harm likely to be suffered by the respondent or child if the provision is included is as great as or greater than the harm attributable to conduct of the respondent which is likely to be suffered by the applicant or child if the provision is not included.

(6) An order under this section shall be limited so as to have effect for a specified period not exceeding six months, but may be extended on one occasion for a further specified period not exceeding six months.

DEFINITIONS

"cohabitant": s.62(1)(a).
"court; the": s.57.
"dwelling-house": s.63(1), (4).
"former cohabitant": s.62(1)(b).
"harm": s.63(1), (3).
"relevant child": s.62(2).

GENERAL NOTE

This section allows occupation orders in favour of cohabitants and former cohabitants to be made where neither party is entitled to occupy the dwelling-house. As with the previous section, the Domestic Violence and Matrimonial Proceedings Act 1976 is reproduced. Orders are to be limited to a maximum duration of six months and may be renewed for a further period of six months. They may only be extended once (contrast the position with spouses and former spouses).

Subs. (1)

The section applies to cohabitants and former cohabitants who occupy a dwelling-house which is the home in which they live or lived together as husband and wife but which neither is entitled to occupy.

As husband and wife. See the General Note to s.62, below.

Estate ... interest ... contract ... enactment. See the General Note to s.30, above.

Subs. (2)

This provides that either cohabitant (or former cohabitant) may apply for an order against the other. For what the order *may* contain, see s.38(3).

For criteria for the exercise of the court's power, see s.38(4), (5).

For duration, see s.38(6).

Subs. (3)

Four regulatory orders may be made.

May. The court has discretion whether or not to make an order.

Enter and remain. See the note on s.37(3), above.

Part of the dwelling-house. See the note on s.37(3), above.

Regulate the occupation. See the note on s.37(3), above.

Defined area. See the note on s.37(3), above.

Subs. (4)

The criteria for the exercise of this jurisdiction are laid down. These include housing needs and resources, financial resources, the effect of the order on the health, safety and well-being of the parties and of any relevant child and the parties' conduct, as well as the balance of harm equation set out in the following subsection.

Housing needs ... resources. See the note on s.33(6), above.

Financial resources. See the note on s.33(6), above.

Likely effect. See the note on s.33(6), above.

Conduct of the parties. See the note on s.33(6), above.

Questions ... subsection (5). I.e., the balance of harm equation.

Subs. (5)

This sets out the balance of harm equation.

Likely to suffer significant harm. See the note on s.35(8), above.

Attributable to ... respondent. See the note on s.35(8), above.

Subs. (6)

Orders last for six months maximum. They may be extended, but only once, for a further period not exceeding six months. No order may last for more than a year.

Supplementary provisions

39.—(1) In this Part an "occupation order" means an order under section 33, 35, 36, 37 or 38.

(2) An application for an occupation order may be made in other family proceedings or without any other family proceedings being instituted.

(3) If—

(a) an application for an occupation order is made under section 33, 35, 36, 37 or 38,and

(b) the court considers that it has no power to make the order under the section concerned, but that it has power to make an order under one of the other sections,

the court may make an order under that other section.

(4) The fact that a person has applied for an occupation order under sections 35 to 38, or that an occupation order has been made, does not affect the right of any person to claim a legal or equitable interest in any property in any subsequent proceedings (including subsequent proceedings under this Part).

DEFINITIONS

"court; the": s.57.

"family proceedings": s.63(1) and (2).

GENERAL NOTE

This section defines an occupation order as an order under ss.33, 35, 36, 37 or 38. It regulates the circumstances in which they can be made. It provides that, if an application for an order is made under any one of these five sections and the court believes that it does not have the power to make such an order under that section, it may nevertheless make an order under one of the other four sections. The section also provides for the effect of an application for an order on subsequent claims to an interest in the property.

Subs. (1)
This subsection defines an occupation order.

Subs. (2)
This subsection enables an application for an occupation order to be made in other family proceedings or without any other proceedings being instituted. This is in line with Children Act-type procedures.
In other family proceedings. Thus, a court hearing a dispute about where a child is to live may settle the occupation of the family home at the same time (it may also make a non-molestation order).

Subs. (3)
This subsection permits the court, on hearing an application for an occupation order made under any one of the five relevant sections, to make an order under any of the other four sections, if it considers that this would be appropriate. The purpose of this is to ensure that the court is not required to dismiss an application for an occupation order simply because it has been made under the wrong section, perhaps because it comes to attention during the hearing that an apparently non-entitled party is in fact entitled, or vice versa.
An application . . . is made. An application has to be made—the court has no powers of its own motion to make an occupation order.
The court may make. I.e., it has discretion.

Subs. (4)
This subsection ensures that neither an application nor an order under ss.35 to 38 of this Act will prevent either party from subsequently claiming an interest in the property in subsequent proceedings, including proceedings under this Part of the Act.

Additional provisions that may be included in certain occupation orders

40.—(1) The court may on, or at any time after, making an occupation order under section 33, 35 or 36—
    (a) impose on either party obligations as to—
            (i) the repair and maintenance of the dwelling-house; or
            (ii) the discharge of rent, mortgage payments or other outgoings affecting the dwelling-house;
    (b) order a party occupying the dwelling-house or any part of it (including a party who is entitled to do so by virtue of a beneficial estate or interest or contract or by virtue of any enactment giving him the right to remain in occupation) to make periodical payments to the other party in respect of the accommodation, if the other party would (but for the order) be entitled to occupy the dwelling-house by virtue of a beneficial estate or interest or contract or by virtue of any such enactment;
    (c) grant either party possession or use of furniture or other contents of the dwelling-house;
    (d) order either party to take reasonable care of any furniture or other contents of the dwelling-house;
    (e) order either party to take reasonable steps to keep the dwelling-house and any furniture or other contents secure.
(2) In deciding whether and, if so, how to exercise its powers under this section, the court shall have regard to all the circumstances of the case including—
    (a) the financial needs and financial resources of the parties; and
    (b) the financial obligations which they have, or are likely to have in the foreseeable future, including financial obligations to each other and to any relevant child.

(3) An order under this section ceases to have effect when the occupation order to which it relates ceases to have effect.

DEFINITIONS
"court; the": s.57.
"dwelling-house": s.63(1), (4).
"mortgage payments": s.63(1).
"occupation order": s.39.
"relevant child": s.62(2).

GENERAL NOTE
This section provides that the court, on making an occupation order under ss.33, 35 or 36, or at any time thereafter, may make an ancillary order imposing certain obligations on either party or granting either party the possession or use of furniture or other contents contained in the dwelling-house. These obligations may relate to the repair and maintenance of the dwelling-house, the discharge of outgoings (for example rent or mortgage payments), the payment of rent to the party who has been ousted, taking reasonable care of the furniture or other contents of the dwelling-house and taking reasonable steps to keep any contents therein secure.

Subs. (1)
This subsection provides for the court, when granting an occupation order under ss.33, 35 or 36, or at any time thereafter, to make ancillary orders relating to the maintenance and repair of the property, and the discharge of rent, mortgage payments and other outgoings by either party. The court can also order the occupying party to pay rent to an entitled respondent who has been ousted, and can make orders relating to the use of furniture and other contents.
At any time thereafter. The ancillary orders need not delay the making of an occupation order; the occupation order can be made immediately, the ancillary orders on an adjournment.
Other outgoings. Including insurance payments.
Beneficial estate, interest, contract, enactment. See the note on s.30, above.
Reasonable care ... reasonable steps to keep secure. This is important where there is any danger that either party, but perhaps in particular an aggrieved and ousted respondent, may damage or destroy contents.

Subs. (2)
This subsection sets out the criteria for the granting of the ancillary orders.

Subs. (3)
This subsection provides that ancillary orders are to lapse automatically when the occupation orders to which they relate cease to have effect.
Occupation order ... ceases to have effect. On which, see s.33(9)(b), (10), s.35(9)(b), (10), s.36(9)(b), (10), s.37(5), and s.38(6).

Additional considerations if parties are cohabitants or former cohabitants

41.—(1) This section applies if the parties are cohabitants or former cohabitants.

(2) Where the court is required to consider the nature of the parties' relationship, it is to have regard to the fact that they have not given each other the commitment involved in marriage.

GENERAL NOTE
This section, which was not in the original Family Law Bill, was added by amendment in the House of Lords. According to the Lord Chancellor (*Hansard*, H.L. Vol. 570, col. 118), cohabitants:
> "have not given each other the commitment involved in marriage. That does not mean to say that they may not have given each other some other kind of commitment, but whatever it is, however like the one in marriage, it is not actually the commitment involved in marriage. They may even decide to stick it out through thick and thin and to have the grit and determination to go on all their lives. But they have not done so in the commitment involved in marriage. ... They do not take vows in public which lead to legal obligations on both of them. Even following divorce, in the married situation the parties may have financial obligations to one another. By contrast cohabitation can involve many different types of commitment, and so much so that I would go so far as to say that the only thing which is certain is that it is not the same as marriage."

The section accordingly provides that where the court is required to consider the nature of the parties' relationship (see s.36(b)(e)), it must have regard to the fact (it is so stated) that they have not given each other the commitment involved in marriage. Earl Russell thought the provision either "useless … or pernicious" (*Hansard*, H.L. Vol. 570, col. 115). It is an ideological statement with its roots in the Daily Mail-inspired opposition to the 1995 Bill. Whether it will assist courts or even whether they will seek assistance in it is dubious. But there are clear dangers that myth will be dressed up as fact and cohabitants be labelled as uncommitted because, for example, she has not taken his surname or they have retained separate bank accounts (*cf* the facts and the court's interpretation of them in *Helby v. Rafferty* [1978] 2 All E.R. 1016).

Non-molestation orders

Non-molestation orders

42.—(1) In this Part a "non-molestation order" means an order containing either or both of the following provisions—

(a) provision prohibiting a person ("the respondent") from molesting another person who is associated with the respondent;

(b) provision prohibiting the respondent from molesting a relevant child.

(2) The court may make a non-molestation order—

(a) if an application for the order has been made (whether in other family proceedings or without any other family proceedings being instituted) by a person who is associated with the respondent; or

(b) if in any family proceedings to which the respondent is a party the court considers that the order should be made for the benefit of any other party to the proceedings or any relevant child even though no such application has been made.

(3) In subsection (2) "family proceedings" includes proceedings in which the court has made an emergency protection order under section 44 of the Children Act 1989 which includes an exclusion requirement (as defined in section 44A(3) of that Act).

(4) Where an agreement to marry is terminated, no application under subsection (2)(a) may be made by virtue of section 62(3)(e) by reference to that agreement after the end of the period of three years beginning with the day on which it is terminated.

(5) In deciding whether to exercise its powers under this section and, if so, in what manner, the court shall have regard to all the circumstances including the need to secure the health, safety and well-being—

(a) of the applicant or, in a case falling within subsection (2)(b), the person for whose benefit the order would be made; and

(b) of any relevant child.

(6) A non-molestation order may be expressed so as to refer to molestation in general, to particular acts of molestation, or to both.

(7) A non-molestation order may be made for a specified period or until further order.

(8) A non-molestation order which is made in other family proceedings ceases to have effect if those proceedings are withdrawn or dismissed.

DEFINITIONS
"associated": ss.62(3), 63(1).
"family proceedings": s.62(1), (2).
"relevant child": s.62(2).

GENERAL NOTE
This section gives the court the power to make non-molestation orders. It follows the precedents of nearly 20 years of legislation, whilst making changes to the law. It extends the *range* of applicants who are eligible for protection so as to include, for example, former spouses, former cohabitants, relatives (a concept that is broadly defined), parents of a child and parties to the same family proceedings. The category of applicants is narrower than that envisaged by the Law Commission ("sexual relationship" is not included) but is still wider than the previous law. It is also significant that non-molestation orders may now be made by the court of *its own motion* as

well as upon application. The Act does not define "molestation". Law Commission consultation received the response that "we know what molestation is and it will only cause problems if it is defined" (see *Minutes*, para. 97 *per* Mrs Justice Hale). Criteria for non-molestation orders are spelt out (see s.42(5)). An order may refer to molestation in general or to particular acts of molestation (see s.42(6)). Orders may be for specified periods or until further order (see s.42(7)).

Subs. (1)

This subsection defines the people whom a respondent may be prohibited from molesting: they are those who are associated with the respondent within the meaning of s.62(3) and any relevant children.

Non-molestation order. It has been held that such an order cannot be granted to an applicant who is living with, and intends to continue living with the respondent (*F v. F* [1989] 2 F.L.R. 451 *per* Judge Nigel Fricker Q.C.). There was nothing in the wording of the 1976 Act to support this conclusion, which it is submitted was wrong. There is no reason why it should be followed in interpreting this section. On orders against mentally ill respondents, see *Wookey v. Wookey* [1991] 3 W.L.R. 135, where it was said that it should not be granted because the respondent would not be capable of complying with it and any breach could not be subject to effective enforcement proceedings since the respondent would have a clear defence to an application for committal for contempt.

Molesting. "Molesting" is not defined in this Act, or elsewhere by statute. "There [is] no evidence of problems having been caused in practice by lack of a statutory definition" and "some concern" that a definition might become "over restrictive or that it could lead to borderline disputes" (*per* Law Commission, para. 3.1). It includes, but is wider than, violence (*Davis v. Johnson* [1979] A.C. 264, 334, *per* Viscount Dilhorne; *Vaughan v. Vaughan* [1973] 3 All E.R. 449; *Horner v. Horner* [1982] Fam. 90). In *Vaughan v. Vaughan*, an ex-husband (who had committed violence in the past) was held to have molested his ex-wife when he called at her house early in the morning and late at night, called at her place of work, and made "a perfect nuisance of himself to her the whole time" (*per* Davies L.J. at p.452). It is important that this conduct frightened her and was known by him so to do. However, in *Johnson v. Walton* [1990] 1 F.L.R. 350, it was said that molestation involving harassment includes an intent to cause distress or harm. It is submitted that to import such intention into molestation is unnecessarily restrictive and that this opinion is wrong. Where there is violence, it is clear that an order does not require any intention by the respondent (see *Wooton v. Wooton* [1984] F.L.R. 871, where the respondent acted violently only during epileptic fits). Other examples of molestation include handing the wife upsetting notes and intercepting her on her way to the station (see *Horner v. Horner* [1982] Fam. 90 (said Ormrod L.J.: "It applies to any conduct which can properly be regarded as such a degree of harassment as to call for the intervention of the court" at p.93)); rifling through a woman's handbag (*Spencer v. Camacho* (1983) 4 F.L.R. 662); writing abusive letters and shouting obscenities (*George v. George* [1986] 2 F.L.R. 347); giving photographs of a former lover to the press (*Johnson v. Walton*). If there is one synonym for "molest", Stephenson L.J. would select "pester" (see *Vaughan v. Vaughan* at p.454). Before an injunction can be granted, there has to be "some evidence" of molestation (see Lawton L.J. in *Spindlow v. Spindlow* [1979] Fam. 52, 60).

Another person who is associated. On the meaning of which, see s.62(3). Attention should be drawn to the wide meaning of "relative": note Dr. Stephen Cretney's observation in his *Evidence to the Special Public Committee on the Family Homes and Domestic Violence Bill*, 1995 (see p.12) that a step-son's former cohabitant becomes eligible to apply for a non-molestation order "because she feels that my well-intentioned behaviour was intended to annoy her" (and thus constitute "molestation", citing *Fearon v. Earl of Aylesford* (1884) 14 Q.B.D. 792, 801 *per* Sir W.B. Brett M.R.).

Relevant child. On the meaning of which, see s.62(2). Given the width of this definition, it is not necessary that the child be one of the family or have any defined relationship with either the applicant or the respondent. Nor is it necessary, as it may have been under the 1976 Act, for the child to be living with the applicant (who may have moved out). It should also be noted that, with leave, children may themselves apply for non-molestation orders (see s.43).

Subs. (2)

This subsection gives the court power to make a non-molestation order either upon application by a person associated with the respondent, or of its own motion in family proceedings. The Law Commission thought "an own motion power might be useful on occasions where the victim is being subjected to threats or intimidation or is for some other reason reluctant to make an application for a non-molestation order herself" (para. 5.2).

Person ... associated with the respondent. Under the Bill proposed by the Law Commission (cl. 17), the police would have had the power to apply for a non-molestation order (and also for an occupation order) on behalf of an "aggrieved person". This followed Australian precedents (see *Family Law: Domestic Violence and Occupation of the Family Home* 1992, Law Com. No. 207, paras. 4.18–5.23). This draft clause was omitted from the Bill but a compromise provision was added at the eleventh hour (see *Hansard*, H.C. Vol. 279, cols. 595–599; H.L. Vol. 573, cols. 1106–1111). This allows for rules to be made to enable others, which may include the police, to initiate action on behalf of victims of domestic violence. Since there is evidence that in cases where criminal action is being pursued, applications by women for legal aid to seek protection under civil law are being refused (see Memorandum by the Association of Directors of Social Services, p.4), the new provision is important. This provision was originally thought by the Government to involve "a novel extension of police powers from a criminal function to a civil function" (*per* Lord Mackay of Clashfern, *Hansard*, H.L. Vol. 561, col. 1256). It would, said the Lord Chancellor, have "imposed significant and unaccustomed responsibilities upon the police for which the service has neither the resources nor the requisite expertise" (see *idem*). In support of the new provision it should be said that the criminal/civil law distinction is, however, somewhat artificial. The police are already empowered under s.46 of the Children Act 1989 to apply for an emergency protection order in respect of a child, despite the fact that the ultimate responsibility lies with local authorities (and see Lord Archer of Sandwell, *Hansard*, H.L. Vol. 561, col. 1260 and Baroness David, *Hansard*, H.L. Vol. 561, col. 1266). Though the Lord Chancellor regards the s.46 power as an "exceptional situation" (*Hansard*, H.L. Vol. 561, col. 1272) and would have preferred to follow the view of the Home Affairs Committee Report on *Domestic Violence* 245–I (February 25, 1993), which described the Law Commission recommendation as "laudable but fundamentally misguided" (para. 118), he was compelled as one of the last minute concessions to offer the compromise which is now s.60. Provision for the police to act on behalf of an aggrieved person is to be left to rules yet to be made. These may give powers of initiation to others than the police (*e.g.* the probation or social services). See further the General Note to s.60, below.

In any family proceedings . . . the court considers. Note the width of "family proceedings" (see s.63(1), (2) and also s.42(3)).

Benefit. It will be observed that the test here is "benefit" and not "harm", as is the case where an occupation order is being considered. And see also s.42(5), where "benefit" is equated with "health, safety and well-being".

Even though no such application . . . . The court (on the meaning of which, see s.57) may make a non-molestation order of its own motion.

Subs. (3)

Family proceedings are defined to include emergency protection orders containing an exclusion requirement, as defined in the new s.44A(3) of the Children Act 1989 (inserted by Sch. 6, para. 3 of this Act). See further, Public Bill Committee, col. 14 *per* Lord Chancellor.

Emergency protection order . . . which includes an exclusion requirement. An emergency protection order which does not include an exclusion requirement is not included within the category of family proceedings. "Family proceedings" do not include Pt. V of the Children Act 1989.

Subs. (4)

This subsection limits applications for non-molestation orders by formerly-engaged applicants to a three year period after termination of the agreement to marry. See also, *Hansard*, H.L. Vol. 564, cols. 1062 and 1067. "Any violence between the couple is likely to occur within three years of the termination of the agreement. That limitation is also likely to assist the courts with any problems of definition and proof if they do not have to deal with agreements which have been terminated many years previously, where the couple may no longer have any greater nexus than other members of the public"(*per* Lord Chancellor, *Hansard*, H.L. Vol. 564, col. 1062).

No application. But this would not preclude the court making an order of its own motion.

Terminated. See the General Note to s.62(3), below.

Subs. (5)

The criteria for the exercise of the court's powers are laid down in this subsection. "A broad statutory criterion" (see *Family Law: Domestic Violence and Occupancy of the Family Home*, Law Commission, No. 207, para. 3.3) is provided. It should be observed that, unlike s.16(2) of the Domestic Proceedings and Magistrates' Courts Act 1978, there is no reference to the respondent's behaviour. This is "only relevant as far as its effect upon the applicant's health, safety and well-being, or that of any children involved, is concerned" (Law Commission, No. 207, para. 3.6). "This fits the general trend in family law towards providing protection from harm rather than punishment or blame" (*idem*).

Health. This includes physical and mental health (see s.63(1)).

In a case falling with subsection (2)(b). I.e., a case where the court makes an order of its own motion.

Subs. (6)

This subsection emphasises the "dual capability" (see Law Commission, No. 207, para. 3.2) of non-molestation orders. They may be general or particular or both. The Law Commission thought rigid standard forms and a rigid use of them undesirable. On the need for common sense plain English forms, see Judge Nigel Fricker Q.C. [1988] Fam. Law 345.

Molestation. As indicated above (see the note on subs. (1)), this is not defined.

In general. Typically, it is expressed in the following terms: "not to assault, molest or otherwise interfere with".

Particular acts. Especially those complained of.

Both. It would be foolhardy only to injunct specific acts, so that where the order sought refers specifically to acts complained of it should in addition normally refer to molestation in general.

Subs. (7)

Non-molestation orders may be made for a specified period or until further order. The Law Commission rejected the idea of different types of orders (short term and long term) (see No. 207, paras. 2.42–2.43).

A non-molestation order. No distinction is drawn on the basis of the class of applicant. Nor is any distinction made between orders made as a result of applications and those granted by courts of their own motion.

A specified period. Caution should be exercised, however, in specifying a period, since a fixed time limit is inevitably arbitrary and can restrict a court's ability to react flexibly to problems within a family.

Until further order. Whilst it is important that a non-molestation order should be capable of continuing beyond the end of a relationship, other orders made on the termination of a relationship may satisfactorily cater for the problem. There may, of course, be a minority of cases where a permanent non-molestation order is necessary to protect the safety or well-being of an applicant: in such cases courts should be encouraged to make "until further order" orders.

Subs. (8)

This subsection provides that, where an order is made in family proceedings which are subsequently withdrawn or dismissed, the order shall cease to have effect. This subsection was moved uncontentiously by the Lord Chancellor at Committee stage of the 1995 Family Homes and Domestic Violence Bill (see Public Bill Committee, col. 15).

Further provisions relating to occupation and non-molestation orders

Leave of court required for applications by children under sixteen

43.—(1) A child under the age of sixteen may not apply for an occupation order or a non-molestation order except with the leave of the court.

(2) The court may grant leave for the purposes of subsection (1) only if it is satisfied that the child has sufficient understanding to make the proposed application for the occupation order or non-molestation order.

DEFINITIONS

"court; the": s.57.
"non-molestation order": s.42(1).
"occupation order": s.39.

GENERAL NOTE

This section provides that a child under the age of 16 years may only apply for an occupation or non-molestation order with the leave of the court, and that the court may grant leave only if it is satisfied that the child has sufficient understanding to make the application. It is modelled on s.10(8) of the Children Act 1989. The provision was moved by the Lord Chancellor at the Public Bill Committee stage of the Family Homes and Domestic Violence Bill 1995 (see Public Bill Committee, cols. 10, 15–16). The uses to which s.10(8) has been put have led to extravagant claims that children can now "divorce" parents (and see M. Freeman in M. Freeman (ed.), *Divorce: Where Next?* (Aldershot: Dartmouth, 1996, p.159). Sir Stephen Brown P. has said that he does not expect applications by children under the 1989 Act to be made frequently (*Re A D (A Minor)* (*Child's wishes*) [1993] Fam. Law 405). Similar caveats are likely to be made in the context of this Act too. There is anecdotal evidence that Legal Aid committees may be reluctant to support applications by children (see [1994] Fam. Law 38). It is, however, important to bear in mind Johnson J.'s remarks in *Re C (a Minor)* (*Leave to seek Section 8 Order*) [1994] 1 F.L.R. 26: "C has been given statutory rights by the Children Act 1989, and I must not seek to impede her in those rights" (at p.27).

Applications under the Children Act 1989 are allocated to a High Court judge: see [1993] 1 F.L.R. 668. The Lord Chancellor has the power to stipulate this under this Act too (see s.57): it may be expected that, if he does not do so, a *Practice Direction* will provide for transfers of such cases to a High Court judge.

Subs. (1)

A child under 16 years requires leave to make an application for an occupation or non-molestation order.

Under the age of sixteen. Children of 16 and 17 years may be married and do not require leave. It is of course possible for a child under 16 years to be married if domiciled in a country which allows marriage at an age of less than 16 (see *Mohamed v. Knott* [1969] 1 Q.B. 1). It seems that such a child would require leave.

Leave of the court. There is thus a filter process. It is more likely that leave will be granted where the proposed application has a reasonable chance of success (see *Re SC* (*Leave to Seek Residence Order*) [1994] 1 F.L.R. 96). Courts have been reluctant to grant leave: see, for example, Johnson J.'s remarks in *Re C* [1994] 1 F.L.R. 26, 29, that to grant leave might "be interpreted as a willingness of the court to entertain applications of children, even children of the age of C [almost 15], in any matter in which they were in disagreement with their parents".

Subs. (2)

Leave may only be granted where the court is satisfied that the child under 16 years has sufficient understanding to make the proposed application.

Sufficient understanding. This involves "much more than instructing a solicitor as to his own views ... He must be able to give instructions on many different matters as the case goes through its stages and to make decisions as the need arises ... The child also will be bound to abide by the rules which govern other parties, including rules as to confidentiality" (*per* Booth J. in *Re H* (*a minor*) (*Role of the Official Solicitor*) [1993] 2 F.L.R. 552). Further evidence of judicial caution are the remarks of Sir Thomas Bingham M.R. in *Re S* (*A Minor*) (*Independent Representation*) [1993] 2 F.L.R. 437, 448. In determining that a boy of 11 years did not have the necessary understanding to seek leave to make an application for an order under s.8 of the Children Act 1989 he stated:

> "The 1989 Act enables and requires a judicious balance to be struck between two considerations. First is the principle, to be honoured and respected, that children are human beings in their own right with individual minds and wills, views and emotions, which should command serious attention. A child's wishes are not to be discounted or dismissed simply because he is a child. He should be free to express them and decision-makers should listen. Second, is the fact that a child is, after all, a child. The reason why the law is particularly solicitous in protecting the interests of children is because they are liable to be vulnerable and impressionable, lacking the maturity to weigh the longer term against the shorter, lacking the insight to know how they will react and the imagination to know how others will react in certain situations, lacking the experience to measure the probable against the possible. Everything of course depends on the individual child in his actual situation. For the purposes of the Act, a babe in arms and a sturdy teenager on the verge of adulthood are both children, but their positions are quite different: for one the second consideration would be dominant, for the other the first principle will come into its own. The process of growing up is ... a continuous one. The judge has to do his best, on the evidence before him to assess the understanding of the individual child in the context of the proceedings in which he seeks to participate".

Even if the court finds the child has "sufficient understanding", it does not follow that it will necessarily grant leave. The court still has to exercise its discretion (note "the court may grant leave"). The Act offers no guidance as to how this discretion should be exercised. The application for an order is a family proceeding but it is not clear whether the application for leave is also a family proceeding. In Children Act cases, conflicting views have been expressed as to whether the paramountcy test in s.1(1) or checklist in s.1(3) govern applications for leave. In *Re C* (*A Minor*) (*Leave To Seek Section 8 Order*) [1994] 1 F.L.R. 26, Johnson J. held that a leave application was governed by s.1(1) (the paramountcy of the child's welfare), but in *Re SC* (*A Minor*) (*Leave to Seek Residence Order*) [1994] 1 F.L.R. 96, Booth J. held that it did not raise any question regarding the upbringing of the child, with the consequence that the child's welfare was not the paramount consideration in determining whether leave should be granted. Though Johnson J.'s view is the better one, it is expected that the more formalistically correct opinion of Booth J. will be followed (see *Re C* [1995] F.L.R. 927). On children's rights and applications, see further C. Lyon and N. Parton in Bob Franklin (ed), *The Handbook of Children's Rights* (London: Routledge, 1995, p.40).

Evidence of agreement to marry

44.—(1) Subject to subsection (2), the court shall not make an order under section 33 or 42 by virtue of section 62(3)(e) unless there is produced to it evidence in writing of the existence of the agreement to marry.

(2) Subsection (1) does not apply if the court is satisfied that the agreement to marry was evidenced by—
  (a) the gift of an engagement ring by one party to the agreement to the other in contemplation of their marriage, or
  (b) a ceremony entered into by the parties in the presence of one or more other persons assembled for the purpose of witnessing the ceremony.

DEFINITION
"court; the": s.57.

GENERAL NOTE
This section sets out, for the purposes of s.62(3)(e), the evidence required to establish the existence of an agreement to marry. It was moved at the Report stage of the Family Homes and Domestic Violence Bill in 1995 (see *Hansard*, H.L. Vol. 564, cols. 1061–1067) after initial resistance by the Lord Chancellor: see Public Law Committee cols. 4–9.

Subs. (1)
  This subsection stipulates the primary evidentiary requirement for an agreement to marry: namely, evidence in writing of the existence of the agreement to marry.
  Evidence in Writing. The agreement itself does not have to be in writing. Evidence in writing can take a number of forms "including correspondence between parties, newspaper announcements, made with the consent of both parties, invitations to an engagement party" *per* Lord Chancellor, *Hansard*, H.L. Vol. 564, col. 1062).

Subs. (2)
  This subsection provides alternative sources of evidence for an agreement to marry: namely, the gift of an engagement ring in contemplation of marriage and a "betrothal" ceremony before a witness.
  Gift of an engagement ring. This does not in itself prove an agreement has been entered into. The Act "does not contemplate the idea that the mere fact that one had an engagement ring from the other would necessarily constitute an agreement to marry, but it is a way in which the court could find that the agreement had been evidenced satisfactorily" (*per* Lord Chancellor, *Hansard*, H.L. Vol. 564, col. 1062).
  One party ... to the other. The gift of an engagement ring by the woman to the man is thus not ruled out as evidence of an agreement to marry.
  Contemplation of their marriage. The gift of an engagement ring and its acceptance must raise a very strong presumption in favour of an agreement to marry.
  A ceremony.... That is of betrothal. Said by the Lord Chancellor to "assist those groups which hold formal or informal engagement ceremonies" (*Hansard*, H.L. Vol. 564, col. 1062).
  One or more. Only one witness is required.
  Persons. Anyone can be a witness. There is no requirement that an official (religious or otherwise) be present.

Ex parte orders

45.—(1) The court may, in any case where it considers that it is just and convenient to do so, make an occupation order or a non-molestation order even though the respondent has not been given such notice of the proceedings as would otherwise be required by rules of court.
  (2) In determining whether to exercise its powers under subsection (1), the court shall have regard to all the circumstances including—
  (a) any risk of significant harm to the applicant or a relevant child, attributable to conduct of the respondent, if the order is not made immediately;
  (b) whether it is likely that the applicant will be deterred or prevented from pursuing the application if an order is not made immediately; and
  (c) whether there is reason to believe that the respondent is aware of the proceedings but is deliberately evading service and that the applicant or a relevant child will be seriously prejudiced by the delay involved—
      (i) where the court is a magistrates' court, in effecting service of proceedings; or
      (ii) in any other case, in effecting substituted service.

(3) If the court makes an order by virtue of subsection (1) it must afford the respondent an opportunity to make representations relating to the order as soon as just and convenient at a full hearing.

(4) If, at a full hearing, the court makes an occupation order ("the full order"), then—

(a) for the purposes of calculating the maximum period for which the full order may be made to have effect, the relevant section is to apply as if the period for which the full order will have effect began on the date on which the initial order first had effect; and

(b) the provisions of section 36(10) or 38(6) as to the extension of orders are to apply as if the full order and the initial order were a single order.

(5) In this section—

"full hearing" means a hearing of which notice has been given to all the parties in accordance with rules of court;

"initial order" means an occupation order made by virtue of subsection (1); and

"relevant section" means section 33(10), 35(10), 36(10), 37(5) or 38(6).

DEFINITIONS

"court; the": s.57.
"full hearing": subs. (5).
"harm": s.63(1), (3).
"initial order": subs. (5).
"non-molestation order": s.42(1).
"occupation order": s.39.
"relevant section": subs. (5).

GENERAL NOTE

This section deals with the power of the court to make *ex parte* orders, and sets out the matters which the court must take into account when making such orders. The Act does not define *ex parte* orders, which can be traced to the judgment of Ormrod L.J. in *Ansah v. Ansah* [1977] Fam. 138. Ormrod L.J. said:

"The power of the court to intervene immediately and without notice in proper cases is essential to the administration of justice. But this power must be used with great caution and only in circumstances in which it is really necessary to act immediately. Such circumstances do undoubtedly tend to occur more frequently in family disputes than in other types of litigation because the parties are often still in close contact with one another and, particularly when a marriage is breaking up, in a state of high emotional tension; but even in such cases the court should only act *ex parte* in an emergency when the interests of justice or the protection of the applicant or a child clearly demands immediate intervention by the court. Such cases should be extremely rare ... Circumstances, of course, may arise where prior notice cannot be given to the other side; for example, cases where one parent has disappeared with the children, or a spouse, usually the wife, is so frightened of the other spouse that some protection must be given against a violent response to service of proceedings, but the court must be fully satisfied that such protection is necessary."

Where an order is sought *ex parte* before a copy of the application has been served on the other party, the affidavit must explain why the application is being made *ex parte* and a copy of any order made *ex parte* must be served with the application and affidavit on the other party at least two days before the further hearing of the application. See CCR Ord. 13, r. 6 (3A). This may be reworded to take account of this legislation. As to the need for full disclosure on *ex parte* applications, see *Behbehani v. Salem* [1989] 2 All E.R. 143. See also *G v. G* [1990] 1 F.L.R. 395. Where conflicting evidence is placed before the court on an application for an ouster order there should be a proper investigation of the evidence by means of cross-examination of the parties (see *Whitlock v. Whitlock* [1989] 1 F.L.R. 209). Note also *Tuck v. Nicholls* [1989] 1 F.L.R. 283 (the court has to be satisfied that the facts established are sufficient to found jurisdiction). Where an ouster order has been obtained *ex parte*, court administrative staff should never turn away a person seeking liberty on the ground that the court list is too full to arrange a hearing. This is a matter for judicial, not administrative, decision, and must always be referred to a judge or other judicial officer (see *G v. G (Ouster: Ex parte Application)* [1990] 1 F.L.R. 395).

Subs. (1)

This subsection deals with the power of the court to make *ex parte* occupation and non-molestation orders.

The court may. It thus retains discretion.

Just and convenient. This is the existing terminology: see the Courts and Legal Services Act 1990, Sched. 18, para. 21.

Such notice ... rules of court. This is currently not less than two days before the hearing of the application (CCR Ord. 13, r.6(3)). It is unlikely that new rules will change this.

Subs. (2)

This subsection prescribes the matters to be considered by the court in deciding whether to make an order *ex parte.* Although "all the circumstances" must be considered, three in particular are specified. It will be noted that s.45(2)(b) ends with, what is likely to be interpreted as, a conjunctive "and". Although in Hale J.'s evidence to the Special Public Committee, which was not contested, this section was said to "reflect" present case law (see Law Comm. No. 207, para. 105), it is submitted that this is not so. A conjunctive interpretation of "and" will restrict the use of *ex parte* orders. The Law Commission (para. 5.7) considered that any one of the three matters listed in (a), (b) and (c) "might be decisive in a particular case". But s.14(2) does not use the word "or" which would have made this clear (and see Written Evidence of Gillian Douglas (at p.17)).

Any risk. The risk must be imminent and genuine however.

Significant Harm. "Harm" is defined in s.63(1). On "significant harm" see note on s.33(7). The Law Commission envisages this covering cases where "there is evidence that the respondent has been violent towards or threatened violence to the applicant or a child, and there is a genuine risk that the violence will be repeated or the threat carried out unless an immediate order is made" (see para. 5(8)(i)).

Deterred or prevented. This was said by the Law Commission to cover the cases (in Ormrod L.J.'s judgment in *Ansah v. Ansah,* quoted above) in which the applicant is "so terrified of the respondent that some protection is necessary to enable her to pursue her remedy, even though the remedy may not necessarily be urgent in itself" (see para. 5(8)(ii)).

And. The Law Commission says the three listed factors are "cumulative" and "any one of them might be decisive in a particular case" (para. 5.7). These two statements are not necessarily consistent: the use of the conjunctive "and" does suggest aggregation rather than reliance on any of the three factors. But see Memorandum by Draftsman (*Written Evidence* in Proceedings of Special Public Committee, H.L. Paper 55 (1995), p.86).

Reason. Note that the provision does not say "reasonable cause", as might have been expected (the Law Commission used "reasonable cause").

Evading service. "Deliberate evasion of service is not infrequently used by respondents in domestic violence cases as a tactic to wear down the applicant's resolution by causing delay and making it even more difficult than it already is to pursue the proceedings against him. For some applicants this can be the last straw, and the proceedings may be withdrawn or abandoned" (*per* Law Commission, para. 5.9).

Substituted Service. See R.S.C. Ord. 65, r.4 and C.C.R. Ord. 7, r.8.

Subs. (3)

This subsection offers the civil liberties balance to *ex parte* orders. The respondent is to be given an opportunity to make representations as soon as is just and convenient. This provision was not in the original Family Homes and Domestic Violence Bill: it was moved by the Lord Chancellor at the Committee stage of that Bill (Public Bill Committee, cols. 15–16).

Subs. (4)

This subsection and the next one were moved by the Lord Chancellor at Report stage (see *Hansard,* H.L. Vol. 570, cols. 121–122). It provides that, in calculating maximum periods of occupation orders, account shall be taken of any *ex parte* order which preceded the full order.

Subs. (5)

Rules of court. These have yet to be made.

Relevant section. Those listed detail occupation orders.

Undertakings

46.—(1) In any case where the court has power to make an occupation order or non-molestation order, the court may accept an undertaking from any party to the proceedings.

(2) No power of arrest may be attached to any undertaking given under subsection (1).

(3) The court shall not accept an undertaking under subsection (1) in any case where apart from this section a power of arrest would be attached to the order.

(4) An undertaking given to a court under subsection (1) is enforceable as if it were an order of the court.

(5) This section has effect without prejudice to the powers of the High Court and the county court apart from this section.

DEFINITIONS
  "court; the": s.57.
  "non-molestation order": s.42(1).
  "occupation order": s.39.
  "relevant child": s.62(2).

GENERAL NOTE
  This section enables the court to accept undertakings from any party to the proceedings. Such an undertaking is to be enforceable in the same way as a court order (see s.46(4)), except that no power of arrest may be attached to an undertaking (see s.46(2)). The court is not to accept an undertaking in circumstances where a power of arrest is appropriate (s.46(3)). This section was not in the Law Commission Draft Bill or in the original Family Homes and Domestic Violence Bill in 1995. The issue was raised in deliberations of the Special Public Bill Committee and the section was introduced by the Lord Chancellor at Committee stage (see Public Bill Committee, cols. 17–21). The section reflects common practice in the county courts and gives magistrates' courts power they have not previously enjoyed. One disadvantage of *ex parte* orders is that the judge/magistrate has no opportunity to try to resolve the parties' differences by agreed undertakings (and see Law Commission, para. 5.6).

Subs. (1)
  An undertaking may be accepted from any party in any case where there is power to make an occupation or non-molestation order. An undertaking has all the force of an order (*Roberts v. Roberts* [1990] 2 F.L.R. 111).
  The court. This now includes magistrates' courts.
  In any case. See ss.33, 35, 36, 37 (occupation orders) and s.42 (non-molestation order).
  May accept. There is no obligation to accept an undertaking.
  Any party. This presumably includes children. On enforcement problems, see *Re S* [1991] Fam. 121 and *R v. Selby Justices ex parte Frame* [1991] 2 All E.R. 344 (a person under 17 years cannot be committed to prison for contempt).

Subs. (2)
  This subsection, following existing case law (see *Carpenter v. Carpenter* [1988] 1 F.L.R. 121) provides that a power of arrest may not be attached to an undertaking. Where a power of arrest is appropriate (as to which, see s.47), the court is not to accept an undertaking, but rather make an order (and presumably attach a power of arrest).
  Power of arrest. On which, see s.47.

Subs. (3)
  The court is not obliged to attach a power of arrest to an *ex parte* order, but may do so if it appears that the respondent has used or threatened violence against the applicant or a relevant child *and* there is a risk of significant harm to the applicant or child if the power of arrest is not attached immediately.

Subs. (2) ... s.45(1)
  The previous subsection which mandates the attachment of powers of arrest does not apply to *ex parte* orders.
  The court may attach. It has a discretion to do so.
  Violence. See the note to s.47(2).
  Significant harm. See s.63(1).
  Attributable to. Note the provision does not say "caused by". "Attributable to" is arguably wider than "caused by". And see *Re B* [1993] 1 F.L.R. 12 for some support for this view.

Subs. (4)
  This subsection provides that undertakings are to be enforceable in the same way as court orders.
  Enforceable as ... an order of the court. Breach of an undertaking constitutes contempt of court. Since an undertaking is volunteered, rather than imposed, the person giving it is presumed to know of it, so that proof of service is not required prior to enforcement. The procedural requirements for the enforcement of an undertaking are not as strict as those applying to the

enforcement of a judgment or an order under RSC Ord. 29, r.1. See *Hussain v. Hussain* [1986] 1 All E.R. 961 (a husband gave an undertaking not to molest his wife in the course of divorce proceedings. An order reciting the undertaking was drawn up, but it did not contain a penal notice and it was never personally served. On a later application by the wife, the judge committed the husband to prison for breach of the undertaking and he purported to dispense with the service of the order. The Court of Appeal was satisfied that the husband was fully aware of the terms of the undertaking and of the consequences of breaking it. It was stressed that, notwithstanding that the undertaking had not been recorded in the formal order of the court, it was the undertaking itself and not the order which required the person giving it to comply with its terms). In *Hussain v. Hussain* it was stressed that where an undertaking is given in lieu of an order, as a matter of general practice the undertaking should be recited in the order of the court, which should be served on the person giving it. Furthermore, the order should be endorsed with a notice explaining the consequences of any breach of the undertaking.

Subs. (5)
The powers of the High Court and county court apart from this section remain.

Arrest for breach of order

47.—(1) In this section "a relevant order" means an occupation order or a non-molestation order.
   (2) If—
   (a) the court makes a relevant order; and
   (b) it appears to the court that the respondent has used or threatened violence against the applicant or a relevant child,
it shall attach a power of arrest to one or more provisions of the order unless satisfied that in all the circumstances of the case the applicant or child will be adequately protected without such a power of arrest.
   (3) Subsection (2) does not apply in any case where the relevant order is made by virtue of section 45(1), but in such a case the court may attach a power of arrest to one or more provisions of the order if it appears to it—
   (a) that the respondent has used or threatened violence against the applicant or a relevant child; and
   (b) that there is a risk of significant harm to the applicant or child, attributable to conduct of the respondent, if the power of arrest is not attached to those provisions immediately.
   (4) If, by virtue of subsection (3), the court attaches a power of arrest to any provisions of a relevant order, it may provide that the power of arrest is to have effect for a shorter period than the other provisions of the order.
   (5) Any period specified for the purposes of subsection (4) may be extended by the court (on one or more occasions) on an application to vary or discharge the relevant order.
   (6) If, by virtue of subsection (2) or (3), a power of arrest is attached to certain provisions of an order, a constable may arrest without warrant a person whom he has reasonable cause for suspecting to be in breach of any such provision.
   (7) If a power of arrest is attached under subsection (2) or (3) to certain provisions of the order and the respondent is arrested under subsection (6)—
   (a) he must be brought before the relevant judicial authority within the period of 24 hours beginning at the time of his arrest; and
   (b) if the matter is not then disposed of forthwith, the relevant judicial authority before whom he is brought may remand him.
   In reckoning for the purposes of this subsection any period of 24 hours, no account is to be taken of Christmas Day, Good Friday or any Sunday.
   (8) If the court has made a relevant order but—
   (a) has not attached a power of arrest under subsection (2) or (3) to any provisions of the order, or
   (b) has attached that power only to certain provisions of the order,

then, if at any time the applicant considers that the respondent has failed to comply with the order, he may apply to the relevant judicial authority for the issue of a warrant for the arrest of the respondent.

(9) The relevant judicial authority shall not issue a warrant on an application under subsection (8) unless—

(a) the application is substantiated on oath; and

(b) the relevant judicial authority has reasonable grounds for believing that the respondent has failed to comply with the order.

(10) If a person is brought before a court by virtue of a warrant issued under subsection (9) and the court does not dispose of the matter forthwith, the court may remand him.

(11) Schedule 5 (which makes provision corresponding to that applying in magistrates' courts in civil cases under sections 128 and 129 of the Magistrates' Courts Act 1980) has effect in relation to the powers of the High Court and a county court to remand a person by virtue of this section.

(12) If a person remanded under this section is granted bail (whether in the High Court or a county court under Schedule 5 or in a magistrates' court under section 128 or 129 of the Magistrates' Courts Act 1980), he may be required by the relevant judicial authority to comply, before release on bail or later, with such requirements as appear to that authority to be necessary to secure that he does not interfere with witnesses or otherwise obstruct the course of justice.

DEFINITIONS
"court; the": s.57.
"harm": s.63(1) and (3).
"non-molestation order": s.42(1).
"occupation order": s.39.
"relevant child": s.62(2).
"relevant judicial authority": s.63(1).

GENERAL NOTE
This section (and Sched. 5) provides for the court's powers to arrest for breach of, and to attach a power of arrest to, an occupation order and a non-molestation order. They extend, and bring into line in all courts, the enforcement procedures formerly to be found in s.18 of the Domestic Proceedings and Magistrates' Courts Act 1978 and s.2 of the Domestic Violence and Matrimonial Proceedings Act 1976. They give the High Court and county court power to remand and power to issue arrest warrants. They also provide for bail requirements to be attached to a remand where necessary in order to ensure that there is no interference with witnesses or to prevent other obstruction of the course of justice (see subs. (12)). The Law Commission sees powers of arrest as "simple, immediate and inexpensive means of enforcement" underlying the "seriousness of the breach to the offending party" (para. 5.13).

Subs. (2)
This subsection requires the court to attach a power of arrest to one or more provisions of the order if the respondent has used or threatened violence against the applicant or a child concerned, unless this is unnecessary for their protection. Thus, there is now a presumption in favour of attaching a power of arrest where violence has been used or threatened: under previous legislation, attaching a power of arrest was to be regarded as exceptional. Even so, admonitions in the past that it was not a "routine remedy" (see *Lewis v. Lewis* [1978] Fam. 60, 63 *per* Ormrod, L.J. and *Widdowson v. Widdowson* (1983) 4 F.L.R. 121, 125 *per* Sir John Arnold P.) retain some force. It is, however, to be expected that there will be more attachments or arrest powers than is currently the case (only 29 per cent of 1976 Act injunctions had powers of arrest attached in 1989: see Law Commission p.44, n.23).

Relevant order. That is, an occupation or non-molestation order (see s.47(1)).

Violence. Violence is not defined in the Act. What constitutes "violence" is a social construction, so that acts of violence deemed legitimate are characterised as a means of control or punishment (see W.J. Goode, "Force and Violence in the Family", *Journal of Marriage and the Family* Vol. 33, p.624 (1971)). Corporal punishment of children comes into this category. Presumably, courts will not label reasonable and moderate corporal chastisement of children as "violence", though what is "reasonable and moderate" is far from clear or value-free and is contingent on any number of variables. It also changes over time. In *Terror and Resistance: A Study of Political*

Violence (Oxford: OUP, 1969), E. Walter defines violence as "destructive harm . . . including not only physical assaults that damage the body, but also . . . the many techniques of inflicting harm by mental or emotional means" (p. 8). It is, he says, "generally understood as unmeasured or exaggerated harm to individuals, either not socially proscribed at all or else beyond established limits". It is often, he adds, "socially defined to include the processes that *originate* as authorised, measured force, but that go beyond the prescribed conditions and limits" (p.12). When the Law Commission justified its rejection of granting magistrates jurisdiction over acts short of violence (this limitation was embodied in the 1978 Act) it argued that "adjudicating on an allegation of psychological damage is a very difficult matter which may involve the assessment of evidence by psychiatrist", a task it conceived as beyond the capabilities of magistrates (see *Family Law: Report on Matrimonial Proceedings in Magistrates' Courts* 1976, Law Com. No. 77, para. 3.12). This view no longer holds (magistrates under this Act will have jurisdiction over "molestation", which they did not have under the 1978 legislation). It would thus be easy to interpret "violence" as not including mental, emotional or psychological abuse, but this would, it is submitted, be wrong. These forms of abuse, as also sexual abuse, constitute "destructive harm" and should be included within the concept of "violence".

The court shall attach. The presumption is in favour of a power of arrest being attached.

One or more provisions of the order. It was held under previous legislation (the 1978 Act) that if magistrates refused to make an exclusion order because the wife was in no "immediate danger", it was inconsistent to attach a power of arrest to the personal protection order (see *McCartney v. McCartney* [1981] Fam. 59). It is equally arguable that if an occupation order is refused, to attach a power of arrest to a non-molestation order is unnecessary.

Adequately protected. It may be that the person against whom violence was used or threatened is now adequately protected (*e.g.* the wife is now in hospital), but a relevant child not so abused hitherto is at risk. It would be an unduly restrictive interpretation of this provision to hold that "violence" and "adequate protection" must relate to the same person. It is difficult to see in what circumstances, short of a violent respondent being in prison, that an applicant or relevant child will be adequately protected without a power of arrest attached to the order.

Subs. (3)

This subsection provides that a power of arrest may be attached to an *ex parte* order where there has been actual or threatened violence and, in addition, there is a risk of significant harm to the applicant or a child if the power of arrest is not attached immediately. The Law Commission reasoned that the "more stringent approach" could be justified because "the court is being asked to grant a power of arrest against someone who has not yet had an opportunity of stating his case" (para. 5.14).

The court may attach. Contrast the language of subs. (2). Here the court has a complete discretion and there is no presumption in favour of a power of arrest. The power of arrest may be attached for a shorter period than the rest of the order (see subs. (4)). But this may be extended (see subs. (5)).

One or more provisions. See the note on subs. (2), above.

Violence. See the note on subs. (2), above.

Significant harm. Harm is defined in s.63(1). "Significant" harm in relation to children is partially explained in s.63(3).

Subs. (4)

The power of arrest may be attached for a shorter period than the other provisions of the order. This provision was moved by the Lord Chancellor at Committee stage of the Family Homes and Domestic Violence Bill 1995 (see Public Bill Committee col. 22).

By virtue of subsection (3). That is, where the application is *ex parte*.

It may provide. The court has complete discretion.

Subs. (5)

A period specified under s.47(4) may be extended on one or more occasions.

Subs. (6)

This subsection provides that once a power of arrest has been attached to an order, a constable may arrest the respondent without a warrant if he has reasonable cause to believe that there has been a breach of the provisions to which the power of arrest was attached.

A constable. There seems to be no requirement that s/he must be in uniform.

May arrest. The constable does not have to arrest even where there is a power of arrest. The arrest must be for a breach of a provision of the order to which the power of arrest is attached (*Bowen v. Bowen* [1990] 2 F.L.R. 93). The arrested person must be given information as to why he is being arrested (*Christie v. Leachinsky* [1947] A.C. 573 and the Police and Criminal Evidence Act 1984, s.28(3)).

Reasonable cause for suspecting. Reasonable suspicion may take into account matters which would not be put into evidence at all or could not form part of a prima facie case (see *Shaaban Bin Hussien v. Chong Fook Kam* [1970] A.C. 942). The burden of showing reasonable cause lies on the constable (*Dallison v. Caffery* [1965] 1 Q.B. 348, 365 *per* Lord Denning M.R).

Subs. (7)
This provides that a respondent who is arrested under a power of arrest must be brought before a judge or justice of the peace within 24 hours, in the calculation of which Sundays, Christmas Day and Good Friday are not included. This confirms the existing law. Additionally, the High Court and county court are given a new power of remand (see also s.18(11) of the DPMCA 1978): this gives these courts powers similar to those already operating in the magistrates' courts (see ss.128 and 129 of the Magistrates' Courts Act 1980).
He shall be brought. Note the mandatory language.
May remand him. See also s.18(11) and Sched. 5.
No account ... or any Sunday. But other Bank Holidays are not ignored.

Subs. (8)
This subsection empowers any court, on application, to issue a warrant for the respondent's arrest for breach of any provisions of an occupation or non-molestation order to which no power of arrest has been attached. This extends to the High Court and county courts a power already enjoyed by magistrates' courts (see the Domestic Proceedings and Magistrates' Courts Act 1978, s.18(4)) and enables these courts to involve the police in the enforcement of orders made under domestic violence legislation, even where no power of arrest has been attached. See, further, Law Commission, No. 207, para. 5.15.
Warrant. For what needs to be proved, see s.47(9); and for the power to remand, see s.47(10).

Subs. (9)
This subsection, derived from s.18(4) of the Domestic Proceedings and Magistrates' Courts Act 1978, provides that an arrest warrant should not be issued under subs. (8) unless certain conditions are satisfied.

Subs. (10)
This subsection enables the court to remand a respondent arrested as a result of an arrest warrant.
Remand. See also Sched. 5.

Subs. (11)
This subsection creates a remand scheme for the High Court and county courts similar to the one that magistrates' courts already operate.

Subs. (12)
This subsection provides that where a person is granted bail, he may be required to comply with whatever requirements the court thinks necessary to secure that he does not interfere with witnesses or otherwise obstruct the course of justice. This subsection was moved by the Lord Chancellor at Committee stage of the Family Homes and Domestic Violence Bill 1995 (see col. 22).

Remand for medical examination and report

48.—(1) If the relevant judicial authority has reason to consider that a medical report will be required, any power to remand a person under section 47(7)(b) or (10) may be exercised for the purpose of enabling a medical examination and report to be made.

(2) If such a power is so exercised, the adjournment must not be for more than 4 weeks at a time unless the relevant judicial authority remands the accused in custody.

(3) If the relevant judicial authority so remands the accused, the adjournment must not be for more than 3 weeks at a time.

(4) If there is reason to suspect that a person who has been arrested—
(a) under section 47(6), or
(b) under a warrant issued on an application made under section 47(8),
is suffering from mental illness or severe mental impairment, the relevant judicial authority has the same power to make an order under section 35 of

the Mental Health Act 1983 (remand for report on accused's mental condition) as the Crown Court has under section 35 of the Act of 1983 in the case of an accused person within the meaning of that section.

DEFINITION
"relevant judicial authority": s.63(1).

GENERAL NOTE
This section gives the court new powers to remand the respondent for medical examination and reports. Time limits are prescribed. The Law Commission's recommendation (No. 207, para. 5.17) followed the view of the Council of Her Majesty's Circuit Judges that it was desirable to have a power to remand for medical examination "the not inconsiderable number of cases where it seems that the arrested person may be suffering from mental ill-health" (*idem*). However, in her evidence to the special Public Committee, Hale J. thought the power would be used "sparingly" (*Proceedings of the Special Public Committee*, H.L. Paper 55, 1995 para. 114).

Subs. (1)
This subsection provides that a remand may be made under s.47 for medical examination and reports.
Has reason. It is difficult to see from where the court will get its evidence and how, if at all, it will be tested. It will not even be necessary for the court initially to find that the respondent is in breach of the original order. Will it have anything to go on save, for example, the respondent's demeanour? Is this firm enough ground ("reason") to take a decision with considerable civil liberties implications?
Medical report. Does this include a psychiatric report? It is not clear. Nor is it clear (perhaps this is to be left to Rules of Court) how the medical examination is to be organised (who will undertake it? where? when? how?). In addition, it is not clear what happens if the respondent refuses a medical examination. Can he be compelled to undergo one? Will he be remanded in custody if he refuses and, if so, for how long? Will he be represented? Is this the sort of situation where the Official Solicitor might be expected to act?
Will be required. Presumably, "is" now required. It is difficult to see why this is couched in the future tense.
Report. It is not clear who will receive a copy of the report. Is the applicant entitled to see it? If she is, is this (knowledge) not likely to constrain the respondent somewhat? Is he likely to tell the doctor/psychiatrist matters that will be reported to his estranged wife? If she is not, of what value is the medical evidence to her? Is she supposed to play a part in the breach proceedings? If so, how is she supposed to conduct the case? If his confidence can be breached, should he be told this in advance?

Subs. (2)
Remands for medical examinations and reports must not exceed four weeks at a time unless the remand is into custody.

Subs. (3)
Remands into custody must not be for more than three weeks at a time.

Subs. (4)
This subsection enables the court to make an order under s.35 of the Mental Health Act 1983, remanding for medical reports a person arrested under a power of arrest or an arrest warrant, where there is reason to suspect that he is suffering from mental illness or severe mental impairment.
Mental illness. This is not defined by statute. In *W v. L* [1974] Q.B. 711, Lawton L.J. said that the words "mental illness" were "ordinary words of the English language. They have no medical significance. They have no particular legal significance ... Ordinary words of the English language should be construed in the way that ordinary sensible people would construe them ... I ask myself, what would the ordinary sensible person have said about the patient's condition ... if he had been informed of his behaviour to the dogs [he hanged a puppy in the garage], the cat [he put this in a gas oven] and his wife [he threatened her with a knife]. In my judgment such a person would have said: "Well, the fellow is obviously mentally ill"". This robust approach will appeal to some, but it amounts to no more than a classification based upon behaviour. Further, the admission that the words have neither medical nor legal significance plays into the hands of critics of psychiatry such as Thomas Szasz and R.D. Laing. To Szasz, "mental illness is a metaphor" used to cover people who are "socially deviant or inept, or in conflict with individuals, groups or institutions" (*Ideology and Insanity*; Harmondsworth: Penguin, 1973, p.114).

Severe mental impairment. This is defined in the Mental Health Act 1983 as "a state of arrested or incomplete development of mind ... which includes significant impairment of intelligence and social functioning and is associated with abnormally aggressive or seriously irresponsible conduct on the part of the person concerned" (s.1(2)).

It will be noted that "psychopathic disorder" and "mental impairment" are omitted.

Accused person. There may be concern that respondents are being treated as if they were criminal defendants.

Same power. This means that remands can be for 28 days at a time or 12 weeks in all. This may be thought excessive in a domestic, as opposed to a criminal context.

An order under section 35. This requires the evidence (oral or written) of an approved medical practitioner, that there is reason to suspect that the accused person [in this context the respondent] is suffering from mental illness, psychopathic disorder, severe mental impairment or mental impairment and that it would be impracticable for a report on his mental condition to be made if he were remanded on bail (see the Mental Health Act 1983, s.35(3)). Courts cannot remand to hospital unless satisfied, on the written or oral evidence of the medical practitioner who would be responsible for making the report or of some other person representing the hospital managers, that arrangements have been made for his admission to hospital within a period of seven days after the remand. Under the Mental Health Act 1983 a remand or a further remand may not be for more than 28 days at a time or for more than 12 weeks in all, and the remand may be terminated if it appears to the court that it is appropriate to do so (Mental Health Act 1983, s.35(7)). Further, a person remanded for report is entitled to obtain, at his own expense, an independent report on his mental condition from a medical practitioner chosen by him and to apply to the court on the basis of it for his remand to be terminated (Mental Health Act 1983, s.35(8)). It should also be noted that a person remanded to hospital for a report on his mental condition retains his common law rights to refuse treatment (the consent to treatment provisions in the 1983 Act do not apply to patients liable to be detained by virtue of s.35) (see s.56(1)(b) of the Mental Health Act 1983).

Variation and discharge of orders

49.—(1) An occupation order or non-molestation order may be varied or discharged by the court on an application by—

(a) the respondent, or

(b) the person on whose application the order was made.

(2) In the case of a non-molestation order made by virtue of section 42(2) (b), the order may be varied or discharged by the court even though no such application has been made.

(3) If a spouse's matrimonial home rights are a charge on the estate or interest of the other spouse or of trustees for the other spouse, an order under section 33 against the other spouse may also be varied or discharged by the court on an application by any person deriving title under the other spouse or under the trustees and affected by the charge.

(4) If, by virtue of section 47(3), a power of arrest has been attached to certain provisions of an occupation order or non-molestation order, the court may vary or discharge the order under subsection (1) in so far as it confers a power of arrest (whether or not any application has been made to vary or discharge any other provision of the order).

DEFINITIONS
   "court; the": s.57.
   "matrimonial home rights": s.30.
   "non-molestation order": s.42(1).
   "occupation order": s.39.

GENERAL NOTE
This section provides for the variation and discharge of occupation orders and non-molestation orders. It prescribes who may apply for such variation and discharge. This section was moved by the Lord Chancellor at the Committee stage of the 1995 Family Homes and Domestic Violence Bill (see Public Bill Committee cols. 11, 22).

Subs. (1)
This provides that orders can be varied or discharged on application of either the respondent or the applicant.

The person on whose application. But not the person on whose behalf. Thus, an order in favour of a child, for which the child did not apply, cannot be varied or discharged on the child's application. It also follows that when provision is made under s.60 for third parties (*e.g.* the police) to act on behalf of victims of domestic violence, the victims will not be able to apply for variation or discharge, only the police will.

Subs. (2)
Where a non-molestation order has been made by the court of its own motion (under s.42(2)(b)), it may be varied or discharged by the court itself even though no application for variation or discharge has been made (see s.49(2)).

Subs. (3)
This subsection makes it clear that a person deriving title and affected by a charge has the capacity to apply for variation and discharge.

Subs. (4)
This subsection enables the court to vary or discharge a power of arrest independently of the order to which it is attached.

Enforcement powers of magistrates' courts

Power of magistrates' court to suspend execution of committal order

50.—(1) If, under section 63(3) of the Magistrates' Courts Act 1980, a magistrates' court has power to commit a person to custody for breach of a relevant requirement, the court may by order direct that the execution of the order of committal is to be suspended for such period or on such terms and conditions as it may specify.

(2) In subsection (1) "a relevant requirement" means—

(a) an occupation order or non-molestation order;

(b) an exclusion requirement included by virtue of section 38A of the Children Act 1989 in an interim care order made under section 38 of that Act; or

(c) an exclusion requirement included by virtue of section 44A of the Children Act 1989 in an emergency protection order under section 44 of that Act.

DEFINITIONS
"non-molestation order": s.42(1).
"occupation order": s.39.
"relevant requirement": subs. (2).

GENERAL NOTE
This section gives a magistrates' court power to suspend execution of a committal order relating to breach of certain requirements. Such a power is already available under the existing law to the High Court and to county courts.

Subs. (1)
Magistrates' courts are given the power to suspend the execution of an order of committal on such terms and conditions as they may specify. This reverses the ruling in *Head v. Head* [1982] 3 All E.R. 14 that a committal order under s.63(3) of the Magistrates' Courts Act 1980 (c. 43) had to take effect from the day it was made.
Relevant requirement. See subs. (2), below.

Subs. (2)
This lists the "relevant requirements".
Exclusion requirement . . . s.38A. See Sched. 6, para. 1.
Exclusion requirement . . . s.44A. See Sched. 6, para. 3.

Power of magistrates' court to order hospital admission or guardianship

51.—(1) A magistrates' court has the same power to make a hospital order or guardianship order under section 37 of the Mental Health Act 1983 or an interim hospital order under section 38 of that Act in the case of a person suffering from mental illness or severe mental impairment who could otherwise be committed to custody for breach of a relevant requirement as a magistrates' court has under those sections in the case of a person convicted of an offence punishable on summary conviction with imprisonment.

(2) In subsection (1) "a relevant requirement" has the meaning given by section 50(2).

DEFINITION
"relevant requirement": subs. (2) and s.50(2).

GENERAL NOTE
This section gives a magistrates' court the power to make a hospital order or a guardianship order under s.37 of the Mental Health Act 1983 or an interim hospital order under s.28 of that Act, instead of a committal to custody, where there has been a breach of an order or exclusion requirement. This conforms with their powers in other proceedings and gives magistrates' courts similar powers to the higher courts in this respect.

Subs. (1)
This subsection governs the circumstances in which magistrates' courts may make hospital orders and guardianship orders in lieu of a committal to custody.

Same power ... hospital order. The court must thus be satisfied, on the written or oral evidence or two medical practitioners, that the offender is suffering from mental illness or severe mental impairment and that the disorder is of "a nature or degree which makes it appropriate for him to be detained in a hospital for medical treatment and, in the case of ... mental impairment [and therefore presumably severe mental impairment], that such treatment is likely to alleviate or prevent a deterioration in his condition, (see the Mental Health Act 1983, s.37(2)(a)(i)). It must also be the most suitable method of disposal (s.37(2)(b)). Further, the court must be satisfied, on the written or oral evidence of the medical practitioner who would be in charge of the treatment of the patient or of some other person representing the hospital managers (who need not be medically qualified), that arrangements have been made for the admission of the offender to a specified hospital within a period of 28 days from the making of the order (Mental Health Act 1983, s.37(4)). One of the two medical practitioners must be approved under s.12(2) of the Mental Health Act 1983 as having special experience in the diagnosis of treatment of mental disorder (see s.54(1) of the 1983 Act). The two doctors giving evidence may be from the same hospital (this contrasts with the position as regards civil admissions, but presumably applies in this domestic context even though the analogy would be with civil cases). Copies of reports must be given to the defendant's representative, if he has one. If he is not represented, the substance of the report must be disclosed to him or, where he is a child or young person, conveyed to his parent or guardian if present in court. A hospital order places the person in hospital for a period of up to six months, which can be renewed for another six months, and for periods of one year at a time. Although the nearest relative has no power to discharge him, this person has the right to apply to a Mental Health Review Tribunal in the period between the expiration of six months and the expiration of 12 months beginning with the date of the order, and in any subsequent period of 12 months (s.69(1)(a)). The patient is not eligible to apply to a tribunal within the first six months of admission (his periods of eligibility correspond to those which apply to his nearest relative).

Same power ... interim hospital order. Interim hospital orders can be made under the Mental Health Act 1983 where (i) a person is convicted before the Crown Court of an offence punishable with imprisonment, other than murder, or by a magistrates' court of an offence punishable on summary conviction with imprisonment, and (ii) the court before or by which he is convicted is satisfied, on the written or oral evidence of two medical practitioners (one of whom is "approved" under s.12 of the Mental Health Act 1983) that (a) he is suffering from mental illness, severe mental impairment, mental impairment or psychopathic disorder; and (b) there is reason to suppose that the mental disorder from which he is suffering is such that it may be appropriate for a hospital order to be made. The interim hospital order authorises the offender's admission to hospital and his detention there (see the Mental Health Act 1983, s.38(1)). The order can only be made where the court is satisfied, on the evidence of the medical practitioner who would be in charge of the treatment or another representative of the hospital managers, that arrangements have been made for the offender's admission to hospital within 28 days. If the court is satisfied, it may, pending the admission, give directions for the offender's conveyance to, and detention in, a place of safety (see s.28(4)). An interim hospital order remains in force for a period not exceeding 12 weeks which the court specifies. It may be renewed for further periods of 28 days after hearing evidence from the responsible medical officer. It cannot remain in force for more than six months in total. It is to terminate if the court makes a hospital order or decides to deal with the offender in some other way (s.38(5)). The power of renewing an interim hospital order may be exercised without the offender being brought before the court, so long as he is legally represented and his solicitor or counsel is given an opportunity of being heard (see s.38(6)). A person given an interim hospital order is subject to the consent to treatment provisions in Pt. IV of the Mental Health Act 1983.

Mental illness. See the note on s.48, above.

Severe mental impairment. See the note on s.48, above.

Relevant requirement. This is defined in s.50(2).

Interim care orders and emergency protection orders

Amendments of Children Act 1989

52. Schedule 6 makes amendments of the provisions of the Children Act 1989 relating to interim care orders and emergency protection orders.

GENERAL NOTE

This section (and Sched. 6) amend the Children Act 1989 so as to enable the court to make an ouster order for the protection of children when making an emergency protection order or interim care order. This will permit the removal of a suspected abuser from the home instead of having to remove the child. There was support for such a provision during debates in Parliament which led to the Children Act 1989 (see *Hansard*, H.C. Standing Committee B, 25 May 1989, cols. 325–329) but supporters of an amendment then tabled failed to get a provision similar to that now in this Act passed. The problem had also troubled the courts (see notably *Nottinghamshire C.C. v. P* [1993] 2 F.L.R. 134). See, further, Law Commission, No. 207, paras. 6.15–6.22. The provision is discussed in detail in the General Note to Sched. 6, below.

Transfer of tenancies

Transfer of certain tenancies

53. Schedule 7 makes provision in relation to the transfer of certain tenancies on divorce etc. or on separation of cohabitants.

GENERAL NOTE

This section (together with Sched. 7) is derived from the power to transfer tenancies in the Matrimonial Homes Act 1983, and extends this power to cohabitants. Schedule 7 enables the court to require the transferee to make a payment to the transferor. It also enables the court to defer the making of such a payment in certain circumstances. See, further, Law Commission, paras. 6.1–6.6. The provision is discussed in detail in the General Note to Sched. 7.

Dwelling-house subject to mortgage

Dwelling-house subject to mortgage

54.—(1) In determining for the purposes of this Part whether a person is entitled to occupy a dwelling-house by virtue of an estate or interest, any right to possession of the dwelling-house conferred on a mortgagee of the dwelling-house under or by virtue of his mortgage is to be disregarded.

(2) Subsection (1) applies whether or not the mortgagee is in possession.

(3) Where a person ("A") is entitled to occupy a dwelling-house by virtue of an estate or interest, a connected person does not by virtue of—

(a) any matrimonial home rights conferred by section 30, or

(b) any rights conferred by an order under section 35 or 36,

have any larger right against the mortgagee to occupy the dwelling-house than A has by virtue of his estate or interest and of any contract with the mortgagee.

(4) Subsection (3) does not apply, in the case of matrimonial home rights, if under section 31 those rights are a charge, affecting the mortgagee, on the estate or interest mortgaged.

(5) In this section "connected person", in relation to any person, means that person's spouse, former spouse, cohabitant or former cohabitant.

DEFINITIONS
  "cohabitant": s.62(1).
  "connected person": subs. (5).
  "dwelling-house": s.63(1), (4).
  "former cohabitant": s.62(1).
  "matrimonial home rights": s.30.
  "mortgage": s.63(1).
  "mortgagee": s.63(1).

GENERAL NOTE
This section substantially reproduces s.8 of the Matrimonial Homes Act 1983 and extends some of its provisions (principally s.8(1) and (2) of the 1983 Act) to cohabitants and former cohabitants. The provisions deal principally with the effect of matrimonial home rights and occupation rights on mortgages and the registration of charges.

Subs. (1)
This provides that, in determining for the purposes of this Act (including Scheds. 1 and 4), whether a spouse, former spouse, cohabitant or former cohabitant is entitled to occupy a dwelling-house by virtue of an estate or interest, there must be disregarded any right to possession of the dwelling-house conferred on a mortgagee of the dwelling-house under or by virtue of his mortgage.
Estate. See the note on s.30, above.
Interest. See the note on s.30, above.

Subs. (2)
The disregarding of the right to possession applies whether the mortgagee is in possession or not.

Subss. (3) and (4)
A spouse, former spouse, cohabitant and former cohabitant have no larger right against the mortgagee to occupy the dwelling-house than does the person with an estate or interest. This is subject to subs. (4): it does not apply where the rights are a charge, affecting the mortgagee, on the estate or interest mortgaged.

Actions by mortgagees: joining connected persons as parties

55.—(1) This section applies if a mortgagee of land which consists of or includes a dwelling-house brings an action in any court for the enforcement of his security.

(2) A connected person who is not already a party to the action is entitled to be made a party in the circumstances mentioned in subsection (3).

(3) The circumstances are that—
(a) the connected person is enabled by section 30(3) or (6) (or by section 30(3) or (6) as applied by section 35(13) or 36(13)), to meet the mortgagor's liabilities under the mortgage;
(b) he has applied to the court before the action is finally disposed of in that court; and
(c) the court sees no special reason against his being made a party to the action and is satisfied—
    (i) that he may be expected to make such payments or do such other things in or towards satisfaction of the mortgagor's liabilities or obligations as might affect the outcome of the proceedings; or
    (ii) that the expectation of it should be considered under section 36 of the Administration of Justice Act 1970.

(4) In this section "connected person" has the same meaning as in section 54.

DEFINITIONS
  "connected person": s.54(5).
  "dwelling house": s.63(1).
  "mortgage": s.63(1).
  "mortgagee": s.63(1).
  "mortgagor": s.63(1).

GENERAL NOTE

This provides that where an action is brought by a mortgagee for enforcement of his security, a spouse, former spouse, cohabitant or former cohabitant is entitled to be made a party where s/he is allowed to meet the mortgagor's liabilities, has applied to do so, and the court sees no special reason against his/her being made a party and is satisfied that s/he may be expected to meet the mortgagor's liabilities so as to affect the outcome of the proceedings or the expectation of it should be considered under s.36 of the Administration of Justice Act 1970 (c. 31).

Actions by mortgagees: service of notice on certain persons

56.—(1) This section applies if a mortgagee of land which consists, or substantially consists, of a dwelling-house brings an action for the enforcement of his security, and at the relevant time there is—

    (a) in the case of unregistered land, a land charge of Class F registered against the person who is the estate owner at the relevant time or any person who, where the estate owner is a trustee, preceded him as trustee during the subsistence of the mortgage; or

    (b) in the case of registered land, a subsisting registration of—

        (i) a notice under section 31(10);

        (ii) a notice under section 2(8) of the Matrimonial Homes Act 1983; or

        (iii) a notice or caution under section 2(7) of the Matrimonial Homes Act 1967.

(2) If the person on whose behalf—

    (a) the land charge is registered, or

    (b) the notice or caution is entered,

is not a party to the action, the mortgagee must serve notice of the action on him.

(3) If—

    (a) an official search has been made on behalf of the mortgagee which would disclose any land charge of Class F, notice or caution within subsection (1)(a) or (b),

    (b) a certificate of the result of the search has been issued, and

    (c) the action is commenced within the priority period,

the relevant time is the date of the certificate.

(4) In any other case the relevant time is the time when the action is commenced.

(5) The priority period is, for both registered and unregistered land, the period for which, in accordance with section 11(5) and (6) of the Land Charges Act 1972, a certificate on an official search operates in favour of a purchaser.

DEFINITIONS

    "Dwelling house": s.63(1).

    "Mortgage": s.63(1).

    "Mortgagee": s.63(1).

    "Priority Period": subs. (5).

GENERAL NOTE

This provides that mortgagees must serve notice on persons who have registered a land charge or entered a notice or caution, where they are bringing an action to enforce their security and those persons are not parties to the action.

Subss. (1) and (2)

This provides that, where a mortgagee of land, which consists (or substantially consists) of a dwelling-house, brings an action for the enforcement of his security, and at the relevant time there is (i) a land charge of Class F registered or any person who, where the estate owner is a trustee, preceded him as trustee during the subsistence of the mortgage (unregistered land); or (ii) a subsisting registration of a notice under s.5(6) (or under previous legislation including a caution under the 1967 Act), notice of the action must be served by the mortgagee on the person on whose behalf the land charge is registered or the notice entered, if that person is not a party to the action (registered land).

Subss. (2) and (3)

This provides that, for the purposes of the foregoing provision as to notice by a mortgagee bringing an action for the enforcement of this security, if there has been issued a certificate of the result of an official search made on behalf of the mortgagee which would disclose any land charge of Class F, or notice or caution above, and the action is commenced within the priority period, the relevant time is the date of that certificate. In any other case the relevant time is the time when the action is commenced.

Subs. (5)

This subsection explains the expression "priority period". It is the period for which, in accordance with s.11(5) and (6) of the Land Charges Act 1972, a certificate on an official search operates in favour of a purchaser.

Jurisdiction and procedure etc.

Jurisdiction of courts

57.—(1) For the purposes of this Part "the court" means the High Court, a county court or a magistrates' court.

(2) Subsection (1) is subject to the provision made by or under the following provisions of this section, to section 59 and to any express provision as to the jurisdiction of any court made by any other provision of this Part.

(3) The Lord Chancellor may by order specify proceedings under this Part which may only be commenced in—

  (a) a specified level of court;
  (b) a court which falls within a specified class of court; or
  (c) a particular court determined in accordance with, or specified in, the order.

(4) The Lord Chancellor may by order specify circumstances in which specified proceedings under this Part may only be commenced in—

  (a) a specified level of court;
  (b) a court which falls within a specified class of court; or
  (c) a particular court determined in accordance with, or specified in, the order.

(5) The Lord Chancellor may by order provide that in specified circumstances the whole, or any specified part of any specified proceedings under this Part is to be transferred to—

  (a) a specified level of court;
  (b) a court which falls within a specified class of court; or
  (c) a particular court determined in accordance with, or specified in, the order.

(6) An order under subsection (5) may provide for the transfer to be made at any stage, or specified stage, of the proceedings and whether or not the proceedings, or any part of them, have already been transferred.

(7) An order under subsection (5) may make such provision as the Lord Chancellor thinks appropriate for excluding specified proceedings from the operation of section 38 or 39 of the Matrimonial and Family Proceedings Act 1984 (transfer of family proceedings) or any other enactment which would otherwise govern the transfer of those proceedings, or any part of them.

(8) For the purposes of subsections (3), (4) and (5), there are three levels of court—

  (a) the High Court;
  (b) any county court; and
  (c) any magistrates' court.

(9) The Lord Chancellor may by order make provision for the principal registry of the Family Division of the High Court to be treated as if it were a county court for specified purposes of this Part, or of any provision made under this Part.

(10) Any order under subsection (9) may make such provision as the Lord Chancellor thinks expedient for the purpose of applying (with or without modifications) provisions which apply in relation to the procedure in county courts to the principal registry when it acts as if it were a county court.

(11) In this section "specified" means specified by an order under this section.

GENERAL NOTE

This section provides generally for a unified jurisdiction between the High Court, county courts and magistrates' courts, except as provided for (see subss. (2), (3)) (and see also subs. (5)).

Contempt proceedings

58. The powers of the court in relation to contempt of court arising out of a person's failure to comply with an order under this Part may be exercised by the relevant judicial authority.

DEFINITIONS

"court; the": s.57.
"relevant judicial authority": s.63(1).

GENERAL NOTE

This section provides that the powers of the court to deal with contempt of court may be exercised by the court concerned. Where the order was made by the High Court, they may be exercised by a judge of that court; where the order was made by a county court, by a judge or district judge of that or any other county court; where the order was made by a magistrates' court, by any magistrates' court. The section was not in the original Family Homes and Domestic Violence Bill, or in the Law Commission recommendations. It was moved by the Lord Chancellor at the Committee stage in the House of Lords of this Bill (see col. 23).

Powers... contempt of court. Breach of an order or an undertaking (see s.46) is a contempt of court. This may be punished by committal to prison. There are no sentencing guidelines (see *Re H* [1986] 1 F.L.R. 558). When there is a reasonable alternative available instead of committal to prison, that alternative should be taken (see *Danchevsky v. Danchevsky* [1975] Fam. 17; *C v. C (contempt: committal)* [1989] Fam. Law 477). Committal orders are orders of last resort (*Ansah v. Ansah* [1977] Fam. 138; *Smith v. Smith* [1988] 1 F.L.R. 179—committal should not be an automatic result of breach of court order; see also *Measham v. Clarke* [1989] 1 F.L.R. 370; and see *Jones v. Jones* [1993] 2 F.L.R. 377, 381—there is little, if any, general principle emerging from Ormrod L.J.'s much-quoted observations in *Ansah* that committal orders for contempt in family cases should be the very last resort: *per* Russell L.J.). Where there are committal and criminal proceedings arising out of the same facts, the committal proceedings should be dealt with swiftly and decisively. However, where one set of proceedings (if allowed to proceed) is likely to prejudice the fairness of the trial of the other proceedings, the discretion to adjourn is only to be exercised when there is a real risk of serious prejudice which might lead to injustice (see *H v. C (Contempt and Criminal Proceedings)* [1993] 1 F.L.R. 787). There may be a disparity of sentence between a magistrates' court dealing with a criminal offence (which is not a sentence imposed for contempt of court) and a judge committing a contemnor. "There is all the difference in the world between assaulting another citizen, reprehensible though that may be, and assaulting a citizen who is notionally accompanied by a constable or an officer of the court for his or her protection... that sort of conduct is wholly unacceptable and must be met with condign punishment" (*Miller v. Juby* [1991] 1 F.L.R. 133 (where the Court of Appeal upheld two consecutive terms of eight months' imprisonment for repeated contempts)).

Magistrates' courts

59.—(1) A magistrates' court shall not be competent to entertain any application, or make any order, involving any disputed question as to a party's entitlement to occupy any property by virtue of a beneficial estate or interest or contract or by virtue of any enactment giving him the right to remain in occupation, unless it is unnecessary to determine the question in order to deal with the application or make the order.

(2) A magistrates' court may decline jurisdiction in any proceedings under this Part if it considers that the case can more conveniently be dealt with by another court.

(3) The powers of a magistrates' court under section 63(2) of the Magistrates' Courts Act 1980 to suspend or rescind orders shall not apply in relation to any order made under this Part.

This section provides that magistrates' courts will not have the power to determine property disputes (see Law Commission, No. 207, para. s.4). It also provides that magistrates are able to decline jurisdiction in any proceedings under the Act. The powers magistrates' courts have to suspend or rescind orders is not to extend to any order made under this Act.

Subs. (1)
This subsection restricts the jurisdiction of magistrates' courts to adjudicate on property questions.
Shall not be competent. Magistrates are therefore required to transfer a case upwards.
Estate ... interest ... contract... enactment. See the notes on s.30, above.
Unless it is necessary. Magistrates can decide disputed questions as to titles if this is a necessary pre-condition to dealing with an application or making an occupation (or non-molestation) order.

Subs. (2)
Magistrates have the power to decline jurisdiction.
More conveniently. Some guidance may be sought in the Children (Allocation of Proceedings) Order 1991 (made under the Children Act 1989), where exceptional gravity, importance or complexity, consolidation with pending proceedings and urgency where no other magistrates' court can take the case are listed (in art. 7) as reasons why a magistrates' court should transfer a case upwards.

Subs. (3)
The powers magistrates' courts have to suspend or rescind orders is not to extend to any order made under this Act.

Provision for third parties to act on behalf of victims of domestic violence

60.—(1) Rules of court may provide for a prescribed person, or any person in a prescribed category, ("a representative") to act on behalf of another in relation to proceedings to which this Part applies.

(2) Rules made under this section may, in particular, authorise a representative to apply for an occupation order or for a non-molestation order for which the person on whose behalf the representative is acting could have applied.

(3) Rules made under this section may prescribe—

(a) conditions to be satisfied before a representative may make an application to the court on behalf of another; and

(b) considerations to be taken into account by the court in determining whether, and if so how, to exercise any of its powers under this Part when a representative is acting on behalf of another.

(4) Any rules made under this section may be made so as to have effect for a specified period and may make consequential or transitional provision with respect to the expiry of the specified period.

(5) Any such rules may be replaced by further rules made under this section.

DEFINITIONS
"non-molestation order": s.42(1).
"occupation order": s.39.

GENERAL NOTE
This section enables rules of court to be made, under which provision may be made for third parties to act on behalf of victims of domestic violence.
This provision was neither in the Family Homes and Domestic Violence Bill of 1995 nor in the Family Law Bill as originally presented to Parliament. The Law Commission (Law Com. No. 207, paras. 5.18–5.23) had recommended that the police be given the power to apply for orders. It envisaged that:
"The police would have power to apply for a civil order where they had attended at or following an incident of molestation or violence, and had reasonable cause to believe that such abuse had occurred. They would then apply for a non-molestation or occupation order

against the aggressor, provided that the people concerned fell within the categories of associated persons ... , and provided that the police consider that this would be an appropriate course of action for them to take. There would be no obligation on the police to take civil proceedings, but the option would be available either as an alternative to or in addition to criminal proceedings." (para. 5.21).

The Law Commission further recommended that the police should be under a duty to consult the victim and to take account of her views in deciding whether to issue and how to conduct any civil proceedings (see para. 5.23).

The House of Commons Home Affairs Committee (H.C. 245, 1993) did not agree. It recognised that there were "arguments on both sides" (para. 118) and was "particularly sensitive to the need for women to have what could be described as a 'powerful friend', especially as legal aid becomes more difficult to obtain ..." (*idem*). It concluded that the proposal was "misguided" and that it would give the police a role for which they are neither "qualified nor resourced" (*idem*).

The original Bills accepted the Home Affairs Committee's conclusion rather than the Law Commission's recommendation. This section was incorporated within the Family Law Bill by an amendment moved at Third Reading in the House of Commons (*Hansard*, H.C. Vol. 279, cols. 595–599). The Government had resisted pressure to include such a provision. Although the proposer of the amendment (Paul Boateng M.P.) saw the need for this provision as "obvious" (see col. 596), it is by no means so. Two dangers are, first, that the provision may disempower women so that private violence is replaced by a form of public paternalism; and, secondly, that potentially it could lead the police into re-defining domestic violence as a civil rather than a criminal matter. On balance, though, it is thought that any new weapon in the battle to conquer violence against women deserves a chance.

The provision does not identify the police as the third party interveners. Instead, intervention is left open to representatives, yet to be specified, to act on behalf of victims. It may be decided that others may be more appropriate representatives: for example, women's aid organisations, refuges, social services, probation. It is coming to be recognised that a co-ordinated response to domestic violence is required. Rules are likely to recognise the need for an inter-agency strategy. This provision also recognises the need to experiment and to set up and monitor pilot schemes (see s.60(4)).

Subs. (2)

The person. It is not clear whether a representative could seek an order on behalf of a child. A child of under 16 years may apply only with leave: it would seem from the wording of this subsection that a representative will only be able to apply where the victim could have applied. If "could have applied" is interpreted as "could have applied without leave", then a representative will be in the same position as the child under 16. Without these words added, a representative would be able to apply for a child under 16 without satisfying the leave requirement. It may be that rules will provide for this problem.

Subs. (3)

Conditions. This may include the agreement of the victim for the representative to take action on her behalf.

Subs. (4)

Specified period. This envisages that the scheme be piloted.

Appeals

61.—(1) An appeal shall lie to the High Court against—

(a) the making by a magistrates' court of any order under this Part, or

(b) any refusal by a magistrates' court to make such an order,

but no appeal shall lie against any exercise by a magistrates' court of the power conferred by section 59(2).

(2) On an appeal under this section, the High Court may make such orders as may be necessary to give effect to its determination of the appeal.

(3) Where an order is made under subsection (2), the High Court may also make such incidental or consequential orders as appear to it to be just.

(4) Any order of the High Court made on an appeal under this section (other than one directing that an application be re-heard by a magistrates' court) shall, for the purposes—

(a) of the enforcement of the order, and

(b) of any power to vary, revive or discharge orders,
be treated as if it were an order of the magistrates' court from which the appeal was brought and not an order of the High Court.

(5) The Lord Chancellor may by order make provision as to the circumstances in which appeals may be made against decisions taken by courts on questions arising in connection with the transfer, or proposed transfer, of proceedings by virtue of any order under section 57(5).

(6) Except to the extent provided for in any order made under subsection (5), no appeal may be made against any decision of a kind mentioned in that subsection.

GENERAL NOTE

This section makes provision for appeals from magistrates' courts to the High Court. There is no appeal against a decision by magistrates to decline jurisdiction under s.59(2). On hearing an appeal the High Court may make orders necessary to give effect to its determination of the appeal and such incidental or consequential orders as appear to it to be just. Orders made by the High Court on appeal are to be treated as if they were orders of the magistrates' court.

General

Meaning of "cohabitants", "relevant child" and "associated persons"

62.—(1) For the purposes of this Part—
  (a) "cohabitants" are a man and a woman who, although not married to each other, are living together as husband and wife; and
  (b) "former cohabitants" is to be read accordingly, but does not include cohabitants who have subsequently married each other.

(2) In this Part, "relevant child", in relation to any proceedings under this Part, means–
  (a) any child who is living with or might reasonably be expected to live with either party to the proceedings;
  (b) any child in relation to whom an order under the Adoption Act 1976 or the Children Act 1989 is in question in the proceedings; and
  (c) any other child whose interests the court considers relevant.

(3) For the purposes of this Part, a person is associated with another person if—
  (a) they are or have been married to each other;
  (b) they are cohabitants or former cohabitants;
  (c) they live or have lived in the same household, otherwise than merely by reason of one of them being the other's employee, tenant, lodger or boarder;
  (d) they are relatives;
  (e) they have agreed to marry one another (whether or not that agreement has been terminated);
  (f) in relation to any child, they are both persons falling within subsection (4); or
  (g) they are parties to the same family proceedings (other than proceedings under this Part).

(4) A person falls within this subsection in relation to a child if—
  (a) he is a parent of the child; or
  (b) he has or has had parental responsibility for the child.

(5) If a child has been adopted or has been freed for adoption by virtue of any of the enactments mentioned in section 16(1) of the Adoption Act 1976, two persons are also associated with each other for the purposes of this Part if—
  (a) one is a natural parent of the child or a parent of such a natural parent; and
  (b) the other is the child or any person—

(i) who has become a parent of the child by virtue of an adoption order or has applied for an adoption order, or

(ii) with whom the child has at any time been placed for adoption.

(6) A body corporate and another person are not, by virtue of subsection (3)(f) or (g), to be regarded for the purposes of this Part as associated with each other.

DEFINITIONS

"child": s.63(1).
"cohabitants": subs. (1)(a).
"court; the": s.57.
"former cohabitants": subs. (1)(b).
"relevant child": subs. (2).

GENERAL NOTE

This section defines cohabitants and former cohabitants for the purpose of Pt. IV of this Act.

This is the first legislation to use the concept of "cohabitant." (Christina Lyon and Michael Freeman: in *Cohabitation Without Marriage* Aldershot Gower (1983)) were the first legal commentators to adopt this terminology, though we described the word as an "ugly expression" (p.5). Many still use the expression "cohabitee", including the latest family law text (see Mary Hayes and Catherine Williams, *Family Law: Principles, Policy and Practice* (1995)).

It is not easy to give a precise definition of what is meant by cohabitation. C.L. Cole (in R. Libby and R. Whitehurst (eds.), *Marriage and Alternatives* (1977)) sees "the cohabitation relationship as a special type of primary relationship in which the partners meet socioemotional, sociosexual, sociophysical and socioeconomic needs and maintenance functions." His view implies that the relationship covers "a relatively large degree of interpersonal commitment in order to meet interpersonal need and support system functions" (p.66).

Historically, there is nothing new about couples "living together" as man and wife without being married (see Freeman and Lyon, *Cohabitation Without Marriage* (1983), pp.6–11; P. Laslett, *Family Life and Illicit Love in Earlier Generations* (1977); S. Parker, *Informal Marriage, Cohabitation and the Law 1750–1984* (1990); L. Stone, *Uncertain Unions* (1992) especially pp.16–17). However, in the last quarter of a century there has been a dramatic increase. Twenty-five years ago it was estimated that about six per cent of couples cohabited before their wedding. By 1979 the *General Household Survey* showed that eight per cent of the single women in the sample over the age of 18 were living with someone as man and wife. It is now 60 per cent (see K. Kiernan and V. Estaugh, *Cohabitation: Extramarital Child-Bearing and Social Policy* (1993). This is reflected in the 1991 Census which shows that cohabitation is most frequent among women aged 20–24 and men aged 25–29 (OPCS, *1991 Census: Household and Family Composition*). Utting comments, "In fact, *most* people in their late twenties have cohabited at some stage in their relatively short lives, compared with fewer than a tenth of those aged 60 or over" (*D. Utting, Family and Parenthood: Supporting Families, Preventing Breakdowns* (1995), p.17). Most cohabitation is between young, childless couples. These relationships rarely last longer than five years and end in marriage or separation. One in seven cohabiting couples, interviewed in 1990 at the start of the longitudinal British Household Panel Survey, were later found to have married within a year. There is evidence that cohabiting couples are four times more likely to split up as married couples (N. Back, J. Gershuny, D. Rose and J. Scott, *Changing Households: The British Household Panel Survey* (1994)). There is also evidence that those who cohabit before marriage are more likely to have divorced within eight years than those who do not live together before they marry. (See J. Haskey, *Population Trends*, 1995, 68.) There are now dependent children in one in three cohabiting households (OPCS, *1991 Census: Household and Family Composition* (1994)). One in 20 dependent children is living in cohabiting couple families and one child in ten aged two years or under is living with a couple who are not married (or not married to each other). There is a discussion of earlier statistical trends in Freeman and Lyon, *Cohabitation Without Marriage* (1983) at pp.56–60.

Cohabitation is notoriously difficult to define. Lord Widgery C.J. commented in *R v. S. W. London Supplementary Benefit Appeal Tribunal ex parte Barnett* (unreported, 1973) that: "We have been invited to give some guidance upon the phrase "cohabitating (*sic*) as man and wife", but for my part it is so well known that nothing I could say about it could possibly assist in its interpretation hereafter." Cohabitation has to be distinguished from the casual encounter, from fornication, adultery and from other relationships which are intended to satisfy only such limited needs as sexual ones. English courts, which once saw a cohabiting woman as little more than a prostitute, have tended to distinguish "permanent" quasi-marital relationships from "casual or intermittent" ones (see *e.g.* James L.J. in *Dyson Holdings v. Fox* [1975] 3 All E.R. 1030). In 1950, a couple who lived together for 20 years were said by the Court of Appeal to be "masquerading ... as husband and wife": to say "that they were members of the same family seems ... an abuse of the English language" (*per* Asquith L.J. in *Gammans v. Ekins* [1950] 2 All E.R. 140, 142). But by 1975 in *Dyson Holdings v. Fox* the Court of Appeal had no difficulty in construing the word "family" to include a woman who had lived with a man for twenty-one years. Significantly, the judges took account of the way that the word "family" had changed its meaning according to the understanding of the ordinary person using the word in its popular sense (*op cit.*, at pp.1033, 1035).

Subs. (1)

For the purposes of this Part. This Act is the only Act as yet to use the concept "cohabitant". Previous legislation has tended to use the archetypal quasi-marital phrase "living together as husband and wife" (also used here) or even "reputed spouse" (see Consumer Credit Act 1974 (c. 39), s.184(5); and Pneumoconiosis etc. (Workers' Compensation) Act 1979 (c. 41), s.3(1)(c)).

A man and a woman. Only heterosexual relationships are thus included, though it is possible that homosexual or lesbian relationships may come within the concept of "associated persons" (see particularly s.2(1)(c)). English law is thus in striking contrast to the law in Denmark, Sweden, Norway and Holland, where gay couples may register their partnership, although in these countries this has lesser effects than marriage.

That earlier history acknowledged same sex unions, even offering a nuptial-type service, is demonstrated by John Boswell, *The Marriage of Likeness: Same-Sex Unions in Pre-Modern Europe* (1995).

English law, at least for the purposes of marriage, holds that "man" and "woman" are biological concepts determined at birth (*Corbett v. Corbett* [1971] P. 83). Transsexuals on this test remain consigned to the sex into which they were born. *Rees v. United Kingdom* (1987) 2 F.L.R. 111 and *Cossey v. United Kingdom* (1991) 2 F.L.R. 492, both challenges to the European Court on Human Rights, hold that the law is not in breach of either Arts. 8 or 12 of the European Convention. For criticisms of the medical basis of the *Corbett* decision see C.M. Armstrong and T. Walton (1990) 140 N.L.J. 1384 and A. Moir and D. Jessell, *Brain Sex* (1989). It remains to be decided whether "man" and "woman" will be so interpreted for the purposes of "cohabitation". It may be argued that *Corbett*, which is out of line with medical and scientific opinion and with more enlightened laws in other countries, should be confined to the facts upon which it was decided and not extended by analogy to other relationships. If this argument is unacceptable, then it may be claimed that a household which includes a transsexual (or presumably consists of transsexuals, though in such a case the couple might meet the "cohabitants" requirement) satisfies the "associated persons" test in s.62(3)(c).

Not married. Presumably this includes a couple who have gone through a ceremony of marriage, whether in this country or overseas, which English law would not recognise as creating a valid marriage. For example, a bigamous marriage, an underage marriage or one which was void for failure to comply with formalities, or a marriage abroad which is void by the *lex loci celebrationis* for failing to comply with local formalities *(Berthiaume v. Dastous* [1930] A.C. 79) or, in a matter of essential validity, a marriage abroad which is void by the law of either party's antenuptial domicile.

To each other. This does not preclude their being married to other persons.

Living together as husband and wife. Thus the couple need no longer live together "in the same household" (*cf.* the Domestic Violence and Matrimonial Proceedings Act 1976, s.1(2)). The Law Commission (No. 207, para 3.18) thought these additional words unnecessary "given that 'living with each other as husband and wife' has been held to connote something more than living in the same household (see *Fuller v. Fuller* [1973] 1 W.L.R. 730) and that cohabitation in the sense of living together as husband and wife can continue although the parties are actually living apart through force of circumstances" (see *Santos v. Santos* [1972] Fam. 247). However, the omission of "in the same household" will focus attention on the meaning of "living together as husband and wife". The phrase is both vague and value-laden. Section 1(2) of the 1976 Act (and we may ignore for these purposes that this had the now-omitted reference to "household") targeted couples living together "on a stable basis" (Official Report, H.C. Standing Committee F, 30 June 1976, col. 5, *per* Jo Richardson M.P.). The courts are likely to regard the stability of the relationship as a constituent element of "living together as husband and wife". But, of course, four in ten marriages are expected to end in divorce and more than one-fifth of today's divorces occur within five years of the wedding, with another quarter dissolving their marriage after five to nine years. Clearly, a couple could live together as husband and wife for a relatively short period. And, as the now-defunct *Handbook* to Supplementary Benefit legislation conceded, "when a couple first live together it may be clear from the start that the relationship is similar to that of husband and wife *e.g.* the woman has taken the man's home and has borne his child ..." (p.28). Nevertheless, in *Helby v. Rafferty* [1978] 3 All E.R. 1016 the Court of Appeal refused to recognise that one cohabitant could be a member of the other cohabitant's family where the relationship had lasted five years. There was in this case "unmarriage-like behaviour" (see below) but, even so, to question the quality of stability in a relationship of five years' duration is puzzling in the light of facts about marriage just adduced.

What, therefore, are the characteristics of a husband and wife relationship that courts expect to find in those who live "as" husband and wife? They are more likely to reach this conclusion if there are children of the relationship. The old *Handbook* (referred to above) stated that "when a couple are caring for a child or children of their union there is a strong presumption that they are living together as husband and wife" (para. 2(12)(e)). The duration of the relationship is also important, although the norm has declined rapidly and in cases today we might expect a few weeks to suffice. The behaviour of the parties has also been significant. To put it at its crudest, have the couple behaved in a marriage-like way? In an early case on what was then called "the cohabitation rule", the National Insurance Commissioner ruled that a man and a woman were cohabiting "if he and she are carrying on a common home in the manner in which husbands and wives do." He went on to say that, "in determining this question it is their general relationship which has to be looked at. Neither their habits with relation to sexual intercourse, nor the manner in which the common household fund ... is spent ... is conclusive" (G 214/50 K.L. Digest of Commissioners' Decisions, H.M.S.O.). In a more recent decision (R (G) 3/71)–though nevertheless still a quarter of a century old—a Commissioner stated: "it is generally accepted that the question of whether a woman is cohabiting with a man as his wife ... requires an examination of three main matters: (i) their relationship in relation to sex; (ii) their relationship in relation to money; (iii) their general relationship." Sex alone cannot be a determining criterion (though there is evidence that the old DHSS administering the cohabitation rule was over-influenced by this incident—see Ruth Lister, *As Man and Wife* (1973), CPAG). On the other hand, it is difficult to see what else the court hinged its jurisdiction on in *McLean v. Nugent* (1980) 1 F.L.R. 26. A relationship had resulted in the birth of a child. She then moved into accommodation away from him because she wanted to end the association. He found her, forced his way in, brutally assaulted her and raped her. The Court of Appeal held that the parties had been living together as husband and wife "because there can be no doubt in fact ... that willy nilly she was living with him as husband and wife" (*per* Ormrod L.J. at p.31). There can be no doubt that this was his intention, but it certainly was not hers. I for one would recoil from the suggestion that what made this association marriage-like was that he raped her. In *Tuck v. Nicholls* [1989] 1 F.L.R. 283, the couple had never lived together although they had had a sexual relationship and a child. They obtained council housing on the basis of this and she spent a couple of nights in the council house with him, whilst continuing to live with her parents. The next time she returned she found him with another woman; there was a violent confrontation and she did not return. The Court of Appeal held that the question to be answered—it was remitted for a rehearing—was whether she had moved into the house. If not, s.1(2) of the Domestic Violence and Matrimonial Proceedings Act 1976 would not apply. Again, this would seem to emphasise the sexual relationship above all else; the implication being that had she moved in for the briefest of periods, she would have been living with him as husband and wife. Looked at another way, the presence of a child might be said to tilt the balance in favour of a conclusion that their relationship was quasi-marital. These two cases show a welcome willingness to protect women from violent partners, but leave the state of the test in some doubt.

The courts have also looked to the financial arrangements existing between the parties as an instance of behaviour indicative of a marriage-like relationship. Thus, in *Crisp v. Mullings, The Times*, July 4, 1975, Russell L.J. was clearly influenced by the "man-and-wife" discussions the parties had in relation to their financial arrangements. By contrast, in *Helby v. Rafferty* [1978] 3 All E.R. 1016, the fact that the parties kept separate bank accounts, although they shared expenses, was a factor deemed relevant by the Court of Appeal in denying Mr Rafferty the status of "family member". Neither of these cases are domestic violence-related, and it may therefore be thought that such questions have only marginal relevance in the context of "living together as husband and wife" for the purposes of this Act. Another incident of behaviour which may be relevant is the way the parties present themselves to the outside world. There are also indications that where stereotypical gender roles are undertaken the courts are more likely to characterise the relationship as "husband and wife-like." *Kokosinski v. Kokosinski* [1980] Fam. 72, where there was 25 years of pre-marital cohabitation followed by a grotesquely short marriage and the "length" of the marriage was in issue, illustrates this well. The wife there was said to have "given the best years of her life to this husband. She has been faithful, loving and hardworking. She has helped him to build what is in every sense a family business. She has managed his home and been a mother to and helped him to bring up a son ... ".

In relation to behaviour the courts have also accepted that, if marriages can be awful, so too can cohabitation! The most striking illustration is the case of *Adeoso v. Adeoso* [1981] 1 All E.R. 107, where the couple's relationship had reached such a low ebb that they slept in separate rooms and communicated only by notes. In deciding for the purposes of an injunction whether they were living together in the same household as if they were husband and wife, the Court of Appeal said that "on an objective view the parties were living together in the flat as if they were husband and wife, their relationship being comparable to a marriage in the last stages of break-down" (p.109) (and see further J.T. Younger 67 Cornell L.R. 45, 94–102 (1981)). More appositely, this couple were living apart as husband and wife!

Cases such as *Adeoso v. Adeoso*, *McClean v. Nugent* and *Tuck v. Nicholls* evince a sympathy towards the plight of the female victim of violent relationships. They also demonstrate that "living together as husband and wife" can be expected to be liberally interpreted by the courts.

Former cohabitants ... accordingly. That is, did they live together as husband and wife?

Cohabitants who have subsequently married each other. These will be treated as married persons (associated persons: see s.62(3)(a)).

Subs. (2)

This subsection defines "relevant child" for the purposes of this Act (see also s.63(1)).

Any child. This is defined in the normal way to mean a person under 18 years. Not included, therefore, are adult offspring who are dependent by reason of disability or handicap. The child does not have to be the child of either of the parties or a child of the family.

Living with. Whether a child whose normal place of residence is not with either party (*e.g.* because he is in boarding school, with foster parents or in care) comes within this paragraph may be doubted, but little turns on it because such a child's interests are likely to be considered "relevant" under para. (c).

An order. *I.e.*, when the question of the child's welfare is already before the court. "It is important that the court hearing proceedings under the Children Act or Adoption Act should have power to protect the child involved in those proceedings against all forms of molestation and abuse" (*per* Law Commission, No. 207, para. 3.27).

Interests ... relevant. This gives, and rightly so, the court complete discretion to protect any other child it considers needs protection. The example given by the Law Commission is the child who has frequent and long periods of staying access with one of the parties (No. 207, para. 3.27). But there seems to be no reason why the provision should be artificially restricted in this way—a child with irregular or rare contact or where the periods of staying access are short also has interests a court might well deem relevant.

Subs. (3)

This section defines "associated persons" for the purposes of this Act (see also s.63(1)). There are *seven* categories of associated persons. The Law Commission recommended that there should be eight categories (para. 3.26). The omitted category is persons who have or have had a sexual relationship with each other, whether or not involving sexual intercourse. The Law Commission conceded that this category was difficult to "define in legislative terms" (para. 3.24). It embraces "people who have been boyfriend and girlfriend in a romantic relationship which might have varying degrees of sexual involvement." It envisaged situations where "there would have been a degree of mutuality and some participation in consensual sexual activity, although not necessarily amounting to sexual intercourse." As an example the Commission cited the "unbalanced stranger who develops an obsession from a distance". The Commission thought that the victims of such obsessions might need protection just as spouses and cohabitants whose relationships have broken down. Parliament did not agree.

The Act, as indeed the Law Commission, takes the policy decision of extending statutory protection only to a named category of persons. The Law Commission conceded that "There is an argument for having no limitations at all, on the basis that it is difficult to see why there should be any restrictions on the ground of relationship or residence if the main aim of the legislation is to provide protection from violence or molestation for people who need it" (para. 3.8). But it countered that "to remove all restrictions would involve the creation of something approaching a new tort of harassment or molestation" (*idem*). This was written before the recent case law developments referred to in the Introduction to this Part of the Act. Those who fall outside the categories listed in s.63(3) may be able to have recourse to the torts of trespass or nuisance or may be able to seek remedies within employment law or property law.

It is the Law Commission's view that:

> Family relationships can ... be appropriately distinguished from other forms of association. In practice many of the same considerations apply to them as to married or cohabiting couples. Thus the proximity of the parties often gives unique opportunities for molestation and abuse to continue; the heightened emotions of all concerned give rise to a particular need for sensitivity and flexibility in the law; there is frequently a possibility that their

relationship will carry on for the foreseeable future; and there is in most cases the likelihood that they will share a common budget, making financial remedies inappropriate. (Law Com. No. 207, para. 3.19).

Para. (a): are or have been married to each other. Protection is thus extended to former spouses (the failure of the previous law adequately to address them caused difficulties in practice). Clearly the parties must be or have been married (though if not so because, for example, the "marriage" is bigamous or is void for some other reason, the parties are likely to be cohabitants or former cohabitants, provided the tests in s.62 are satisfied). "Married" includes those who have actually polygamously married (see s.63(5)).

Para. (b): cohabitants or former cohabitant. For the meaning of which, see s.62(1) and the commentary thereto.

Para. (c): live or have lived in the same household. According to the Law Commission, this is intended to include "people who live in the same household, other than on a purely commercial basis" (No. 207, para. 3.21). Thus, it could "exclude a student renting the spare bedroom or a live-in nanny employed to care for children" (*idem*). The Law Commission recognises that the approach adopted may involve "distinctions which at first sight seem strange. For example, remedies may be available to three or four friends sharing a flat if they are all joint tenants, but not between the one who takes a tenancy and sublets to his friends" (para. 3.22). Its response is that "however similar the factual circumstances may appear, the legal relationship of landlord and tenant is quite unlike that of equal household shares" (*idem*). The Act preserves this distinction. The words used in s.62(3)(c) are designed to target "anyone who is associated with the respondent by virtue of a family relationship or something closely akin to such a relationship" (para. 3.19). An anticipated problem situation is the gay relationship. In the past, the courts have evinced a reluctance to categorise one gay person as a member of another gay person's family: see *Harrogate B.C.* v. *Simpson* [1986] 2 F.L.R. 91. But the Law Commission is in no doubt that the language used here embraces gay relationships: in rejecting the model it initially preferred, the Commission says it "might exclude people who have a genuine need for protection in circumstances which most people would regard as family relationships in the broader sense. We have in mind instances such as two people who have lived together on a long term basis whether as close friends or in a homosexual relationship" (para. 3.19). Whether it is right to believe this view is congruent with public opinion is dubious, but this is an area where legislation and judicial interpretation of it may legitimately lead, rather than slavishly follow, instinctual public feeling. The better view is that gay couples may be associated persons for the purposes of this Act.

The same household. This has become a term of art in matrimonial law. See *Hopes* v. *Hopes* [1948] 2 All E.R. 920; *Mouncer* v. *Mouncer* [1972] 1 W.L.R. 321. These cases establish that people can live in different households although they are actually living in the same house. As the Law Commission puts it (Law Com. No. 207, para. 3.21):

> "The crucial test is the degree of community life which goes on. If the parties shut themselves up in separate rooms and cease to have anything to do with each other, they live in separate households. But if they share domestic chores and shopping, eat meals together or share the same living room, they are living in the same household, however strained their relations may be."

Employee, tenant, lodger, boarder. In these instances, remedies exist in labour and property law and possibly within the law of tort.

Para. (d): relatives. This is defined in s.63. Note the breadth of the definition which widens "relative" to include those whose relationship is the result of a cohabitation. So, for example, for the purpose of this Act the brother of a woman's cohabitant is her relative. The Law Commission was satisfied of the need to cover such cases (see para. 3.23).

Para. (e): agreed to marry. This extends protection to engaged or formerly engaged couples who have neither cohabited nor lived together in the same household. This class of persons may be a minority (see Kiernan and Estaugh, *Cohabitation: Extra-Marital Child-Bearing and Social Policy* (1993)—60 per cent of marrying couples have cohabited before their marriage) but it is clearly one which is worthy of protection. On proof of an agreement to marry, see s.44. Occupation orders (s.33) and non-molestation orders (s.42) may not be made in favour of an engaged or formerly engaged person unless the agreement to marry is evidenced in writing (s.44(1))—note that the agreement itself does not have to be in writing. It is clear that an engagement to marry may be evidenced in a number of written manifestations, ranging from a newspaper announcement (so long as this is with the consent of both parties), written or printed invitations to an engagement party or correspondence between the parties (and see Lord Mackay, *Hansard*, H.L. Vol. 564, col. 1062). Alternatively, it may be evidenced by the gift of an engagement ring by one party to the agreement to the other in contemplation of marriage (nor does the Act stipulate that the donor must be the man), or by a ceremony entered into by the parties in the presence of one or more other persons assembled for the purpose of witnessing the ceremony (s.44(2)). The court has to be satisfied (on a balance of probabilities) that the gift of an engagement ring is evidence of an agreement to marry: the gift in itself will not necessarily constitute an agreement to marry. The recognition of betrothal ceremonies, formal agreements to marry that still exist among certain ethnic minority groups, is the third category of evidence.

Terminated. Applications must be made before the third anniversary of the termination of the agreement to marry (s.33(2) and s.42(4)).

Para. (f): any child ... both persons. They must either be parents or have parental responsibility in relation to the child or under (g) below be parties to the same family proceedings.

Para. (g): parties to the same family proceedings. "Family proceedings" are defined in s.63(1) and (2). Of the many useful applications, one may be cited. It will now be possible in adoption proceedings, in appropriate circumstances (*e.g.* a violent birth father), to restrain contact with the child. *Cf. Re D* [1991] Fam. 137. And see Law Commission at No. 207, para. 3.25.

Subs. (4)

Parent of the child. The concept of "parent" is complex and by no means free of doubt. Since the Family Law Reform Act 1987 (c. 42), s.1, the term "parent" has included both parents of the child, whether they are married to each other or not. An unmarried father does not automatically have parental responsibility, but he is a parent. Thus unmarried parents who have neither lived together as husband and wife nor lived in the same household can be "associated persons", with the consequence that non-molestation orders can be made.

The "reproduction revolution" has complicated the determination of who a parent is. Section 27(1) of the Human Fertilisation and Embryology Act 1990 (c. 37) provides that "the woman who is carrying or who has carried a child as a result of the placing in her of an embryo or of sperm and eggs, and no other woman, is to be treated as the mother of the child" (and this is for *all* purposes—see s.29(1) of the same Act). The woman who gives birth to a child is thus the child's mother, whether or not the child is genetically related to her. If she is a surrogate for a married couple and one of the couple is genetically related to the child, a court may make an order in favour of the commissioning couple "providing for a child to be treated in law as the child of the parties to a marriage" (s.30 of the Human Fertilisation and Embryology Act 1990, and avoiding the problem of *Re W* [1991] 1 F.L.R. 385). Once an order is made, the child becomes the child of the commissioning parents, and the woman who gave birth is no longer recognised by law as the mother. Where a *married* woman is impregnated with the sperm from a man who is not her husband, s.28 of the 1990 Act provides that her husband shall be treated as the child's father for all purposes, unless he has not consented to the assisted conception. Where he has not consented, the common law presumption of legitimacy applies, unless rebutted by evidence to the contrary (see s.28(5)(a)). In the case of *unmarried* couples, a man who is not the child's genetic father is treated by law as the father, provided that the methods used to assist conception were carried out in the course of treatment services provided for her and a man together, by a person to whom a licence applies (*i.e.* one issued by the Human Fertilisation and Embryology Authority) (see s.28(3)). Where a woman conceives through donor insemination using DIY methods, the father is the donor.

Parental responsibility. This is "defined" in s.3(1) of the Children Act 1989 (c. 41) as "All the rights, duties, powers, responsibility and authority which by law a parent of a child has in relation to the child and his property". A mother always has parental responsibility. When a child's father and mother were married to each other at the time of the child's birth, each has parental responsibility for the child (s.2(1) of the Children Act 1989). "Were married" includes the situation of the "putative marriage" (*e.g.* a bigamous marriage where one of the parties reasonably believed the marriage was valid: see the Legitimacy Act 1976 (c. 31), s.1). It also includes cases of legitimation by subsequent marriage (s.2 of the Legitimacy Act states that such parents are treated as if they were married to each other at the time of the child's birth). Parents of adopted children are also deemed to be married to each other at the time of the child's birth (Family Law Reform Act 1987, s.1(3)(c)). Where a child's mother and father were not married to each other at the time of his/her birth, only the mother has parental responsibility for the child (s.2(2) of the Children Act 1989). But the father may acquire it "in accordance with the provisions of [the Children] Act." He may do this in one of five ways:

1. By making an agreement with the mother (s.4(1)(b) of the 1989 Act).
2. By the court making a parental responsibility order under s.4(1)(a) of the 1989 Act. The child's welfare is the paramount consideration: *Re G* [1994] 1 F.L.R. 504. The court should ask itself: "can [he] show that he is a father to the child, not in the biological sense, but in the sense that he has established or is likely to establish such a real family tie with the child that he should now be afforded the corresponding legal tie?" *per* Ward J. in *D v. Hereford and Worcester County Council* [1991] 1 F.L.R. 205, 212. In *Re H* [1991] 1 F.L.R. 214, Balcombe L.J. said that in determining whether to make an order

the court should take account of the degree of commitment the father had shown to the child, the degree of attachment that existed between father and child, and the reasons why the father was applying for the order. But this is not to be treated as quasi-statutory (*Re G* [1994] 1 F.L.R. 504, 507). Acrimony between mother and father is not a reason for denying the father parental responsibility (*Re P* [1994] 1 F.L.R. 578). Where the purpose in seeking the order is to frustrate a local authority's long term plans for a child, it should be refused (see *W v. Ealing L.B.C* [1993] 2 F.L.R. 788).

3. By obtaining a residence order under s.8 of the Children Act 1989. Where a court makes a residence order in favour of an unmarried father, it must also make an order giving him parental responsibility under s.4 of that Act (see s.12(1) of the Children Act 1989). If the residence order is brought to an end, he retains parental responsibility.

4. By being appointed as the child's guardian by the court (see s.5(1) of the Children Act 1989).

5. By being appointed as the child's guardian by the mother or another guardian, but this will take effect only after the mother's death.

Subs. (5)

Freed for adoption. Namely, under s.18 of the Adoption Act 1976.

Any of the enactments mentioned in s.16(1) ... Namely, s.18 of the Adoption Act 1976 or, in Scotland, s.14 of the Children Act 1975.

Interpretation of Part IV

63.—(1) In this Part—

"adoption order" has the meaning given by section 72(1) of the Adoption Act 1976;

"associated", in relation to a person, is to be read with section 62(3) to (6);

"child" means a person under the age of eighteen years;

"cohabitant" and "former cohabitant" have the meaning given by section 62(1);

"the court" is to be read with section 57;

"development" means physical, intellectual, emotional, social or behavioural development;

"dwelling-house" includes (subject to subsection (4))—

    (a) any building or part of a building which is occupied as a dwelling,

    (b) any caravan, house-boat or structure which is occupied as a dwelling,

and any yard, garden, garage or outhouse belonging to it and occupied with it;

"family proceedings" means any proceedings—

    (a) under the inherent jurisdiction of the High Court in relation to children; or

    (b) under the enactments mentioned in subsection (2);

"harm"—

    (a) in relation to a person who has reached the age of eighteen years, means ill-treatment or the impairment of health; and

    (b) in relation to a child, means ill-treatment or the impairment of health or development;

"health" includes physical or mental health;

"ill-treatment" includes forms of ill-treatment which are not physical and, in relation to a child, includes sexual abuse;

"matrimonial home rights" has the meaning given by section 30;

"mortgage", "mortgagor" and "mortgagee" have the same meaning as in the Law of Property Act 1925;

"mortgage payments" includes any payments which, under the terms of the mortgage, the mortgagor is required to make to any person;

"non-molestation order" has the meaning given by section 42(1);

"occupation order" has the meaning given by section 39;

"parental responsibility" has the same meaning as in the Children Act 1989;

"relative", in relation to a person, means—

    (a) the father, mother, stepfather, stepmother, son, daughter, stepson, stepdaughter, grandmother, grandfather, grandson or granddaughter of that person or of that person's spouse or former spouse, or

    (b) the brother, sister, uncle, aunt, niece or nephew (whether of the full blood or of the half blood or by affinity) of that person or of that person's spouse or former spouse,

and includes, in relation to a person who is living or has lived with another person as husband and wife, any person who would fall within paragraph (a) or (b) if the parties were married to each other;

"relevant child", in relation to any proceedings under this Part, has the meaning given by section 62(2);

"the relevant judicial authority", in relation to any order under this Part, means—

    (a) where the order was made by the High Court, a judge of that court;

    (b) where the order was made by a county court, a judge or district judge of that or any other county court; or

    (c) where the order was made by a magistrates' court, any magistrates' court.

(2) The enactments referred to in the definition of "family proceedings" are—

(a) Part II;

(b) this Part;

(c) the Matrimonial Causes Act 1973;

(d) the Adoption Act 1976;

(e) the Domestic Proceedings and Magistrates' Courts Act 1978;

(f) Part III of the Matrimonial and Family Proceedings Act 1984;

(g) Parts I, II and IV of the Children Act 1989;

(h) section 30 of the Human Fertilisation and Embryology Act 1990.

(3) Where the question of whether harm suffered by a child is significant turns on the child's health or development, his health or development shall be compared with that which could reasonably be expected of a similar child.

(4) For the purposes of sections 31, 32, 53 and 54 and such other provisions of this Part (if any) as may be prescribed, this Part is to have effect as if paragraph (b) of the definition of "dwelling-house" were omitted.

(5) It is hereby declared that this Part applies as between the parties to a marriage even though either of them is, or has at any time during the marriage been, married to more than one person.

GENERAL NOTE

This is the interpretation section. Other interpretations are to be found in s.62(1) ("cohabitants", "former cohabitants"), s.62(3) (the meaning of "associated persons"), s.63(2) (the meaning of "relevant child"), s.39 (the meaning of "occupation order"), s.42(1) ("non-molestation order"), s.57 (the meaning of "the court") and s.63(1) (the meaning of "family proceedings"). This section (see s.63(5)) also makes it clear that the Act applies to a husband and wife who entered into a marriage under a law which permits polygamy.

Subs. (1)

Child. But note s.43 for applications by children. Those aged 16 and 17 may apply for orders without leave: those under 16 years require leave.

Development. See also s.62(1). The definition of "development" is that to be found in s.31(9) of the Children Act 1989, on which see M.D.A. Freeman in Allan Levy (ed.), *Refocus on Child Abuse* (London: Hawksmere, 1994, p.18).

Harm. See also s.63(1), (3). Note that (b) is based on the Children Act 1989, s.31(9).

Sexual abuse. This is not further defined in the Act. Nor is there a universally accepted definition of what constitutes "sexual abuse". It seems the standard of proof is higher than in other civil cases: see *Re W* [1994] 1 F.L.R. 419.

Relative. The width of this definition should be noted.

Subs. (3)

This subsection is taken from the Children Act 1989 s.31(10).

A similar child. According to the Lord Chancellor (*Hansard*, H.L. Vol. 503, col. 354—debating the Children Bill), this means a child with the same physical attributes as the child concerned, and not a child of the same background. On this test, the development of a four year old child has to be compared with that of other four year olds, and not with other four year olds from similar backgrounds. This would mean that a child from a deprived background is expected to achieve intellectual growth and emotional maturity comparable to children who come from well-ordered, materially comfortable and stimulating environments. However, the *Guidance*, issued under the Children Act 1989, says we "may" need "to take account of environmental, social and cultural characteristics of the child" (see Vol. 1, para. 3.20). Neither view has legal authority: that expressed by the Department of Health in the *Guidance* is, it is submitted, preferable. Whatever the problem, the phrase does at least make us compare *this* child with children like him or her, that is with children who have the same attributes. Thus, to take an example, the development of a deaf four year old boy is to be compared with what is to be expected of other four year old boys who are deaf, and not with other four year olds. But the value of this may be more apparent than real, for much depends upon other factors: *e.g.* when was he diagnosed as deaf? Are his parents also deaf? How is he being educated? If we take account only of the characteristics of the child, as the subsection requires, a deaf child of deaf parents is like a deaf child of hearing parents, but, of course, he is not. His rearing, socialisation and education will have taken place in a different environment: has parents, with experience of living with deafness, may well have attitudes to hearing problems and to the education of the deaf which are very different from parents who have not themselves experienced the disability. However laudatory the goal—in emphasising the special needs of children with disabilities—reliance on the concept of "similar child" overlooks the essential individuality of families and their problems. By concentrating on the child, it also ignores the impact of interaction between the child and his or her parents. The courts have only interpreted the concept of "similar child" in the unusual circumstance of a school refusal case. In *Re O* [1992] 2 F.L.R. 7, "similar child" was said to mean "a child of equivalent intellectual and social development, who has gone to school, and not merely an average child who may or may not be at school".

Subs. (4)

Dwelling-house has a narrower meaning (it does not include a caravan, house-boat or structure occupied as a dwelling) for the purposes of the provisions specified. We have been assured that a tree (*e.g.* one occupied by a protestors on the Newbury bypass) is not a structure (*per* Lord Chancellor, *Hansard*, H.L. Vol. 570, col. 122).

Subs. (5)

For the purposes of this Act "married" includes those polygamously married, whether actually or potentially so. This is a liberal provision but it has implications that have not been thought through. It should cause no problems where there is only one spouse but, where there is more than one, the provision may cause difficulties, particularly with matrimonial home rights and occupation orders.

Part V

INTRODUCTION

Part V contains supplemental provisions including, in s.64, provision for the separate representation of children in any matter under Pts. II or IV of this Act, the Matrimonial Causes Act 1973 or the Domestic Proceedings and Magistrates Court Act 1978. This section was moved late in the Bill's progress (see *Hansard*, H.C. Vol. 279, cols. 581–586).

Section 63 is the definition/interpretation section of this Part of the Act. In particular, it defines "harm" for the purposes of ss.33(7) and 35(8) and "relative" for the purposes of s.62(3)(d). "Family proceedings" are also defined both for this Part of the Act and in relation to Pt. II of the Act. The definition of these is modelled on that in s.8(4) of the Children Act 1989. "Relevant judicial authority" is also defined.

Section 65 makes provision for rule-making power under the Act.

Section 66, together with Scheds. 8, 9, and 10 provides a large number of consequential amendments, makes transitional provisions and provides for savings, and repeals a number of statutes or parts thereof. Repealed in total are the Domestic Violence and Matrimonial Proceedings Act 1976, the Domestic Proceedings and Magistrates' Court Act 1978 and the Matrimonial Homes Act 1983.

Section 67 is the short title, commencement and extent provision. Sections 65 and 67 are in force. The remaining provisions will come into force on such day or days as the Lord Chancellor may by order appoint. The Act basically extends to England and Wales only. Exceptions, which include s.17 (dealing with pension assets in Scotland), are listed in s.67(4).

SUPPLEMENTAL

Provision for separate representation for children

64.—(1) The Lord Chancellor may by regulations provide for the separate representation of children in proceedings in England and Wales which relate to any matter in respect of which a question has arisen, or may arise, under—
  (a) Part II;
  (b) Part IV;
  (c) the 1973 Act; or
  (d) the Domestic Proceedings and Magistrates' Courts Act 1978.
  (2) The regulations may provide for such representation only in specified circumstances.

GENERAL NOTE

This provision, which was moved at the Third Reading of the Bill in the House of Commons (see *Hansard*, H.C. Vol. 279, cols. 582–586), permits the Lord Chancellor to provide by regulations for the separate representation of children in a wide range of civil proceedings, including applications for occupation and non-molestation orders. As the law stands (see s.37 of the Children Act 1989), there is provision for the appointment of a guardian *ad litem* in civil proceedings only where it appears to the court that it may be necessary for a care or supervision order to be made in respect of the child. Under the new provision, the courts will not be constrained in this way. In addition, it should be pointed out that in certain cases there will be a welfare officer's report and in such circumstances it may not be thought necessary to provide for the representation envisaged by this section. The subsection permits the regulations to provide for separate representation of children "only in specified circumstances". They may well provide that separate representation is not necessary where a court welfare officer is involved. But on the difference of functions between the two, see Butler-Sloss L.J. in *Re S* [1992] 2 F.C.R. 554:
"The functions are not identical although they do have many features in common: each has a duty to report to the court; each has a duty to consider the welfare or interests of the child; each may be cross-examined on any report which they give. However, a child welfare officer is not a party to proceedings whereas a GAL is.... Nevertheless, each has a similar duty to the court, which is to advise the court as to what is best for the child independently of the other parties to the proceedings, and each of them is independent of all the other parties to the proceedings. The reports of both should be given the same consideration by the court.".
See also *Re W (Welfare Reports)* [1995] 2 F.L.R. 142.
"Children" is not defined (it is only defined for the purposes of Pt. IV of this Act and s.64 is contained in Pt. V). But the reference to "children" in s.64(1) should, it may be assumed, refer to persons under 18 years, unless the context implies otherwise.

Rules, regulations and orders

65.—(1) Any power to make rules, orders or regulations which is conferred by this Act is exercisable by statutory instrument.
  (2) Any statutory instrument made under this Act may—
  (a) contain such incidental, supplemental, consequential and transitional provision as the Lord Chancellor considers appropriate; and
  (b) make different provision for different purposes.
  (3) Any statutory instrument containing an order, rules or regulations made under this Act, other than an order made under section 5(8) or 67(3), shall be subject to annulment by a resolution of either House of Parliament.
  (4) No order shall be made under section 5(8) unless a draft of the order has been laid before, and approved by a resolution of, each House of Parliament.

(5) This section does not apply to rules of court made, or any power to make rules of court, for the purposes of this Act.

GENERAL NOTE
Rules, orders and regulations may be made by statutory instrument. Statutory instruments are subject to annulment by either Houses of Parliament.

Consequential amendments, transitional provisions and repeals

66.—(1) Schedule 8 makes minor and consequential amendments.

(2) Schedule 9 provides for the making of other modifications consequential on provisions of this Act, makes transitional provisions and provides for savings.

(3) Schedule 10 repeals certain enactments.

GENERAL NOTE
This provides for consequential amendments (see Sched. 8), repeals (see Sched. 10) and makes transitional provisions (see Sched. 9).
Attention should be drawn to Sched. 9, para. 5, which preserves existing legislation in relation to decrees granted before this Act comes into operation and provides that nothing in any provision in Pt. II of this Act applies to proceedings begun before the Act comes into operation. Also significant is Sched. 9, para. 1, which covers parties living apart at the beginning of the transitional period, defined as the period of two years beginning with the day on which s.3 (dealing with the circumstances in which divorce and separation orders are made) is brought into force. See, further, the commentary on Sched. 9.

Short title, commencement and extent

67.—(1) This Act may be cited as the Family Law Act 1996.

(2) Section 65 and this section come into force on the passing of this Act.

(3) The other provisions of this Act come into force on such day as the Lord Chancellor may by order appoint; and different days may be appointed for different purposes.

(4) This Act, other than section 17, extends only to England and Wales, except that—

(a) in Schedule 8—
  (i) the amendments of section 38 of the Family Law Act 1986 extend also to Northern Ireland;
  (ii) the amendments of the Judicial Proceedings (Regulation of Reports) Act 1926 extend also to Scotland; and
  (iii) the amendments of the Maintenance Orders Act 1950, the Civil Jurisdiction and Judgments Act 1982, the Finance Act 1985 and sections 42 and 51 of the Family Law Act 1986 extend also to both Northern Ireland and Scotland; and

(b) in Schedule 10, the repeal of section 2(1)(b) of the Domestic and Appellate Proceedings (Restriction of Publicity) Act 1968 extends also to Scotland.

GENERAL NOTE
This section contains the short title (s.67(1)), the commencement details (s.67(2), (3)) (the Act is expected to come into operation at the beginning of 1999), and the extent of the Act (see s.67(4)).

SCHEDULES

Section 9(6)   SCHEDULE 1

ARRANGEMENTS FOR THE FUTURE

The first exemption

1. The circumstances referred to in section 9(7)(a) are that—
(a) the requirements of section 11 have been satisfied;

(b) the applicant has, during the period for reflection and consideration, taken such steps as are reasonably practicable to try to reach agreement about the parties' financial arrangements; and

(c) the applicant has made an application to the court for financial relief and has complied with all requirements of the court in relation to proceedings for financial relief but—

(i) the other party has delayed in complying with requirements of the court or has otherwise been obstructive; or

(ii) for reasons which are beyond the control of the applicant, or of the other party, the court has been prevented from obtaining the information which it requires to determine the financial position of the parties.

The second exemption

2. The circumstances referred to in section 9(7)(b) are that—

(a) the requirements of section 11 have been satisfied;

(b) the applicant has, during the period for reflection and consideration, taken such steps as are reasonably practicable to try to reach agreement about the parties' financial arrangements;

(c) because of—

(i) the ill health or disability of the applicant, the other party or a child of the family (whether physical or mental), or

(ii) an injury suffered by the applicant, the other party or a child of the family, the applicant has not been able to reach agreement with the other party about those arrangements and is unlikely to be able to do so in the foreseeable future; and

(d) a delay in making the order applied for under section 3—

(i) would be significantly detrimental to the welfare of any child of the family; or

(ii) would be seriously prejudicial to the applicant.

The third exemption

3. The circumstances referred to in section 9(7)(c) are that—

(a) the requirements of section 11 have been satisfied;

(b) the applicant has found it impossible to contact the other party; and

(c) as a result, it has been impossible for the applicant to reach agreement with the other party about their financial arrangements.

The fourth exemption

4. The circumstances referred to in section 9(7)(d) are that—

(a) the requirements of section 11 have been satisfied;

(b) an occupation order or a non-molestation order is in force in favour of the applicant or a child of the family, made against the other party;

(c) the applicant has, during the period for reflection and consideration, taken such steps as are reasonably practicable to try to reach agreement about the parties' financial arrangements;

(d) the applicant has not been able to reach agreement with the other party about those arrangements and is unlikely to be able to do so in the foreseeable future; and

(e) a delay in making the order applied for under section 3—

(i) would be significantly detrimental to the welfare of any child of the family; or

(ii) would be seriously prejudicial to the applicant.

Court orders and agreements

5.—(1) Section 9 is not to be read as requiring any order or agreement to have been carried into effect at the time when the court is considering whether arrangements for the future have been made by the parties.

(2) The fact that an appeal is pending against an order of the kind mentioned in section 9(2)(a) is to be disregarded.

Financial arrangements

6. In section 9 and this Schedule "financial arrangements" has the same meaning as in section 34(2) of the 1973 Act.

Negotiated agreements

7. In section 9(2)(b) "negotiated agreement" means a written agreement between the parties as to future arrangements—

(a) which has been reached as the result of mediation or any other form of negotiation involving a third party; and
(b) which satisfies such requirements as may be imposed by rules of court.

Declarations

8.—(1) Any declaration of a kind mentioned in section 9—
(a) must be in a prescribed form;
(b) must, in prescribed cases, be accompanied by such documents as may be prescribed; and
(c) must, in prescribed cases, satisfy such other requirements as may be prescribed.
(2) The validity of a divorce order or separation order made by reference to such a declaration is not to be affected by any inaccuracy in the declaration.

Interpretation

9. In this Schedule—
"financial relief" has such meaning as may be prescribed; and
"prescribed" means prescribed by rules of court.

DEFINITIONS
"child of the family": s.24(1).
"financial arrangements": para. 6.
"health": s.63(1).
"party": s.24(1).
"period for reflection and consideration": s.7(1), (2).

GENERAL NOTE
This schedule supplements s.9. It sets out the circumstances in which a court may declare that an order for separation or divorce may be made even though evidence of arrangements for the future cannot be produced to the court. In all cases arrangements regarding children must be satisfied. The Schedule also defines certain terms ("financial arrangements", "negotiated agreements"), which are used in s.9.

Para. 1
The first exemption applies where the other party has failed to comply with court requirements or has otherwise been obstructive, or where for reasons beyond the applicant's control the court has been prevented from obtaining the information it requires to determine the parties' financial position. The obligation to make a full and frank disclosure, firmly entrenched in the law (see *Livesey (formerly Jenkins) v. Livesey* [1985] A.C. 424, 436 *per* Lord Brandon of Oakbrook) remains. But for the so-called millionaires' defence see *Van G v. Van G* [1995] 1 F.L.R. 328.

Para. 2
The second exemption applies where ill-health, disability or injury (of the applicant, other party or a child of the family) has prevented, and is likely to prevent for the foreseeable future, agreement about financial arrangements and a delay in making a divorce or separation order would be significantly detrimental to the welfare of any child of the family or seriously prejudicial to the applicant.

Para. 3
The third exemption applies where the applicant has found it impossible to contact the other party and, as a result, it has been impossible to reach an agreement about financial arrangements. Note that the emphasis is on the applicant finding it impossible to contact the other party, not on its being impossible in any objective sense.

Para. 4
The fourth exemption applies where there is an occupation order or non-molestation order in force. The applicant must have taken such steps as are reasonably practicable to reach agreement about financial arrangements and have failed to do so until now and be likely to fail to do so in the foreseeable future. Further, it must be the case that a delay in making a divorce or separation order would be significantly detrimental to the welfare of any child of the family or be seriously prejudicial.

Para. 5
Section 9 requires an order or agreement to be produced to the court before a divorce or separation order can be made. This paragraph makes it clear that such an order or agreement need not be in effect. The fact that an appeal is pending against a court order is to be disregarded.

Para. 6

"Financial arrangements" means provisions governing the rights and liabilities of the parties to a marriage (including a marriage which has been dissolved or annulled) towards one another when living separately in respect of the making or securing of payments or the disposition or use of any property, including such rights and liabilities with respect to the maintenance or education of any child, whether or not the child of the family.

Para. 7

This defines a "negotiated agreement".

Para. 8

This details the formal requirements of declarations. A divorce or separation order may not be impugned by "any inaccuracy" in the declaration.

Section 15   SCHEDULE 2

FINANCIAL PROVISION

Introductory

1. Part II of the 1973 Act (financial provision and property adjustment orders) is amended as follows.

The orders

2. For section 21 (definitions) substitute—

"Financial provision and property adjustment orders

21.—(1) For the purposes of this Act, a financial provision order is—

  (a) an order that a party must make in favour of another person such periodical payments, for such term, as may be specified (a "periodical payments order");

  (b) an order that a party must, to the satisfaction of the court, secure in favour of another person such periodical payments, for such term, as may be specified (a "secured periodical payments order");

  (c) an order that a party must make a payment in favour of another person of such lump sum or sums as may be specified (an "order for the payment of a lump sum").

(2) For the purposes of this Act, a property adjustment order is—

  (a) an order that a party must transfer such of his or her property as may be specified in favour of the other party or a child of the family;

  (b) an order that a settlement of such property of a party as may be specified must be made, to the satisfaction of the court, for the benefit of the other party and of the children of the family, or either or any of them;

  (c) an order varying, for the benefit of the parties and of the children of the family, or either or any of them, any marriage settlement;

  (d) an order extinguishing or reducing the interest of either of the parties under any marriage settlement.

(3) Subject to section 40 below, where an order of the court under this Part of this Act requires a party to make or secure a payment in favour of another person or to transfer property in favour of any person, that payment must be made or secured or that property transferred—

  (a) if that other person is the other party to the marriage, to that other party; and

  (b) if that other person is a child of the family, according to the terms of the order—

    (i) to the child; or

    (ii) to such other person as may be specified, for the benefit of that child.

(4) References in this section to the property of a party are references to any property to which that party is entitled either in possession or in reversion.

(5) Any power of the court under this Part of this Act to make such an order as is mentioned in subsection (2)(b) to (d) above is exercisable even though there are no children of the family.

(6) In this section—

    "marriage settlement" means an ante-nuptial or post-nuptial settlement made on the parties (including one made by will or codicil);

    "party" means a party to a marriage; and

    "specified" means specified in the order in question."

Financial provision: divorce and separation

3. Insert, before section 23—

"Financial provision orders: divorce and separation
22A.—(1) On an application made under this section, the court may at the appropriate time make one or more financial provision orders in favour of—
(a) a party to the marriage to which the application relates; or
(b) any of the children of the family.
(2) The "appropriate time" is any time—
(a) after a statement of marital breakdown has been received by the court and before any application for a divorce order or for a separation order is made to the court by reference to that statement;
(b) when an application for a divorce order or separation order has been made under section 3 of the 1996 Act and has not been withdrawn;
(c) when an application for a divorce order has been made under section 4 of the 1996 Act and has not been withdrawn;
(d) after a divorce order has been made;
(e) when a separation order is in force.
(3) The court may make—
(a) a combined order against the parties on one occasion,
(b) separate orders on different occasions,
(c) different orders in favour of different children,
(d) different orders from time to time in favour of the same child,
but may not make, in favour of the same party, more than one periodical payments order, or more than one order for payment of a lump sum, in relation to any marital proceedings, whether in the course of the proceedings or by reference to a divorce order or separation order made in the proceedings.
(4) If it would not otherwise be in a position to make a financial provision order in favour of a party or child of the family, the court may make an interim periodical payments order, an interim order for the payment of a lump sum or a series of such orders, in favour of that party or child.
(5) Any order for the payment of a lump sum made under this section may—
(a) provide for the payment of the lump sum by instalments of such amounts as may be specified in the order; and
(b) require the payment of the instalments to be secured to the satisfaction of the court.
(6) Nothing in subsection (5) above affects—
(a) the power of the court under this section to make an order for the payment of a lump sum; or
(b) the provisions of this Part of this Act as to the beginning of the term specified in any periodical payments order or secured periodical payments order.
(7) Subsection (8) below applies where the court—
(a) makes an order under this section ("the main order") for the payment of a lump sum; and
(b) directs—
    (i) that payment of that sum, or any part of it, is to be deferred; or
    (ii) that that sum, or any part of it, is to be paid by instalments.
(8) In such a case, the court may, on or at any time after making the main order, make an order ("the order for interest") for the amount deferred, or the instalments, to carry interest (at such rate as may be specified in the order for interest)—
(a) from such date, not earlier than the date of the main order, as may be so specified;
(b) until the date when the payment is due.
(9) This section is to be read subject to any restrictions imposed by this Act and to section 19 of the 1996 Act.

Restrictions affecting section 22A
22B.—(1) No financial provision order, other than an interim order, may be made under section 22A above so as to take effect before the making of a divorce order or separation order in relation to the marriage, unless the court is satisfied—
(a) that the circumstances of the case are exceptional; and
(b) that it would be just and reasonable for the order to be so made.
(2) Except in the case of an interim periodical payments order, the court may not make a financial provision order under section 22A above at any time while the period for reflection and consideration is interrupted under section 7(8) of the 1996 Act.

(3) No financial provision order may be made under section 22A above by reference to the making of a statement of marital breakdown if, by virtue of section 5(3) or 7(9) of the 1996 Act (lapse of divorce or separation process), it has ceased to be possible—

(a) for an application to be made by reference to that statement; or

(b) for an order to be made on such an application.

(4) No financial provision order may be made under section 22A after a divorce order has been made, or while a separation order is in force, except—

(a) in response to an application made before the divorce order or separation order was made; or

(b) on a subsequent application made with the leave of the court.

(5) In this section, "period for reflection and consideration" means the period fixed by section 7 of the 1996 Act."

Financial provision: nullity of marriage

4. For section 23 substitute—

"Financial provision orders: nullity

23.—(1) On or after granting a decree of nullity of marriage (whether before or after the decree is made absolute), the court may, on an application made under this section, make one or more financial provision orders in favour of—

(a) either party to the marriage; or

(b) any child of the family.

(2) Before granting a decree in any proceedings for nullity of marriage, the court may make against either or each of the parties to the marriage—

(a) an interim periodical payments order, an interim order for the payment of a lump sum, or a series of such orders, in favour of the other party;

(b) an interim periodical payments order, an interim order for the payment of a lump sum, a series of such orders or any one or more other financial provision orders in favour of each child of the family.

(3) Where any such proceedings are dismissed, the court may (either immediately or within a reasonable period after the dismissal) make any one or more financial provision orders in favour of each child of the family.

(4) An order under this section that a party to a marriage must pay a lump sum to the other party may be made for the purpose of enabling that other party to meet any liabilities or expenses reasonably incurred by him or her in maintaining himself or herself or any child of the family before making an application for an order under this section in his or her favour.

(5) An order under this section for the payment of a lump sum to or for the benefit of a child of the family may be made for the purpose of enabling any liabilities or expenses reasonably incurred by or for the benefit of that child before the making of an application for an order under this section in his favour to be met.

(6) An order under this section for the payment of a lump sum may—

(a) provide for the payment of that sum by instalments of such amount as may be specified in the order; and

(b) require the payment of the instalments to be secured to the satisfaction of the court.

(7) Nothing in subsections (4) to (6) above affects—

(a) the power under subsection (1) above to make an order for the payment of a lump sum; or

(b) the provisions of this Act as to the beginning of the term specified in any periodical payments order or secured periodical payments order.

(8) The powers of the court under this section to make one or more financial provision orders are exercisable against each party to the marriage by the making of—

(a) a combined order on one occasion, or

(b) separate orders on different occasions,

but the court may not make more than one periodical payments order, or more than one order for payment of a lump sum, in favour of the same party.

(9) The powers of the court under this section so far as they consist in power to make one or more orders in favour of the children of the family—

(a) may be exercised differently in favour of different children; and

(b) except in the case of the power conferred by subsection (3) above, may be exercised from time to time in favour of the same child; and

(c) in the case of the power conferred by that subsection, if it is exercised by the making of a financial provision order of any kind in favour of a child, shall include power to make, from time to time, further financial provision orders of that or any other kind in favour of that child.

(10) Where an order is made under subsection (1) above in favour of a party to the marriage on or after the granting of a decree of nullity of marriage, neither the order nor any settlement made in pursuance of the order takes effect unless the decree has been made absolute.

(11) Subsection (10) above does not affect the power to give a direction under section 30 below for the settlement of an instrument by conveyancing counsel.

(12) Where the court—

(a) makes an order under this section ("the main order") for the payment of a lump sum; and

(b) directs—

(i) that payment of that sum or any part of it is to be deferred; or

(ii) that that sum or any part of it is to be paid by instalments,

it may, on or at any time after making the main order, make an order ("the order for interest") for the amount deferred or the instalments to carry interest at such rate as may be specified by the order for interest from such date, not earlier than the date of the main order, as may be so specified, until the date when payment of it is due.

(13) This section is to be read subject to any restrictions imposed by this Act."

Property adjustment orders: divorce and separation

5. Insert, before section 24—

"Property adjustment orders: divorce and separation

23A.—(1) On an application made under this section, the court may, at any time mentioned in section 22A(2) above, make one or more property adjustment orders.

(2) If the court makes, in favour of the same party to the marriage, more than one property adjustment order in relation to any marital proceedings, whether in the course of the proceedings or by reference to a divorce order or separation order made in the proceedings, each order must fall within a different paragraph of section 21(2) above.

(3) The court shall exercise its powers under this section, so far as is practicable, by making on one occasion all such provision as can be made by way of one or more property adjustment orders in relation to the marriage as it thinks fit.

(4) Subsection (3) above does not affect section 31 or 31A below.

(5) This section is to be read subject to any restrictions imposed by this Act and to section 19 of the 1996 Act.

Restrictions affecting section 23A

23B.—(1) No property adjustment order may be made under section 23A above so as to take effect before the making of a divorce order or separation order in relation to the marriage unless the court is satisfied—

(a) that the circumstances of the case are exceptional; and

(b) that it would be just and reasonable for the order to be so made.

(2) The court may not make a property adjustment order under section 23A above at any time while the period for reflection and consideration is interrupted under section 7(8) of the 1996 Act.

(3) No property adjustment order may be made under section 23A above by virtue of the making of a statement of marital breakdown if, by virtue of section 5(3) or 7(5) of the 1996 Act (lapse of divorce or separation process), it has ceased to be possible—

(a) for an application to be made by reference to that statement; or

(b) for an order to be made on such an application.

(4) No property adjustment order may be made under section 23A above after a divorce order has been made, or while a separation order is in force, except—

(a) in response to an application made before the divorce order or separation order was made; or

(b) on a subsequent application made with the leave of the court.

(5) In this section, "period for reflection and consideration" means the period fixed by section 7 of the 1996 Act."

Property adjustment orders: nullity

6. For section 24, substitute—

"Property adjustment orders: nullity of marriage

24.—(1) On or after granting a decree of nullity of marriage (whether before or after the decree is made absolute), the court may, on an application made under this section, make one or more property adjustment orders in relation to the marriage.

(2) The court shall exercise its powers under this section, so far as is practicable, by making on one occasion all such provision as can be made by way of one or more property adjustment orders in relation to the marriage as it thinks fit.

(3) Subsection (2) above does not affect section 31 or 31A below.

(4) Where a property adjustment order is made under this section on or after the granting of a decree of nullity of marriage, neither the order nor any settlement made in pursuance of the order is to take effect unless the decree has been made absolute.

(5) That does not affect the power to give a direction under section 30 below for the settlement of an instrument by conveyancing counsel.

(6) This section is to be read subject to any restrictions imposed by this Act."

Period of secured and unsecured payments orders

7.—(1) In section 28(1) (duration of a continuing financial provision order in favour of a party to a marriage), for paragraphs (a) and (b) substitute—

"(a) a term specified in the order which is to begin before the making of the order shall begin no earlier—

(i) where the order is made by virtue of section 22A(2)(a) or (b) above, unless sub-paragraph (ii) below applies, than the beginning of the day on which the statement of marital breakdown in question was received by the court;

(ii) where the order is made by virtue of section 22A(2)(b) above and the application for the divorce order was made following cancellation of an order preventing divorce under section 10 of the 1996 Act, than the date of the making of that application;

(iii) where the order is made by virtue of section 22A(2)(c) above, than the date of the making of the application for the divorce order; or

(iv) in any other case, than the date of the making of the application on which the order is made;

(b) a term specified in a periodical payments order or secured periodical payments order shall be so defined as not to extend beyond—

(i) in the case of a periodical payments order, the death of the party by whom the payments are to be made; or

(ii) in either case, the death of the party in whose favour the order was made or the remarriage of that party following the making of a divorce order or decree of nullity."

(2) In section 29 (duration of continuing financial provision order in favour of a child of the family) insert after subsection (1)—

"(1A) The term specified in a periodical payments order or secured periodical payments order made in favour of a child shall be such term as the court thinks fit.

(1B) If that term is to begin before the making of the order, it may do so no earlier than—

(a) in the case of an order made by virtue of section 22A(2)(a) or (b) above, except where paragraph (b) below applies, the beginning of the day on which the statement of marital breakdown in question was received by the court;

(b) in the case of an order made by virtue of section 22A(2)(b) above where the application for the divorce order was made following cancellation of an order preventing divorce under section 10 of the 1996 Act, the date of the making of that application;

(c) in the case of an order made by virtue of section 22A(2)(c) above, the date of the making of the application for the divorce order; or

(d) in any other case, the date of the making of the application on which the order is made."

Variations etc. following reconciliations

8. Insert after section 31—

"Variation etc. following reconciliations

31A.—(1) Where, at a time before the making of a divorce order—

(a) an order ("a paragraph (a) order") for the payment of a lump sum has been made under section 22A above in favour of a party,

(b) such an order has been made in favour of a child of the family but the payment has not yet been made, or

(c) a property adjustment order ("a paragraph (c) order") has been made under section 23A above,

the court may, on an application made jointly by the parties to the marriage, vary or discharge the order.

(2) Where the court varies or discharges a paragraph (a) order, it may order the repayment of an amount equal to the whole or any part of the lump sum.

(3) Where the court varies or discharges a paragraph (c) order, it may (if the order has taken effect)—

(a) order any person to whom property was transferred in pursuance of the paragraph (c) order to transfer—

(i) the whole or any part of that property, or

(ii) the whole or any part of any property appearing to the court to represent that property,

in favour of a party to the marriage or a child of the family; or

(b) vary any settlement to which the order relates in favour of any person or extinguish or reduce any person's interest under that settlement.

(4) Where the court acts under subsection (3) it may make such supplemental provision (including a further property adjustment order or an order for the payment of a lump sum) as it thinks appropriate in consequence of any transfer, variation, extinguishment or reduction to be made under paragraph (a) or (b) of that subsection.

(5) Sections 24A and 30 above apply for the purposes of this section as they apply where the court makes a property adjustment order under section 23A or 24 above.

(6) The court shall not make an order under subsection (2), (3) or (4) above unless it appears to it that there has been a reconciliation between the parties to the marriage.

(7) The court shall also not make an order under subsection (3) or (4) above unless it appears to it that the order will not prejudice the interests of—

(a) any child of the family; or

(b) any person who has acquired any right or interest in consequence of the paragraph (c) order and is not a party to the marriage or a child of the family."

GENERAL NOTE

This Schedule amends Pt. III of the Matrimonial Causes Act 1973 relating to financial provision and property adjustment orders.

Para. 2

The definitions section of the 1973 Act (s.21) is replaced by a new s.21.

Para. 3

Section 22, maintenance pending suit, is replaced (see Sched. 10). But see new s.22A(2)(a). Section 22 is not replaced but there are new ss.22A and 22B.

Section 22A sets out when ("the appropriate time") the court may make a financial provision order (see s.22A(2)); the orders it may make (see s.22A(3), and also s.21), including an interim periodical payment order and an interim order for the payment of a lump sum (s.22A(4)). An order for a lump sum payment may provide for the payment of this by instalments, which may be secured (s.22A(5)). Instalment payments may attract interest (s.22A(8)).

Section 22B provides that no financial provision order, other than an interim order, may take effect before a divorce order or separation order is made unless the circumstances are exceptional and it would be just and reasonable for the order to be so made (see s.22B(1)). Other restrictions imposed on the making of a s.22A order are,

(i) during the interruption of a period of reflection and consideration (s.22B(2));

(ii) when it is no longer possible for an application to be made by reference to the statement of marital breakdown or for an order to be made on such an application (s.22B(3)); and

(iii) after a divorce order (or while a separation order is in force) except where the application antedated the order or the court gives leave (s.22B(4)).

Para. 4

Section 23 of the 1973 Act is replaced by a new s.23. The new s.23 applies to financial provisions on nullity only (divorce and separation financial provision orders are now to be found in s.22A). There is provision for lump sums to be paid by instalments or for instalments to be secured (s.23(6)).

Para. 5

This paragraph substitutes a new s.23A to replace s.24 of the 1973 Act insofar as it dealt with property adjustment orders on divorce.

A property adjustment order may be made at the same time as a financial provision may be made (s.23A(1)). The property adjustment orders available are listed in s.21(2). More than one property adjustment order may be made but, if in favour of the same party, they must be different types of order (*e.g.* a transfer and a settlement) (s.23A(2)). The goal is to make the orders at the same time (s.23A(3)).

Section 23B provides that no property adjustment order may be made to take effect before a divorce or separation order is made unless the court is satisfied the circumstances are exceptional and it would be just and reasonable for the order to be so made (s.23B(1)). Other restrictions on property adjustment orders parallel the restrictions on financial provision orders (on which see s.22B, s.23B(2) to (4)).

Para. 6

This paragraph substitutes a revised s.24 of the 1973 Act. It provides for property adjustment orders on nullity of marriage.

The property adjustment orders are found in s.21(2). If more than one order is made, the court is to endeavour to make all the orders at the same time (s.24(2)) (this is without prejudice to variation powers in s.31 and s.31A). Orders (and settlements) are not to take effect unless the decree is made absolute (see s.24(4)).

Para. 7

Section 28(1) of the 1973 Act improves limits on the term a court may specify in a periodical payments or secured periodical payments order. These terms are replaced by those in para. 7(1)(a) and (b).

Section 29 of the 1973 Act is also amended. The duration of a periodical or secured periodical payments order in favour of a child is to be such term as the court thinks fit. Limits are imposed on this discretion by s.29(1B).

Para. 8

This paragraph adds a new s.31A to the Matrimonial Causes Act 1973. The court is given the power, on a joint application by the parties, to vary or discharge a lump sum order in favour of a party or a child (where the payment has not been made) or a property adjustment order, at any time before the making of a divorce order. As the heading is "*Variations etc following reconciliations*", we may assume that it is intended that such variations may be sought in such circumstances only. But the paragraph is silent as to the circumstances in which an application may be made. Circumstances are, however, specified for other orders under this paragraph: thus, where there is a variation or discharge the court may order repayment but not unless there has been a reconciliation (see s.31A(2), (b)).

Section 19(5)   SCHEDULE 3

STAY OF PROCEEDINGS

Introductory

1. Schedule 1 to the Domicile and Matrimonial Proceedings Act 1973 (which relates to the staying of matrimonial proceedings) is amended as follows.

Interpretation

2. In paragraph 1, for "The following five paragraphs" substitute "Paragraphs 2 to 6 below".
3. For paragraph 2 substitute—
"2.—(1) "Matrimonial proceedings" means—
(a) marital proceedings;
(b) proceedings for nullity of marriage;
(c) proceedings for a declaration as to the validity of a marriage of the petitioner; or
(d) proceedings for a declaration as to the subsistence of such a marriage.
(2) "Marital proceedings" has the meaning given by section 20 of the Family Law Act 1996.
(3) "Divorce proceedings" means marital proceedings that are divorce proceedings by virtue of that section."
4. Insert, after paragraph 4—
"4A.—(1) "Statement of marital breakdown" has the same meaning as in the Family Law Act 1996.
(2) "Relevant statement" in relation to any marital proceedings, means—
(a) the statement of marital breakdown with which the proceedings commenced; or

(b) if the proceedings are for the conversion of a separation order into a divorce order under section 4 of the Family Law Act 1996, the statement of marital breakdown by reference to which the separation order was made."

Duty to furnish particulars of concurrent proceedings

5. For paragraph 7 substitute—

"7.—(1) While marital proceedings are pending in the court with respect to a marriage, this paragraph applies—

    (a) to the party or parties to the marriage who made the relevant statement; and

    (b) in prescribed circumstances where the statement was made by only one party, to the other party.

(2) While matrimonial proceedings of any other kind are pending in the court with respect to a marriage and the trial or first trial in those proceedings has not begun, this paragraph applies—

    (a) to the petitioner; and

    (b) if the respondent has included a prayer for relief in his answer, to the respondent.

(3) A person to whom this paragraph applies must give prescribed information about any proceedings which—

    (a) he knows to be continuing in another jurisdiction; and

    (b) are in respect of the marriage or capable of affecting its validity or subsistence.

(4) The information must be given in such manner, to such persons and on such occasions as may be prescribed."

Obligatory stays in divorce cases

6.—(1) Paragraph 8 is amended as follows.

(2) For the words before paragraph (a) of sub-paragraph (1) substitute—

"(1) This paragraph applies where divorce proceedings are continuing in the court with respect to a marriage.

(2) Where it appears to the court, on the application of a party to the marriage—".

(3) In sub-paragraph (1), in the words after paragraph (d), for "proceedings" substitute "divorce proceedings".

(4) For sub-paragraph (2) substitute—

"(3) The effect of such an order is that, while it is in force—

    (a) no application for a divorce order in relation to the marriage may be made either by reference to the relevant statement or by reference to any subsequent statement of marital breakdown; and

    (b) if such an application has been made, no divorce order may be made on that application."

Discretionary stays

7.—(1) Paragraph 9 is amended as follows.

(2) For sub-paragraph (1), substitute—

"(1) Sub-paragraph (1A) below applies where—

    (a) marital proceedings are continuing in the court; or

    (b) matrimonial proceedings of any other kind are continuing in the court, if the trial or first trial in the proceedings has not begun.

(1A) The court may make an order staying the proceedings if it appears to the court—

    (a) that proceedings in respect of the marriage, or capable of affecting its validity or subsistence, are continuing in another Jurisdiction; and

    (b) that the balance of fairness (including convenience) as between the parties to the marriage is such that it is appropriate for proceedings in that jurisdiction to be disposed of before further steps are taken in the proceedings to which the order relates."

(3) For sub-paragraph (3) substitute—

"(3) Where an application for a stay is pending under paragraph 8 above, the court shall not make an order under sub-paragraph (1A) staying marital proceedings in relation to the marriage."

(4) In sub-paragraph 4, after "pending in the court," insert "other than marital proceedings,".

(5) After sub-paragraph (4), insert—

"(5) The effect of an order under sub-paragraph (1A) for a stay of marital proceedings is that, while it is in force—

    (a) no application for a divorce order or separation order in relation to the marriage may be made either by reference to the relevant statement or by reference to any subsequent statement of marital breakdown; and

(b) if such an application has been made, no divorce order or separation order shall be made on that application."

Discharge of orders

8. In paragraph 10, for sub-paragraph (2), substitute—
　"(1A) Where the court discharges an order staying any proceedings, it may direct that the whole or a specified part of any period while the order has been in force—
　　(a) is not to count towards any period specified in section 5(3) or 7(9) of the Family Law Act 1996; or
　　(b) is to count towards any such period only for specified purposes.
　(2) Where the court discharges an order under paragraph 8 above, it shall not again make such an order in relation to the marriage except in a case where the obligation to do so arises under that paragraph following receipt by the court of a statement of marital breakdown after the discharge of the order."

Ancillary matters

9.—(1) Paragraph 11 is amended as follows.
(2) For sub-paragraph (1) substitute—
　"(1) Sub-paragraphs (2) and (3) below apply where a stay of marital proceedings or proceedings for nullity of marriage—
　　(a) has been imposed by reference to proceedings in a related jurisdiction for divorce, separation or nullity of marriage, and
　　(b) is in force.
　(1A) In this paragraph—
　　"lump sum order", in relation to a stay, means an order—
　　(a) under section 22A or 23, 31 or 31A of the Matrimonial Causes Act 1973 which is an order for the payment of a lump sum for the purposes of Part II of that Act, or
　　(b) made in any equivalent circumstances under Schedule 1 to the Children Act 1989 and of a kind mentioned in paragraph 1(2)(a) or (b) of that Schedule,
　　so far as it satisfies the condition mentioned in sub-paragraph (1C) below;
　　"the other proceedings", in relation to a stay, means the proceedings in another jurisdiction by reference to which the stay was imposed;
　　"relevant order", in relation to a stay, means—
　　　(a) any financial provision order (including an interim order), other than a lump sum order;
　　　(b) any order made in equivalent circumstances under Schedule 1 to the Children Act 1989 and of a kind mentioned in paragraph 1(2)(a) or (b) of that Schedule;
　　　(c) any section 8 order under the Act of 1989; and
　　　(d) except for the purposes of sub-paragraph (3) below, any order restraining a person from removing a child out of England and Wales or out of the care of another person,
　　so far as it satisfies the condition mentioned in sub-paragraph (1C) below.
　(1C) The condition is that the order is, or (apart from this paragraph) could be, made in connection with the proceedings to which the stay applies."
(3) In sub-paragraph (2)—
(a) for "any proceedings are stayed" substitute "this paragraph applies in relation to a stay";
(b) in paragraph (a), and in the first place in paragraph (c), omit "in connection with the stayed proceedings"; and
(c) in paragraphs (b) and (c), for "made in connection with the stayed proceedings" substitute "already made".
(4) In sub-paragraph (3)—
(a) for "any proceedings are stayed" substitute "this paragraph applies in relation to a stay";
(b) in paragraph (a), for "made in connection with the stayed proceedings" substitute "already made";
(c) in paragraphs (b) and (c), omit "in connection with the stayed proceedings".
(5) In sub-paragraph (3A), for the words before "any order made" substitute—
　"Where a secured periodical payments order within the meaning of the Matrimonial Causes Act 1973—
　　(a) has been made under section 22A(1)(b) or 23(1)(b) or (2)(b) of that Act, but
　　(b) ceases to have effect by virtue of sub-paragraph (2) or (3) above,".
(6) For sub-paragraph (4), substitute—
　"(4) Nothing in sub-paragraphs (2) and (3) above affects any relevant order or lump sum order or any power to make such an order in so far as—

(a) where the stay applies to matrimonial proceedings other than marital proceedings, the order has been made or the power may be exercised following the receipt by the court of a statement of marital breakdown;

(b) where the stay is of marital proceedings, the order has been made or the power may be exercised in matrimonial proceedings of any other kind; or

(c) where the stay is of divorce proceedings only, the order has been made or the power may be exercised—

(i) in matrimonial proceedings which are not marital proceedings, or

(ii) in marital proceedings in which an application has been made for a separation order."

(7) In sub-paragraph (5)(c), for the words from "in connection" onwards substitute "where a stay no longer applies".

GENERAL NOTE

This Schedule amends Sched. 1 of the Domicile and Matrimonial Proceedings Act 1973, which deals with the staying of matrimonial proceedings, where the matter ought to proceed in another jurisdiction. These remain obligatory stays where proceedings are continuing in another part of the British Isles (see para. 6), and discretionary stays, where there are proceedings elsewhere than the British Isles. See further, the commentary on s.19, above.

Section 32 SCHEDULE 4

PROVISIONS SUPPLEMENTARY TO SECTIONS 30 AND 31

Interpretation

1.—(1) In this Schedule—

(a) any reference to a solicitor includes a reference to a licensed conveyancer or a recognised body, and

(b) any reference to a person's solicitor includes a reference to a licensed conveyancer or recognised body acting for that person.

(2) In sub-paragraph (1)—

"licensed conveyancer" has the meaning given by section 11(2) of the Administration of Justice Act 1985;

"recognised body" means a body corporate for the time being recognised under section 9 (incorporated practices) or section 32 (provision of conveyancing by recognised bodies) of that Act.

Restriction on registration where spouse entitled to more than one charge

2. Where one spouse is entitled by virtue of section 31 to a registrable charge in respect of each of two or more dwelling-houses, only one of the charges to which that spouse is so entitled shall be registered under section 31(10) or under section 2 of the Land Charges Act 1972 at any one time, and if any of those charges is registered under either of those provisions the Chief Land Registrar, on being satisfied that any other of them is so registered, shall cancel the registration of the charge first registered.

Contract for sale of house affected by registered charge to include term requiring cancellation of registration before completion

3.—(1) Where one spouse is entitled by virtue of section 31 to a charge on an estate in a dwelling-house and the charge is registered under section 31(10) or section 2 of the Land Charges Act 1972, it shall be a term of any contract for the sale of that estate whereby the vendor agrees to give vacant possession of the dwelling-house on completion of the contract that the vendor will before such completion procure the cancellation of the registration of the charge at his expense.

(2) Sub-paragraph (1) shall not apply to any such contract made by a vendor who is entitled to sell the estate in the dwelling-house freed from any such charge.

(3) If, on the completion of such a contract as is referred to in sub-paragraph (1), there is delivered to the purchaser or his solicitor an application by the spouse entitled to the charge for the cancellation of the registration of that charge, the term of the contract for which sub-paragraph (1) provides shall be deemed to have been performed.

(4) This paragraph applies only if and so far as a contrary intention is not expressed in the contract.

(5) This paragraph shall apply to a contract for exchange as it applies to a contract for sale.

(6) This paragraph shall, with the necessary modifications, apply to a contract for the grant of a lease or underlease of a dwelling-house as it applies to a contract for the sale of an estate in a dwelling-house.

Cancellation of registration after termination of marriage, etc.

4.—(1) Where a spouse's matrimonial home rights are a charge on an estate in the dwelling-house and the charge is registered under section 31(10) or under section 2 of the Land Charges Act 1972, the Chief Land Registrar shall, subject to sub-paragraph (2), cancel the registration of the charge if he is satisfied—

(a) by the production of a certificate or other sufficient evidence, that either spouse is dead, or

(b) by the production of an official copy of a decree or order of a court, that the marriage in question has been terminated otherwise than by death, or

(c) by the production of an order of the court, that the spouse's matrimonial home rights constituting the charge have been terminated by the order.

(2) Where—

(a) the marriage in question has been terminated by the death of the spouse entitled to an estate in the dwelling–house or otherwise than by death, and

(b) an order affecting the charge of the spouse not so entitled had been made under section 33(5),

then if, after the making of the order, registration of the charge was renewed or the charge registered in pursuance of sub-paragraph (3), the Chief Land Registrar shall not cancel the registration of the charge in accordance with sub-paragraph (1) unless he is also satisfied that the order has ceased to have effect.

(3) Where such an order has been made, then, for the purposes of sub-paragraph (2), the spouse entitled to the charge affected by the order may—

(a) if before the date of the order the charge was registered under section 31(10) or under section 2 of the Land Charges Act 1972, renew the registration of the charge, and

(b) if before the said date the charge was not so registered, register the charge under section 31(10) or under section 2 of the Land Charges Act 1972.

(4) Renewal of the registration of a charge in pursuance of sub-paragraph (3) shall be effected in such manner as may be prescribed, and an application for such renewal or for registration of a charge in pursuance of that sub-paragraph shall contain such particulars of any order affecting the charge made under section 33(5) as may be prescribed.

(5) The renewal in pursuance of sub-paragraph (3) of the registration of a charge shall not affect the priority of the charge.

(6) In this paragraph "prescribed" means prescribed by rules made under section 16 of the Land Charges Act 1972 or section 144 of the Land Registration Act 1925, as the circumstances of the case require.

Release of matrimonial home rights

5.—(1) A spouse entitled to matrimonial home rights may by a release in writing release those rights or release them as respects part only of the dwelling-house affected by them.

(2) Where a contract is made for the sale of an estate or interest in a dwelling-house, or for the grant of a lease or underlease of a dwelling-house, being (in either case) a dwelling-house affected by a charge registered under section 31 (10) or under section 2 of the Land Charges Act 1972, then, without prejudice to sub-paragraph (1), the matrimonial home rights constituting the charge shall be deemed to have been released on the happening of whichever of the following events first occurs—

(a) the delivery to the purchaser or lessee, as the case may be, or his solicitor on completion of the contract of an application by the spouse entitled to the charge for the cancellation of the registration of the charge; or

(b) the lodging of such an application at Her Majesty's Land Registry.

Postponement of priority of charge

6. A spouse entitled by virtue of section 31 to a charge on an estate or interest may agree in writing that any other charge on, or interest in, that estate or interest shall rank in priority to the charge to which that spouse is so entitled.

GENERAL NOTE

This Schedule reproduces, with consequential amendments, ss.3, 4, 5 and 6 of the Matrimonial Homes Act 1983. These sections deal with the conveyancing aspects of a spouse's rights of occupation in the matrimonial home. The concept "matrimonial home rights" replace that of "rights of occupation", which was used in the 1983 Act.

Para. 1

This provides for the interpretation of various expressions used in the Schedule.

Para. 2

This reproduces s.3 of the 1983 Act. It provides that where a spouse is entitled to a registrable charge in respect of each of two or more dwelling-houses, only one of those charges may be registered. If more than one charge is registered, the Chief Land Registrar must cancel the registration of the charge first registered.

Para. 3

This reproduces s.4 of the 1983 Act, without substantive change. It protects the purchaser of a dwelling-house in respect of which the vendor's spouse is entitled to matrimonial home rights, by making it an implied term of the contract that the vendor will procure cancellation of any registered charge in any case where vacant possession is to be given on occupation. This paragraph applies only if and so far as a contrary intention is not expressed in the contract. It applies to a contract for exchange as it applies to a contract for sale. It also applies (with necessary modifications) to a contract for the grant of a lease or underlease of a dwelling-house, as it applies to a contract for the sale of an estate in a dwelling-house.

Para. 4

This reproduces s.5 of the 1983 Act, without substantive change. It provides for the cancellation of registered charges after the termination of the marriage, and for the renewal of registration in cases where an order has been made under s.33(5), extending matrimonial home rights beyond the end of the marriage. The renewal does not affect the priority of the charge.

Para. 5

This reproduces in amended form ss.1 and 2 of the 1983 Act. It provides that a spouse with matrimonial home rights may, by a release in writing, release those rights, or release them as respects part only of the dwelling-house affected by them. Where a contract is made for the sale of an estate or interest in a dwelling-house, or for the grant of a lease or underlease of a dwelling-house, being (in either case) a dwelling-house affected by a charge registered under s.2 of the Land Charges Act 1972 or s.31(10) of this Act, then, without prejudice to sub-para. (1), the matrimonial home rights constituting the charge shall, have been deemed to have been released on the happening of whichever of the following events first occurs, namely, the delivery to the purchaser or lessee or his solicitor on completion of the contract of an application by the spouse entitled to the charge for the cancellation of the registration charge, or the lodging of such an application at Her Majesty's Land Registry.

Para. 6

This reproduces s.6(3) of the 1983 Act. It provides that a spouse, entitled by virtue of s.31 to a charge on an estate or interest, may agree in writing that any other charge on, or interest in, that estate or interest ranks in priority to the charge to which that spouse is so entitled.

Section 47(11)   SCHEDULE 5

POWERS OF HIGH COURT AND COUNTY COURT TO REMAND

Interpretation

1. In this Schedule "the court" means the High Court or a county court and includes—
(a) in relation to the High Court, a judge of that court, and
(b) in relation to a county court, a judge or district judge of that court.

Remand in custody or on bail

2.—(1) Where a court has power to remand a person under section 47, the court may—
(a) remand him in custody, that is to say, commit him to custody to be brought before the court at the end of the period of remand or at such earlier time as the court may require, or
(b) remand him on bail—

(i) by taking from him a recognizance (with or without sureties) conditioned as provided in sub-paragraph (3), or

(ii) by fixing the amount of the recognizances with a view to their being taken subsequently in accordance with paragraph 4 and in the meantime committing the person to custody in accordance with paragraph (a).

(2) Where a person is brought before the court after remand, the court may further remand him.

(3) Where a person is remanded on bail under sub-paragraph (1), the court may direct that his recognizance be conditioned for his appearance—

(a) before that court at the end of the period of remand, or

(b) at every time and place to which during the course of the proceedings the hearing may from time to time be adjourned.

(4) Where a recognizance is conditioned for a person's appearance in accordance with sub-paragraph (1)(b), the fixing of any time for him next to appear shall be deemed to be a remand; but nothing in this sub-paragraph or sub-paragraph (3) shall deprive the court of power at any subsequent hearing to remand him afresh.

(5) Subject to paragraph 3, the court shall not remand a person under this paragraph for a period exceeding 8 clear days, except that—

(a) if the court remands him on bail, it may remand him for a longer period if he and the other party consent, and

(b) if the court adjourns a case under section 48(1), the court may remand him for the period of the adjournment.

(6) Where the court has power under this paragraph to remand a person in custody it may, if the remand is for a period not exceeding 3 clear days, commit him to the custody of a constable.

Further remand

3.—(1) If the court is satisfied that any person who has been remanded under paragraph 2 is unable by reason of illness or accident to appear or be brought before the court at the expiration of the period for which he was remanded, the court may, in his absence, remand him for a further time; and paragraph 2(5) shall not apply.

(2) Notwithstanding anything in paragraph 2(1), the power of the court under sub-paragraph (1) to remand a person on bail for a further time may be exercised by enlarging his recognizance and those of any sureties for him to a later time.

(3) Where a person remanded on bail under paragraph 2 is bound to appear before the court at any time and the court has no power to remand him under sub-paragraph (1), the court may in his absence enlarge his recognizance and those of any sureties for him to a later time; and the enlargement of his recognizance shall be deemed to be a further remand.

Postponement of taking of recognizance

4. Where under paragraph 2(1)(b)(ii) the court fixes the amount in which the principal and his sureties, if any, are to be bound, the recognizance may thereafter be taken by such person as may be prescribed by rules of court, and the same consequences shall follow as if it had been entered into before the court.

GENERAL NOTE

This Schedule establishes a scheme for the remand of persons arrested pursuant to a power of arrest or warrant granted by the High Court and county courts. It is based on the existing scheme in the magistrates' court established by ss.128 and 129 of the Magistrates' Courts Act 1980.

Paragraph 1 is a definition paragraph.

Paragraphs 2, 3 and 4 provide that the court may remand the person arrested either in custody or on bail by taking from him a recognizance, with or without sureties, and impose certain time limits. It should be noted that where the court adjourns a case it can remand in custody for a period exceeding eight days. There are provisions for further remand.

Section 52   SCHEDULE 6

AMENDMENTS OF CHILDREN ACT 1989

1. After section 38 of the Children Act 1989 insert—

"Power to include exclusion requirement in interim care order
    38A.—(1) Where—

    (a) on being satisfied that there are reasonable grounds for believing that the circumstances with respect to a child are as mentioned in section 31(2)(a) and (b)(i), the court makes an interim care order with respect to a child, and

    (b) the conditions mentioned in subsection (2) are satisfied,

the court may include an exclusion requirement in the interim care order.

    (2) The conditions are—

    (a) that there is reasonable cause to believe that, if a person ("the relevant person") is excluded from a dwelling-house in which the child lives, the child will cease to suffer, or cease to be likely to suffer, significant harm, and

    (b) that another person living in the dwelling-house (whether a parent of the child or some other person)—

        (i) is able and willing to give to the child the care which it would be reasonable to expect a parent to give him, and

        (ii) consents to the inclusion of the exclusion requirement.

    (3) For the purposes of this section an exclusion requirement is any one or more of the following—

    (a) a provision requiring the relevant person to leave a dwelling-house in which he is living with the child,

    (b) a provision prohibiting the relevant person from entering a dwelling-house in which the child lives, and

    (c) a provision excluding the relevant person from a defined area in which a dwelling-house in which the child lives is situated.

    (4) The court may provide that the exclusion requirement is to have effect for a shorter period than the other provisions of the interim care order.

    (5) Where the court makes an interim care order containing an exclusion requirement, the court may attach a power of arrest to the exclusion requirement.

    (6) Where the court attaches a power of arrest to an exclusion requirement of an interim care order, it may provide that the power of arrest is to have effect for a shorter period than the exclusion requirement.

    (7) Any period specified for the purposes of subsection (4) or (6) may be extended by the court (on one or more occasions) on an application to vary or discharge the interim care order.

    (8) Where a power of arrest is attached to an exclusion requirement of an interim care order by virtue of subsection (5), a constable may arrest without warrant any person whom he has reasonable cause to believe to be in breach of the requirement.

    (9) Sections 47(7), (11) and (12) and 48 of, and Schedule 5 to, the Family Law Act 1996 shall have effect in relation to a person arrested under subsection (8) of this section as they have effect in relation to a person arrested under section 47(6) of that Act.

    (10) If, while an interim care order containing an exclusion requirement is in force, the local authority have removed the child from the dwelling-house from which the relevant person is excluded to other accommodation for a continuous period of more than 24 hours, the interim care order shall cease to have effect in so far as it imposes the exclusion requirement.

Undertakings relating to interim care orders

    38B.—(1) In any case where the court has power to include an exclusion requirement in an interim care order, the court may accept an undertaking from the relevant person.

    (2) No power of arrest may be attached to any undertaking given under subsection (1).

    (3) An undertaking given to a court under subsection (1)—

    (a) shall be enforceable as if it were an order of the court, and

    (b) shall cease to have effect if, while it is in force, the local authority have removed the child from the dwelling-house from which the relevant person is excluded to other accommodation for a continuous period of more than 24 hours.

    (4) This section has effect without prejudice to the powers of the High Court and county court apart from this section.

    (5) In this section "exclusion requirement" and "relevant person" have the same meaning as in section 38A."

  2. In section 39 of the Children Act 1989 (discharge and variation etc. of care orders and supervision orders) after subsection (3) insert—

    "(3A) On the application of a person who is not entitled to apply for the order to be discharged, but who is a person to whom an exclusion requirement contained in the order applies, an interim care order may be varied or discharged by the court in so far as it imposes the exclusion requirement.

(3B) Where a power of arrest has been attached to an exclusion requirement of an interim care order, the court may, on the application of any person entitled to apply for the discharge of the order so far as it imposes the exclusion requirement, vary or discharge the order in so far as it confers a power of arrest (whether or not any application has been made to vary or discharge any other provision of the order)."

3. After section 44 of the Children Act 1989 insert—

"Power to include exclusion requirement in emergency protection order

44A.—(1) Where—

(a) on being satisfied as mentioned in section 44(1)(a), (b) or (c), the court makes an emergency protection order with respect to a child, and

(b) the conditions mentioned in subsection (2) are satisfied,

the court may include an exclusion requirement in the emergency protection order.

(2) The conditions are—

(a) that there is reasonable cause to believe that, if a person ("the relevant person") is excluded from a dwelling-house in which the child lives, then—

(i) in the case of an order made on the ground mentioned in section 44(1)(a), the child will not be likely to suffer significant harm, even though the child is not removed as mentioned in section 44(1)(a)(i) or does not remain as mentioned in section 44(1)(a)(ii), or

(ii) in the case of an order made on the ground mentioned in paragraph (b) or (c) of section 44(1), the enquiries referred to in that paragraph will cease to be frustrated, and

(b) that another person living in the dwelling-house (whether a parent of the child or some other person)—

(i) is able and willing to give to the child the care which it would be reasonable to expect a parent to give him, and

(ii) consents to the inclusion of the exclusion requirement.

(3) For the purposes of this section an exclusion requirement is any one or more of the following—

(a) a provision requiring the relevant person to leave a dwelling-house in which he is living with the child,

(b) a provision prohibiting the relevant person from entering a dwelling-house in which the child lives, and

(c) a provision excluding the relevant person from a defined area in which a dwelling-house in which the child lives is situated.

(4) The court may provide that the exclusion requirement is to have effect for a shorter period than the other provisions of the order.

(5) Where the court makes an emergency protection order containing an exclusion requirement, the court may attach a power of arrest to the exclusion requirement.

(6) Where the court attaches a power of arrest to an exclusion requirement of an emergency protection order, it may provide that the power of arrest is to have effect for a shorter period than the exclusion requirement.

(7) Any period specified for the purposes of subsection (4) or (6) may be extended by the court (on one or more occasions) on an application to vary or discharge the emergency protection order.

(8) Where a power of arrest is attached to an exclusion requirement of an emergency protection order by virtue of subsection (5), a constable may arrest without warrant any person whom he has reasonable cause to believe to be in breach of the requirement.

(9) Sections 47(7), (11) and (12) and 48 of, and Schedule 5 to, the Family Law Act 1996 shall have effect in relation to a person arrested under subsection (8) of this section as they have effect in relation to a person arrested under section 47(6) of that Act.

(10) If, while an emergency protection order containing an exclusion requirement is in force, the applicant has removed the child from the dwelling-house from which the relevant person is excluded to other accommodation for a continuous period of more than 24 hours, the order shall cease to have effect in so far as it imposes the exclusion requirement.

Undertakings relating to emergency protection orders

44B.—(1) In any case where the court has power to include an exclusion requirement in an emergency protection order, the court may accept an undertaking from the relevant person.

(2) No power of arrest may be attached to any undertaking given under subsection (1).

(3) An undertaking given to a court under subsection (1)—

(a) shall be enforceable as if it were an order of the court, and

    (b) shall cease to have effect if, while it is in force, the applicant has removed the child from the dwelling-house from which the relevant person is excluded to other accommodation for a continuous period of more than 24 hours.

    (4) This section has effect without prejudice to the powers of the High Court and county court apart from this section.

    (5) In this section "exclusion requirement" and "relevant person" have the same meaning as in section 44A."

4. In section 45 of the Children Act 1989 (duration of emergency protection orders and other supplemental provisions), insert after subsection (8)—

    "(8A) On the application of a person who is not entitled to apply for the order to be discharged, but who is a person to whom an exclusion requirement contained in the order applies, an emergency protection order may be varied or discharged by the court in so far as it imposes the exclusion requirement.

    (8B) Where a power of arrest has been attached to an exclusion requirement of an emergency protection order, the court may, on the application of any person entitled to apply for the discharge of the order so far as it imposes the exclusion requirement, vary or discharge the order in so far as it confers a power of arrest (whether or not any application has been made to vary or discharge any other provision of the order)."

5. In section 105(1) of the Children Act 1989 (interpretation), after the definition of "domestic premises", insert—

    "dwelling-house" includes—

        (a) any building or part of a building which is occupied as a dwelling;

        (b) any caravan, house-boat or structure which is occupied as a dwelling;

    and any yard, garden, garage or outhouse belonging to it and occupied with it;".

GENERAL NOTE

This Schedule makes important amendments to the Children Act 1989. They enable the court to attach ouster orders (exclusion requirements) to interim care orders and emergency protection orders, so as to permit the removal of the suspected abuser from the home instead of having to remove the child. The Schedule can be traced back to a debate at the Committee stage of the Children Bill in the House of Commons (*Official Report* (H.C.) Standing Committee 13, May 25, 1989, cols. 325–329), to the difficulties courts and local authorities have encountered (see notably *Nottinghamshire C.C. v. P* [1994] Fam. 18, although inherent jurisdiction has since been successfully invoked in *Re S* [1994] 1 F.L.R. 623 and in *Devon C.C. v. S* [1994] 1 F.L.R. 355), and to the Law Commission's report (No. 207, paras. 6.15–6.22), the recommendations of which constitute the basis of the new legislation.

The Schedule provides for exclusion requirements to be included within interim care orders and emergency protection orders. Ouster of the abuser is not, therefore, a free-standing remedy. It is supplementary to an emergency protection order or an interim care order. It follows that the court is able to regulate contact, medical examinations, treatment and assessment during the order in exactly the same way as it has done under the Children Act 1989 (see ss.38(6)–(8), 43, 44(6)).

New Section 38A

Subs. (1)

This provides that, if the criteria for making an interim care order under the Children Act 1989 are satisfied and there is reasonable cause to believe that the likelihood of harm to the child will not arise if the suspected abuser is excluded, then an order may be made ousting or prohibiting him.

Satisfied. The court does not have to be satisfied that the grounds for an interim care order exist, in fact, but simply that there are reasonable grounds for believing that they do (*Re B (A Minor) (Care Order: Criteria)* [1993] 1 F.L.R. 815). The court also held in *Re B* that evidence which might not be sufficient to satisfy the court at a final hearing may be acceptable to discharge the lower standard for an interim care order. Note that an application for an interim care order is not a trial run for a final hearing: accordingly, evidence, and the cross-examination of witnesses, should be restricted to the issues essential to the interim stage (see *Hampshire C.C. v. S* [1993] 1 F.L.R. 559 and *Re W (Interim Care Order)* [1994] 2 F.L.R. 892).

Reasonable grounds. See also *Re B (A Minor) (Care Order: Criteria)* [1993] 1 F.L.R. 815.

Circumstances ... in s.31(2)(a) and (b)(i). That is, that the child is suffering or likely to suffer significant harm and the harm, or its likelihood, is attributable to the care given or likely to be given, not being what it would be reasonable to expect a parent to give.

Interim care order. The making of an interim care order was described in *Re G* (Minors) (*Interim Care Order*) [1993] 2 F.L.R. 839 as "an essentially impartial step, favouring neither one side nor the other" (*per* Waite L.J. at p.845). Whether an interim care order with an exclusion requirement could be similarly so described is doubtful. Waite L.J. went on to describe an interim care order as a neutral method of preserving the status quo. Again, to characterise such an order with an exclusion requirement in this way would be wrong.

The conditions ... in subsection (2). These must be satisfied in addition to satisfaction (on which see above) that there are reasonable grounds for an interim care order.

The court may. It thus has a discretion not to include an exclusion requirement even where both (a) and (b) are satisfied. It should be stressed that s.1(5) of the Children Act 1989 (the court shall not make an order "unless it considers that doing so would be better for the child than making no order at all") applies to interim care orders even if it does not strictly apply to the exclusion requirement (which is an added-on extra rather than an order). But it is suggested that the spirit of s.1(5), if not the letter, should not be ignored by courts carrying out their duties under this section.

Exclusion requirement. As to which, see s.38A(3). Note that a power of arrest may be attached (see s.38A(5)).

Subs. (2)

This subsection sets out the conditions that must be satisfied before an exclusion requirement can be attached to an interim care order.

Reasonable cause to believe. On this, see *Re B (A Minor) (Care Order: Criteria)* [1993] 1 F.L.R. 815 (it was likely that a girl of four years had been sexually abused, but it was not clear who the perpetrator was. An assessment was crucial to that question and the girl would remain at risk of significant harm if it was not carried out. An aunt was prepared to care for the girl—she had sought an interim residence order—but the aunt refused to countenance the possibility that the father had sexually abused the girl. This, said the court, would seriously impair the assessment and, if the assessment did not continue or was rendered valueless, there were reasonable grounds for believing that significant harm would be suffered by the girl which would be attributable to the care likely to be given to her by the aunt).

Relevant person. This is not defined in the Act, deliberately so (despite s.38B(5) giving the expression the same "meaning" in that section as it has here). The person can be any person and not just a parent or relative. Commonly, the person may be a boy-friend of the mother.

Dwelling-house. This is defined in Sched. 6, para. 5.

Lives. It is suggested that this should be liberally interpreted so that it covers the home where the child normally lives. A child currently with his/her mother in a refuge in these terms "lives" in his/her home, not the refuge. Similarly, a child living with a relative or foster parent or at boarding school. It is submitted that any other interpretation would not cure the mischief behind this provision: the sex abuser, for example, would be encouraged to drive the child out in order himself to remain in the home.

Cease to suffer ... cease to be likely to suffer. The object of this is perfectly clear, if rather naïve (a child who has been sexually abused is unlikely to cease to suffer significant harm merely because her abuser is no longer living with her). The same applies to emotional abuse, which oddly Mrs Justice Hale does not think is anyway appropriately dealt with by an interim care order: see *Minutes of Proceedings of the Special Public Committee,* H.L. Paper 55, 1995 para. 131).

Significant harm. This is defined in the Children Act 1989, s.31(9) and (10). See also M.D.A. Freeman in Allan Levy (ed.), *Refocus on Child Abuse* (London: Hawksmere, 1994 p.18); M. Adcock, R. White and A. Hollows, *Significant Harm* (Croydon: Significant Publications, 1991).

Another person living in the dwelling-house. And not therefore a relative, for example, living elsewhere, even presumably one prepared to take up residence in the child's dwelling-house. *Cf.* the facts of *Re B (A Minor) (Care Order: Criteria)* [1993] 1 F.L.R. 815 above.

Parent. This is not defined in the Children Act 1989. For the meaning of "parent" in the context of assisted reproduction, see the Human Fertilisation and Embryology Act 1990.

Some other person. Who need not have (and will not acquire by reason of an exclusion requirement) parental responsibility. It may be assumed that in most cases this person will be a close relative (for example, an aunt or grandmother), but the concept is not so limited. It could be anybody.

The care. The Children Act 1989 does not define "care". In *Re B (A Minor) (Care Order: Criteria)* [1993] 1 F.L.R. 815, Douglas Brown J. says it "goes beyond physical care and includes the emotional care which a reasonable parent would give the child" (p.820). And he adds, most pertinently for this context, "in the case of a child who has probably been sexually abused, that includes listening to the child and monitoring its words and actions so that a professional assessment can be carried out" (*idem*).

A parent. Note the indefinite article (as in s.31(2) of the Children Act 1989). The test is care that a parent, not this child's parent, would reasonably give.

Consents. This is a positive act, different from "not objecting". As the Law Commission states (No. 207, para. 6.20): "clearly, the co-operation of the person caring for the child is essential to the success of the order ... the provision of consent would be some indication to the court that this person is willing and able to provide reasonable care for the child in the meantime".

Subs. (3)
This lists what an exclusion requirement can include.
Relevant person. See the note above under s.38A(2).
Dwelling-house. See the note above under s.38A(2). Note that there is no power to exclude the relevant person from only part of the dwelling-house.
Defined area. On which, see the precedents under the Domestic Violence and Matrimonial Proceedings Act 1976, such as *Tuck v. Nicholls* [1989] 1 F.L.R. 283 (and see the discussion in relation to s.33(3) of this Act).

Subs. (4)
This subsection enables the court to specify a shorter duration period for the exclusion requirement than for the interim care order. See Law Commission, No. 207, para. 6.21.
Shorter period. Interim care orders last for eight weeks and are extendable for four weeks at a time (see the Children Act 1989, s.38(4) and (5)).

Subs. (5)
This provides that a power of arrest may be attached to an exclusion requirement in an interim care order. This is to provide "immediate protection for the child which would achieve the overall objective of avoiding the need to remove him from home" *per* Law Commission, No. 207, para. 6.22. This is the first use of the power of arrest concept in children's protective legislation.

Subs. (6)
This provides that the power of arrest provision may be of shorter duration than the exclusion requirement.

Subs. (7)
This provides that periods stipulated for the exclusion requirement and for the power of arrest may be extended on an application to vary or discharge the interim care order.
Vary ... discharge interim care order. On which, see the Children Act 1989, s.38.

Subs. (8)
This provides for arrest without warrant by a police officer who has reasonable cause to believe that the person concerned is in breach of an exclusion requirement.
Constable. Who need not be in uniform.

Subs. (9)
This extends relevant provisions on arrest for breach of an order in this Act to arrest for breach of an exclusion requirement in the Children Act 1989.

Subs. (10)
This subsection provides that the exclusion requirement will lapse automatically if the local authority removes the child from the dwelling-house concerned for 24 hours. See Law Commission, No. 207, para. 6.19.
Have removed. It is difficult to see what putting this in the past tense achieves. If the lapse is to be automatic it will take effect when the local authority removes the child.

New Section 38B
This section provides that an undertaking may be accepted by the court in lieu of imposing an exclusion requirement. The undertaking is enforceable as a court order but a power of arrest may not be attached to it. Parties have the same right to challenge an exclusion requirement as they have to challenge the interim care order to which it is supplementary.

Subs. (1)
This provides that, where an exclusion requirement may be imposed, an undertaking may be accepted.
Exclusion requirement. See s.38A.
Undertaking. See the note on s.46(1).

Subs. (2)
No power of arrest may be attached to an undertaking. This confirms existing law. See further, the note on s.46(2), above.

Subs. (3)

This provides that undertakings may be enforced as court orders and cease to have effect if the local authority removes the child from the house from which the abuser has been excluded for 24 hours.

An order of the court. And, therefore, by committal for contempt of court. See, further, the note on s.46(4), above.

Subs. (4)

This provides that s.38B is without prejudice to the powers of the High Court and county court apart from this section; in particular it is without prejudice to their inherent jurisdiction.

Para. 2

The insertion of new subsections in s.39 of the Children Act 1989 ensures that the parties have the same right to challenge an exclusion requirement and the attachment of a power of arrest as they have to challenge the interim care order to which they are supplementary.

Para. 3

New Section 44A

Subs. (1)

This subsection, together with subss. (2) and (3) provides that, if the criteria for making an emergency protection order under the Children Act 1989 are satisfied, and there is reasonable cause to believe that the likelihood of harm to the child will not arise, or that the investigating authorities' access to the child's home will no longer be frustrated, if the suspected person is excluded from the dwelling-house, then an order may be made ousting or prohibiting the suspected person from that dwelling-house or its vicinity. There must also be another person in the household who is willing and able to provide reasonable care for the child, and who consents to the order being made.

The court. This may be a single justice on an *ex parte* application.

May include. The court has a discretion not to include an exclusion requirement. On the relevance of s.1(5) of the Children Act 1989, see the note on new s.38A, above.

Subs. (2)

Likely to suffer significant harm. Evidence of harm occurring at the time of the application or in the past is not sufficient unless it gives reasonable cause to believe that it is likely to occur in the future. "Likely" means there is a real possibility, one that cannot sensibly be ignored, having regard to the nature and gravity of the feared harm in the particular case (see *Re H and R (Child Sexual Abuse: Standard of Proof)* [1996] 1 F.L.R. 80).

Cease to be frustrated. "The hypothesis of the grounds at s.44(1)(b) and (c) is that this combination of factors is evidence of an emergency or the likelihood of an emergency. The court will have to decide whether the refusal of access to the child was unreasonable if the person refusing had explained to him the reason for the enquiries and the request for access, the request itself was reasonable, and he had failed to respond positively in some other suitable way ..." (See *Guidance To The Children Act, Court Orders* (London: H.M.S.O. 1991) Vol. 1, para. 4.39).

Reasonable to expect a parent. Not this child's parent or indeed this person. The test is what could be expected of a reasonable parent.

Consents. See the note on new s.38A(2), above.

Subs. (3)

This lists what an exclusion requirement may contain. See further the commentary on new s.38A(3).

Subs. (4)

The exclusion requirement may have effect for a shorter period than other provisions of the emergency protection order.

Shorter period. An emergency protection order may be granted for up to eight days. This may be extended once for up to seven days (see the Children Act 1989, s.45(1), (5), (6)).

Subs. (5)

The exclusion requirement may have a power of arrest attached to it. See also the note on new s.38A(5), above.

Subs. (6)

The power of arrest provision may be of shorter duration than the exclusion requirement itself.

Subs. (7)
This provides that periods stipulated for the exclusion requirement and for the power of arrest may be extended on an application to vary or discharge the emergency order.
Discharge. See ss.45(8)–(11) of the Children Act 1989.

Subs. (8)
This provides for arrest without warrant by a police officer who has reasonable cause to believe that the person concerned is in breach of an exclusion requirement.
Constable. Who need not be in uniform.
Reasonable cause. The burden of reasonable cause lies on the constable (*Dallison v. Caffery* [1965 1 Q.B. 348, 365, *per* Lord Denning M.R.).

Subs. (9)
This extends relevant provisions on arrest for breach of an order in the Family Law Act to arrest for breach of an exclusion requirement in the Children Act 1989.

Subs. (10)
This provides that the exclusion requirement will lapse automatically if the local authority (or other applicant—it can only be the NSPCC) removes the child from the dwelling-house concerned for more than 24 hours.

New Section 44B
This section provides that an undertaking may be accepted by the court in lieu of imposing an exclusion requirement. The undertaking is enforceable as a court order, but may not have a power of arrest attached to it. Like a requirement, it lapses if the applicant has removed the child from the dwelling-house from which the relevant person has been excluded for 24 hours.

Para. 4
This ensures that the parties have the same right to challenge an exclusion requirement as they have to challenge the emergency protection order to which it is supplementary. They also have the same right to challenge a power of arrest attached to an exclusion requirement of an emergency protection order.

Section 53   SCHEDULE 7

Transfer of certain tenancies on divorce etc. or on separation of cohabitants

Part I

General

Interpretation

1. In this Schedule—
   "cohabitant", except in paragraph 3, includes (where the context requires) former cohabitant;
   "the court" does not include a magistrates' court,
   "landlord" includes—
      (a) any person from time to time deriving title under the original landlord; and
      (b) in relation to any dwelling-house, any person other than the tenant who is, or (but for Part VII of the Rent Act 1977 or Part II of the Rent (Agriculture) Act 1976) would be, entitled to possession of the dwelling-house;
   "Part II order" means an order under Part II of this Schedule;
   "a relevant tenancy" means—
      (a) a protected tenancy or statutory tenancy within the meaning of the Rent Act 1977;
      (b) a statutory tenancy within the meaning of the Rent (Agriculture) Act 1976;
      (c) a secure tenancy within the meaning of section 79 of the Housing Act 1985; or
      (d) an assured tenancy or assured agricultural occupancy within the meaning of Part I of the Housing Act 1988;
   "spouse", except in paragraph 2, includes (where the context requires) former spouse; and
   "tenancy" includes sub-tenancy.

Cases in which the court may make an order

2.—(1) This paragraph applies if one spouse is entitled, either in his own right or jointly with the other spouse, to occupy a dwelling-house by virtue of a relevant tenancy.

(2) At any time when it has power to make a property adjustment order under section 23A (divorce or separation) or 24 (nullity) of the Matrimonial Causes Act 1973 with respect to the marriage, the court may make a Part II order.

3.—(1) This paragraph applies if one cohabitant is entitled, either in his own right or jointly with the other cohabitant, to occupy a dwelling-house by virtue of a relevant tenancy.

(2) If the cohabitants cease to live together as husband and wife, the court may make a Part II order.

4. The court shall not make a Part II order unless the dwelling-house is or was—

(a) in the case of spouses, a matrimonial home; or

(b) in the case of cohabitants, a home in which they lived together as husband and wife.

Matters to which the court must have regard

5. In determining whether to exercise its powers under Part II of this Schedule and, if so, in what manner, the court shall have regard to all the circumstances of the case including—

(a) the circumstances in which the tenancy was granted to either or both of the spouses or cohabitants or, as the case requires, the circumstances in which either or both of them became tenant under the tenancy;

(b) the matters mentioned in section 33(6)(a), (b) and (c) and, where the parties are cohabitants and only one of them is entitled to occupy the dwelling-house by virtue of the relevant tenancy, the further matters mentioned in section 36(6)(e), (f), (g) and (h); and

(c) the suitability of the parties as tenants.

PART II

ORDERS THAT MAY BE MADE

References to entitlement to occupy

6. References in this Part of this Schedule to a spouse or a cohabitant being entitled to occupy a dwelling-house by virtue of a relevant tenancy apply whether that entitlement is in his own right or jointly with the other spouse or cohabitant.

Protected, secure or assured tenancy or assured agricultural occupancy

7.—(1) If a spouse or cohabitant is entitled to occupy the dwelling-house by virtue of a protected tenancy within the meaning of the Rent Act 1977, a secure tenancy within the meaning of the Housing Act 1985 or an assured tenancy or assured agricultural occupancy within the meaning of Part I of the Housing Act 1988, the court may by order direct that, as from such date as may be specified in the order, there shall, by virtue of the order and without further assurance, be transferred to, and vested in, the other spouse or cohabitant—

(a) the estate or interest which the spouse or cohabitant so entitled had in the dwelling-house immediately before that date by virtue of the lease or agreement creating the tenancy and any assignment of that lease or agreement, with all rights, privileges and appurtenances attaching to that estate or interest but subject to all covenants, obligations, liabilities and incumbrances to which it is subject; and

(b) where the spouse or cohabitant so entitled is an assignee of such lease or agreement, the liability of that spouse or cohabitant under any covenant of indemnity by the assignee express or implied in the assignment of the lease or agreement to that spouse or cohabitant.

(2) If an order is made under this paragraph, any liability or obligation to which the spouse or cohabitant so entitled is subject under any covenant having reference to the dwelling-house in the lease or agreement, being a liability or obligation falling due to be discharged or performed on or after the date so specified, shall not be enforceable against that spouse or cohabitant.

(3) If the spouse so entitled is a successor within the meaning of Part IV of the Housing Act 1985, his former spouse or former cohabitant (or, if a separation order is in force, his spouse) shall be deemed also to be a successor within the meaning of that Part.

(4) If the spouse or cohabitant so entitled is for the purpose of section 17 of the Housing Act 1988 a successor in relation to the tenancy or occupancy, his former spouse or former cohabitant (or, if a separation order is in force, his spouse) is to be deemed to be a successor in relation to the tenancy or occupancy for the purposes of that section.

(5) If the transfer under sub-paragraph (1) is of an assured agricultural occupancy, then, for the purposes of Chapter III of Part I of the Housing Act 1988—

(a) the agricultural worker condition is fulfilled with respect to the dwelling-house while the spouse or cohabitant to whom the assured agricultural occupancy is transferred continues to be the occupier under that occupancy, and

   (b) that condition is to be treated as so fulfilled by virtue of the same paragraph of Schedule 3 to the Housing Act 1988 as was applicable before the transfer.

   (6) In this paragraph, references to a separation order being in force include references to there being a judicial separation in force.

Statutory tenancy within the meaning of the Rent Act 1977

8.—(1) This paragraph applies if the spouse or cohabitant is entitled to occupy the dwelling-house by virtue of a statutory tenancy within the meaning of the Rent Act 1977.

   (2) The court may by order direct that, as from the date specified in the order—

   (a) that spouse or cohabitant is to cease to be entitled to occupy the dwelling-house; and

   (b) the other spouse or cohabitant is to be deemed to be the tenant or, as the case may be, the sole tenant under that statutory tenancy.

   (3) The question whether the provisions of paragraphs 1 to 3, or (as the case may be) paragraphs 5 to 7 of Schedule 1 to the Rent Act 1977, as to the succession by the surviving spouse of a deceased tenant, or by a member of the deceased tenant's family, to the right to retain possession are capable of having effect in the event of the death of the person deemed by an order under this paragraph to be the tenant or sole tenant under the statutory tenancy is to be determined according as those provisions have or have not already had effect in relation to the statutory tenancy.

Statutory tenancy within the meaning of the Rent (Agriculture) Act 1976

9.—(1) This paragraph applies if the spouse or cohabitant is entitled to occupy the dwelling-house by virtue of a statutory tenancy within the meaning of the Rent (Agriculture) Act 1976.

   (2) The court may by order direct that, as from such date as may be specified in the order—

   (a) that spouse or cohabitant is to cease to be entitled to occupy the dwelling-house; and

   (b) the other spouse or cohabitant is to be deemed to be the tenant or, as the case may be, the sole tenant under that statutory tenancy.

   (3) A spouse or cohabitant who is deemed under this paragraph to be the tenant under a statutory tenancy is (within the meaning of that Act) a statutory tenant in his own right, or a statutory tenant by succession, according as the other spouse or cohabitant was a statutory tenant in his own right or a statutory tenant by succession.

PART III

SUPPLEMENTARY PROVISIONS

Compensation

10.—(1) If the court makes a Part II order, it may by the order direct the making of a payment by the spouse or cohabitant to whom the tenancy is transferred ("the transferee") to the other spouse or cohabitant ("the transferor").

   (2) Without prejudice to that, the court may, on making an order by virtue of sub-paragraph (1) for the payment of a sum—

   (a) direct that payment of that sum or any part of it is to be deferred until a specified date or until the occurrence of a specified event, or

   (b) direct that that sum or any part of it is to be paid by instalments.

   (3) Where an order has been made by virtue of sub-paragraph (1), the court may, on the application of the transferee or the transferor—

   (a) exercise its powers under sub-paragraph (2), or

   (b) vary any direction previously given under that sub-paragraph,

at any time before the sum whose payment is required by the order is paid in full.

   (4) In deciding whether to exercise its powers under this paragraph and, if so, in what manner, the court shall have regard to all the circumstances including—

   (a) the financial loss that would otherwise be suffered by the transferor as a result of the order;

   (b) the financial needs and financial resources of the parties; and

   (c) the financial obligations which the parties have, or are likely to have in the foreseeable future, including financial obligations to each other and to any relevant child.

   (5) The court shall not give any direction under sub-paragraph (2) unless it appears to it that immediate payment of the sum required by the order would cause the transferee financial hardship which is greater than any financial hardship that would be caused to the transferor if the direction were given.

Liabilities and obligations in respect of the dwelling-house

11.—(1) If the court makes a Part II order, it may by the order direct that both spouses or cohabitants are to be jointly and severally liable to discharge or perform any or all of the liabilities and obligations in respect of the dwelling-house (whether arising under the tenancy or otherwise) which—

(a) have at the date of the order fallen due to be discharged or performed by one only of them; or

(b) but for the direction, would before the date specified as the date on which the order is to take effect fall due to be discharged or performed by one only of them.

(2) If the court gives such a direction, it may further direct that either spouse or cohabitant is to be liable to indemnify the other in whole or in part against any payment made or expenses incurred by the other in discharging or performing any such liability or obligation.

Date when order made between spouses is to take effect

12.—(1) In the case of a decree of nullity of marriage, the date specified in a Part II order as the date on which the order is to take effect must not be earlier than the date on which the decree is made absolute.

(2) In the case of divorce proceedings or separation proceedings, the date specified in a Part II order as the date on which the order is to take effect is to be determined as if the court were making a property adjustment order under section 23A of the Matrimonial Causes Act 1973 (regard being had to the restrictions imposed by section 23B of that Act).

Remarriage of either spouse

13.—(1) If after the making of a divorce order or the grant of a decree annulling a marriage either spouse remarries, that spouse is not entitled to apply, by reference to the making of that order or the grant of that decree, for a Part II order.

(2) For the avoidance of doubt it is hereby declared that the reference in sub-paragraph (1) to remarriage includes a reference to a marriage which is by law void or voidable.

Rules of court

14.—(1) Rules of court shall be made requiring the court, before it makes an order under this Schedule, to give the landlord of the dwelling-house to which the order will relate an opportunity of being heard.

(2) Rules of court may provide that an application for a Part II order by reference to an order or decree may not, without the leave of the court by which that order was made or decree was granted, be made after the expiration of such period from the order or grant as may be prescribed by the rules.

Saving for other provisions of Act

15.—(1) If a spouse is entitled to occupy a dwelling-house by virtue of a tenancy, this Schedule does not affect the operation of sections 30 and 31 in relation to the other spouse's matrimonial home rights.

(2) If a spouse or cohabitant is entitled to occupy a dwelling-house by virtue of a tenancy, the court's powers to make orders under this Schedule are additional to those conferred by sections 33, 35 and 36.

GENERAL NOTE

This Schedule is derived from the power to transfer tenancies in the Matrimonial Homes Act 1983. It extends the power to cohabitants and former cohabitants. The Schedule enables the court to require the transferee to make a payment to the transferor, and also enables the court to defer the making of such a payment in certain circumstances.

Para. 1

This provides for the interpretation of various expressions used in the Schedule.

Para. 2

This reproduces Sched. 1, para. 1 of the Matrimonial Homes Act 1983.

Para. 3

This empowers the court to make a transfer of a relevant tenancy between cohabitants who have ceased to live together as husband and wife.

Para. 4

This makes if clear that a transfer can only be made in respect of a matrimonial home, or in the case of cohabitants, a home in which they lived together as husband and wife.

Para. 5

This sets out the criteria which the court must apply when deciding whether to make an order. See further Law Com. No. 207, para. 6.9.

Para. 6

This makes it clear that any references to a spouse or a cohabitant being entitled to occupy applies whether the entitlement is in his/her own right or jointly with the other spouse or cohabitant.

Para. 7

This is derived from Sched. 1, para. 2 of the Matrimonial Homes Act 1983. Its provisions have been extended to cover cohabitants as well as spouses.

Para. 8

This extends para. 3 of Sched. 1 of the Matrimonial Homes Act 1983 and enables transfers between cohabitants in addition to spouses.

Para. 9

This is derived from Sched. 1, para. 4 of the Matrimonial Homes Act 1983. It is extended to cover cohabitants as well as spouses.

Para. 10

This gives the court power to order one party to compensate the other for any financial loss suffered as a consequence of the tenancy being transferred to the other spouse or cohabitant. The court is directed, when considering compensation, to have particular regard to the financial loss to the transferor if no compensation is awarded, the parties' financial needs and resources and any financial obligations which the parties have or are likely to have in the foreseeable future. See, further, Law Com. No. 207, para. 6.12.

Para. 11

This follows the provisions of para. 5 of Sched. 1 of the Matrimonial Homes Act 1983. It extends them to cohabitants.

Para. 12

This follows the provision of para. 6 of Sched. 1 of the Matrimonial Homes Act 1983. It provides that a transfer order cannot take effect before a decree of nullity of marriage is made absolute. It further provides that in the case of divorce or separation, the date specified as the date on which the order is to take effect is to be determined as if the court were making a property adjustment order.

Para. 13

This reproduces para. 7 of Sched. 1 of the Matrimonial Homes Act 1983. It provides that no spouse can apply for a transfer after remarriage. It makes it clear that a reference to remarriage includes a marriage which by law is void or voidable.

Para. 14

Paragraph 14(1) reproduces para. 8(1) of Sched. 1 of the Matrimonial Homes Act 1983. It provides for rules to be made giving the landlord an opportunity to be heard before a transfer order is made.

Paragraph 14(2) follows para. 8(2) of Sched. 1 of the Matrimonial Homes Act 1983.

Para. 15

This makes savings for other provisions of the Act.

Section 66(1)   SCHEDULE 8

MINOR AND CONSEQUENTIAL AMENDMENTS

PART I

AMENDMENTS CONNECTED WITH PART II

The Wills Act 1837 (c. 26)

1. In section 18A(1) of the Wills Act 1837 (effect of dissolution or annulment of marriage on wills), for "a decree" substitute "an order or decree".

The Judicial Proceedings (Regulation of Reports) Act 1926 (c. 61)

2. In section 1(1)(b) of the Judicial Proceedings (Regulation of Reports) Act 1926 (restriction on reporting) after "in relation to" insert "any proceedings under Part II of the Family Law Act 1996 or otherwise in relation to".

The Maintenance Orders Act 1950 (c. 37)

3. In section 16 of the Maintenance Orders Act 1950 (orders to which Part II of that Act applies)—
   (a) in subsection (2)(a)(i), for "23(1), (2) and (4)" substitute "22A, 23"; and
   (b) in subsection (2)(c)(v), after "Matrimonial Causes Act 1973" insert "(as that Act had effect immediately before the passing of the Family Law Act 1996)".

The Matrimonial Causes Act 1973 (c. 18)

4. The 1973 Act is amended as follows.

5. In section 8 (intervention of Queen's Proctor)—
   (a) for "a petition for divorce" substitute "proceedings for a divorce order";
   (b) in subsection (1)(b), omit "or before the decree nisi is made absolute"; and
   (c) in subsection (2), for "a decree nisi in any proceedings for divorce" substitute "the making of a divorce order".

6. For section 15 (application of provisions relating to divorce to nullity proceedings) substitute—

"Decrees of nullity to be decrees nisi
   15. Every decree of nullity of marriage shall in the first instance be a decree nisi and shall not be made absolute before the end of six weeks from its grant unless—
   (a) the High Court by general order from time to time fixes a shorter period; or
   (b) in any particular case, the court in which the proceedings are for the time being pending from time to time by special order fixes a shorter period than the period otherwise applicable for the time being by virtue of this section.

Intervention of Queen's Proctor
   15A.—(1) In the case of a petition for nullity of marriage—
   (a) the court may, if it thinks fit, direct all necessary papers in the matter to be sent to the Queen's Proctor, who shall under the directions of the Attorney-General instruct counsel to argue before the court any question in relation to the matter which the court considers it necessary or expedient to have fully argued;
   (b) any person may at any time during the progress of the proceedings or before the decree nisi is made absolute give information to the Queen's Proctor on any matter material to the due decision of the case, and the Queen's Proctor may thereupon take such steps as the Attorney-General considers necessary or expedient.
   (2) If the Queen's Proctor intervenes or shows cause against a decree nisi in any proceedings for nullity of marriage, the court may make such order as may be just as to the payment by other parties to the proceedings of the costs incurred by him in so doing or as to the payment by him of any costs incurred by any of those parties by reason of his so doing.
   (3) Subsection (3) of section 8 above applies in relation to this section as it applies in relation to that section.

Proceedings after decree nisi: general powers of court

15B.—(1) Where a decree of nullity of marriage has been granted under this Act but not made absolute, then, without prejudice to section 15A above, any person (excluding a party to the proceedings other than the Queen's Proctor) may show cause why the decree should not be made absolute by reason of material facts not having been brought before the court; and in such a case the court may—

(a) notwithstanding anything in section 15 above (but subject to section 41 below) make the decree absolute; or

(b) rescind the decree; or

(c) require further inquiry; or

(d) otherwise deal with the case as it thinks fit.

(2) Where a decree of nullity of marriage has been granted under this Act and no application for it to be made absolute has been made by the party to whom it was granted, then, at any time after the expiration of three months from the earliest date on which that party could have made such an application, the party against whom it was granted may make an application to the court, and on that application the court may exercise any of the powers mentioned in paragraphs (a) to (d) of subsection (1) above."

7. In section 19(4) (application of provisions relating to divorce to proceedings under section 19)—

(a) for "1(5), 8 and 9" substitute "15, 15A and 15B"; and

(b) for "divorce" in both places substitute "nullity of marriage".

8. In section 24A(1) (orders for sale of property), for "section 23 or 24 of this Act" substitute "any of sections 22A to 24 above".

9.—(1) Section 25 (matters to which the court is to have regard) is amended as follows.

(2) In subsection (1), for "section 23, 24 or 24A" substitute "any of sections 22A to 24A".

(3) In subsection (2)—

(a) for "section 23(1)(a), (b) or (c)" substitute "section 22A or 23 above to make a financial provision order in favour of a party to a marriage or the exercise of its powers under section 23A,";

(b) in paragraph (g), after "parties" insert ", whatever the nature of the conduct and whether it occurred during the marriage or after the separation of the parties or (as the case may be) dissolution or annulment of the marriage,"; and

(c) in paragraph (h), omit "in the case of proceedings for divorce or nullity of marriage,".

(4) In subsection (3), for "section 23(1)(d), (e) or (f), (2) or (4)" substitute "section 22A or 23 above to make a financial provision order in favour of a child of the family or the exercise of its powers under section 23A,".

(5) In subsection (4), for "section 23(1)(d), (e) or (f), (2) or (4), 24 or 24A" substitute "any of sections 22A to 24A".

(6) After subsection (4) insert—

"(5) In relation to any power of the court to make an interim periodical payments order or an interim order for the payment of a lump sum, the preceding provisions of this section, in imposing any obligation on the court with respect to the matters to which it is to have regard, shall not require the court to do anything which would cause such a delay as would, in the opinion of the court, be inappropriate having regard—

(a) to any immediate need for an interim order;

(b) to the matters in relation to which it is practicable for the court to inquire before making an interim order; and

(c) to the ability of the court to have regard to any matter and to make appropriate adjustments when subsequently making a financial provision order which is not interim."

10.—(1) Section 25A (requirement to consider need to provide for "a clean break") is amended as follows.

(2) In subsection (1), for the words from the beginning to "the marriage" substitute—

"If the court decides to exercise any of its powers under any of sections 22A to 24A above in favour of a party to a marriage (other than its power to make an interim periodical payments order or an interim order for the payment of a lump sum)".

(3) In subsection (1), for "the decree" substitute "a divorce order or decree of nullity".

(4) For subsection (3) substitute—

"(3) If the court—

(a) would have power under section 22A or 23 above to make a financial provision order in favour of a party to a marriage ("the first party"), but

(b) considers that no continuing obligation should be imposed on the other party to the marriage ("the second party") to make or secure periodical payments in favour of the first party, it may direct that the first party may not at any time after the direction takes effect, apply to the court for the making against the second party of any periodical payments order or secured periodical payments order and, if the first party has already applied to the court for the making of such an order, it may dismiss the application.

(3A) If the court—

(a) exercises, or has exercised, its power under section 22A at any time before making a divorce order, and

(b) gives a direction under subsection (3) above in respect of a periodical payments order or a secured periodical payments order,

it shall provide for the direction not to take effect until a divorce order is made."

11. In each of sections 25B(2) and (3), 25C(1) and (3) and 25D(1)(a), (2)(a), (c) and (e) (benefits under a pension scheme on divorce, etc.) for "section 23" substitute "section 22A or 23".

12. In section 26(1) (commencement of proceedings for ancillary relief), for the words from the beginning to "22 above" substitute—

"(1) If a petition for nullity of marriage has been presented, then, subject to subsection (2) below, proceedings".

13.—(1) Section 27 (financial provision orders etc. in case of failure to provide proper maintenance) is amended as follows.

(2) In subsection (5)—

(a) after "an order requiring the respondent" insert "—

(a)"; and

(b) at the end insert ", or

(b) to pay to the applicant such lump sum or sums as the court thinks reasonable."

(3) For subsection (6) substitute—

"(6) Subject to the restrictions imposed by the following provisions of this Act, if on an application under this section the applicant satisfies the court of any ground mentioned in subsection (1) above, the court may make one or more financial provision orders against the respondent in favour of the applicant or a child of the family."

(4) In subsection (7), for "(6)(c) or (f)" substitute "(6)".

14.—(1) Section 28 (duration of continuing financial provision order in favour of a party to a marriage) is amended as follows.

(2) In subsection (1A), for the words from the beginning to "nullity of marriage" substitute—

"(1A) At any time when—

(a) the court exercises, or has exercised, its power under section 22A or 23 above to make a financial provision order in favour of a party to a marriage,

(b) but for having exercised that power, the court would have power under one of those sections to make such an order, and

(c) an application for a divorce order or a petition for a decree of nullity of marriage is outstanding or has been granted in relation to the marriage,".

(3) Insert, after subsection (1A)—

"(1B) If the court—

(a) exercises, or has exercised, its power under section 22A at any time before making a divorce order, and

(b) gives a direction under subsection (1A) above in respect of a periodical payments order or a secured periodical payments order,

it shall provide for the direction not to take effect until a divorce order is made."

(4) In subsection (2), for the words from "on or after" to "nullity of marriage" substitute "at such a time as is mentioned in subsection (1A)(c) above".

(5) In subsection (3)—

(a) for "a decree" substitute "an order or decree"; and

(b) for "that decree" substitute "that order or decree".

15. In section 29(1) (duration of a continuing financial provision order in favour of a child of the family), for "under section 24(1)(a)" substitute "such as is mentioned in section 21 (2)(a)".

16.—(1) Section 31 (variation etc. of orders) is amended as follows.

(2) In subsection (2)—

(a) after "following orders" insert "under this Part of this Act";

(b) for paragraph (d) substitute—

"(d) an order for the payment of a lump sum in a case in which the payment is to be by instalments;";

(c) in paragraph (dd), for "23(1)(c)" substitute "21(1)(c)";

(d) after paragraph (dd) insert—

"(de) any other order for the payment of a lump sum, if it is made at a time when no divorce order has been made, and no separation order is in force, in relation to the marriage;";

(e) for paragraph (e) substitute—
"(e) any order under section 23A of a kind referred to in section 21(2)(b), (c) or (d) which is made on or after the making of a separation order;
(ea) any order under section 23A which is made at a time when no divorce order has been made, and no separation order is in force in relation to the marriage;".
(3) In subsection (4)—
(a) for the words from "for a settlement" to "24(1)(c) or (d)", substitute "referred to in subsection (2)(e)"; and
(b) for paragraphs (a) and (b) substitute "on an application for a divorce order in relation to the marriage".
(4) After subsection (4) insert—
"(4A) In relation to an order which falls within subsection (2)(de) or (ea) above ("the subsection (2) order"—
(a) the powers conferred by this section may be exercised—
(i) only on an application made before the subsection (2) order has or, but for paragraph (b) below, would have taken effect; and
(ii) only if, at the time when the application is made, no divorce order has been made in relation to the marriage and no separation order has been so made since the subsection (2) order was made; and
(b) an application made in accordance with paragraph (a) above prevents the subsection (2) order from taking effect before the application has been dealt with.
(4B) No variation—
(a) of a financial provision order made under section 22A above, other than an interim order, or
(b) of a property adjustment order made under section 23A above,
shall be made so as to take effect before the making of a divorce order or separation order in relation to the marriage, unless the court is satisfied that the circumstances of the case are exceptional, and that it would be just and reasonable for the variation to be so made."
(5) In subsection (5)—
(a) insert, at the beginning, "Subject to subsections (7A) to (7F) below and without prejudice to any power exercisable by virtue of subsection (2)(d), (dd) or (e) above or otherwise than by virtue of this section,"; and
(b) for "section 23", in each place, substitute "section 22A or 23".
(6) In subsection (7)(a)—
(a) for "on or after" to "consider" substitute "in favour of a party to a marriage, the court shall, if the marriage has been dissolved or annulled, consider"; and
(b) after "sufficient" insert "(in the light of any proposed exercise by the court, where the marriage has been dissolved, of its powers under subsection (7B) below)".
(7) After subsection (7), insert—
"(7A) Subsection (7B) below applies where, after the dissolution of a marriage, the court—
(a) discharges a periodical payments order or secured periodical payments order made in favour of a party to the marriage; or
(b) varies such an order so that payments under the order are required to be made or secured only for such further period as is determined by the court.
(7B) The court has power, in addition to any power it has apart from this subsection, to make supplemental provision consisting of any of—
(a) an order for the payment of a lump sum in favour of a party to the marriage;
(b) one or more property adjustment orders in favour of a party to the marriage;
(c) a direction that the party in whose favour the original order discharged or varied was made is not entitled to make any further application for—
(i) a periodical payments or secured periodical payments order, or
(ii) an extension of the period to which the original order is limited by any variation made by the court.
(7C) An order for the payment of a lump sum made under subsection (7B) above may—
(a) provide for the payment of that sum by instalments of such amount as may be specified in the order; and
(b) require the payment of the instalments to be secured to the satisfaction of the court.
(7D) Subsections (7) and (8) of section 22A above apply where the court makes an order for the payment of a lump sum under subsection (7B) above as they apply where it makes such an order under section 22A above.
(7E) If under subsection (7B) above the court makes more than one property adjustment order in favour of the same party to the marriage, each of those orders must fall within a different paragraph of section 21(2) above.

(7F) Sections 24A and 30 above apply where the court makes a property adjustment order under subsection (7B) above as they apply where it makes such an order under section 23A above."

17. In section 32(1) (payment of certain arrears to be unenforceable), for the words from "an order" to "financial provision order" substitute "any financial provision order under this Part of this Act or any interim order for maintenance".

18. For section 33(2) (repayment of sums paid under certain orders) substitute—

"(2) This section applies to the following orders under this Part of this Act—

(a) any periodical payments order;

(b) any secured periodical payments order; and

(c) any interim order for maintenance, so far as it requires the making of periodical payments."

19.—(1) Section 33A (consent orders) is amended as follows.

(2) In subsection (2), after "applies", in the first place, insert "(subject, in the case of the powers of the court under section 31A above, to subsections (6) and (7) of that section)".

(3) In subsection (3), in the definition of "order for financial relief", for "an order under any of sections 23, 24, 24A or 27 above" substitute "any of the following orders under this Part of this Act, that is to say, any financial provision order, any property adjustment order, any order for the sale of property or any interim order for maintenance".

20. In section 35 (alteration of maintenance agreements), after subsection (6), insert—

"(7) Subject to subsection (5) above, references in this Act to any such order as is mentioned in section 21 above shall not include references to any order under this section."

21. In section 37(1) (avoidance of transactions intended to prevent or reduce financial relief), for "22, 23, 24, 27, 31 (except subsection (6))" substitute "22A to 24, 27, 31 (except subsection (6)), 31A".

22. In section 47(2) (relief in cases of polygamous marriages—

(a) in paragraph (a), after "any" insert the words "divorce order, any separation order under the 1996 Act or any"; and

(b) in paragraph (d), after "this Act" insert "or the 1996 Act" and for "such decree or order" substitute "a statement of marital breakdown or any such order or decree".

23. Omit section 49 (under which a person who is alleged to have committed adultery with a party to a marriage is required to be made a party to certain proceedings).

24.—(1) Section 52(1) (interpretation) is amended as follows.

(2) After "In this Act", insert—

" "the 1996 Act" means the Family Law Act 1996;".

(3) After the definition of "maintenance assessment" insert—

" "statement of marital breakdown" has the same meaning as in the Family Law Act 1996."

25. In section 52(2)(a), for "with section 21 above" substitute "(subject to section 35(7) above) with section 21 above and—

(i) in the case of a financial provision order or periodical payments order, as including (except where the context otherwise requires) references to an interim periodical payments order under section 22A or 23 above; and

(ii) in the case of a financial provision order or order for the payment of a lump sum, as including (except where the context otherwise requires) references to an interim order for the payment of a lump sum under section 22A or 23 above;".

The Domicile and Matrimonial Proceedings Act 1973 (c. 45)

26. For section 5(5) of the Domicile and Matrimonial Proceedings Act 1973 (jurisdiction in cases of change of domicile or habitual residence) substitute—

"(5) The court shall have jurisdiction to entertain proceedings for nullity of marriage (even though it would not otherwise have jurisdiction) at any time when marital proceedings, as defined by section 20 of the Family Law Act 1996, are pending in relation to the marriage."

The Inheritance (Provision for Family and Dependants) Act 1975 (c. 63)

27.—(1) The Inheritance (Provision for Family and Dependants) Act 1975 (meaning of reasonable financial provision) is amended as follows.

(2) In section 1(2)(a), for the words from "the marriage" to "in force" substitute ", at the date of death, a separation order under the Family Law Act 1996 was in force in relation to the marriage".

(3) In section 3(2) (matters to which the court is to have regard)—

(a) for "decree of judicial separation" substitute "separation order under the Family Law Act 1996"; and

(b) for "a decree of divorce" substitute "a divorce order".

(4) In section 14 (provision where no financial relief was granted on divorce)—

(a) in subsection (1), for the words from "a decree" to first "granted" substitute "a divorce order or separation order has been made under the Family Law Act 1996 in relation to a marriage or a decree of nullity of marriage has been made absolute";

(b) in subsection (1)(a), for "section 23" and "section 24" substitute, respectively, "section 22A or 23" and "section 23A or 24";

(c) after paragraph (b), for the words from "the decree of divorce" to the end substitute ", as the case may be, the divorce order or separation order had not been made or the decree of nullity had not been made absolute"; and

(d) in subsection (2), for "decree of judicial separation" and "the decree" substitute, respectively, "separation order" and "the order".

(5) In section 15(1) (restriction imposed in divorce proceedings on applications under that Act), for the words from the beginning to "thereafter" substitute—

"At any time when the court—

(a) has jurisdiction under section 23A or 24 of the Matrimonial Causes Act 1973 to make a property adjustment order in relation to a marriage; or

(b) would have such jurisdiction if either the jurisdiction had not already been exercised or an application for such an order were made with the leave of the court,".

(6) In section 15, for subsections (2) to (4) substitute—

"(2) An order made under subsection (1) above with respect to any party to a marriage has effect in accordance with subsection (3) below at any time—

(a) after the marriage has been dissolved;

(b) after a decree of nullity has been made absolute in relation to the marriage; and

(c) while a separation order under the Family Law Act 1996 is in force in relation to the marriage and the separation is continuing.

(3) If at any time when an order made under subsection (I) above with respect to any party to a marriage has effect the other party to the marriage dies, the court shall not entertain any application made by the surviving party to the marriage for an order under section 2 of this Act."

(7) In section 19(2)(b) (effect and duration of certain orders), for the words from "the marriage" to "in force" substitute ", at the date of death, a separation order under the Family Law Act 1996 was in force in relation to the marriage with the deceased".

(8) In section 25 (interpretation), in the definition of "former wife" and "former husband", for "a decree", in the first place, substitute "an order or decree".

The Domestic Proceedings and Magistrates' Courts Act 1978 (c. 22)

28.—(1) Section 28(1) of the Domestic Proceedings and Magistrates' Courts Act 1978 (powers of High Court in respect of orders under Part I) is amended as follows.

(2) After "this Act" insert—

"(a) a statement of marital breakdown under section 5 of the Family Law Act 1996 with respect to the marriage has been received by the court but no application has been made under that Act by reference to that statement, or

(b)".

(3) For the words from "then" to "lump sum" substitute "then, except in the case of an order for the payment of a lump sum, any court to which an application may be made under that Act by reference to that statement or, as the case may be,".

The Housing Act 1980 (c. 51)

29. In section 54(2) of the Housing Act 1980 (prohibition of assignment of shorthold tenancy under that section) for "section 24" substitute "sections 23A or 24".

The Supreme Court Act 1981 (c. 54)

30. In section 18 of the Supreme Court Act 1981 (restrictions on appeals to Court of Appeal), in paragraph (d) of subsection (1) omit "divorce or" and after that paragraph insert—

"(dd) from a divorce order;".

The Civil Jurisdiction and Judgments Act 1982 (c. 27)

31. In section 18(6)(a) of the Civil Jurisdiction and Judgments Act 1982 (decrees of judicial separation), for "a decree" substitute "an order or decree".

The Matrimonial and Family Proceedings Act 1984 (c. 42)

32.—(1) The Matrimonial and Family Proceedings Act 1984 is amended as follows.

(2) In section 17(1) (financial relief in the case of overseas divorces etc.), tor the words from "any" where it first occurs to the end substitute "one or more orders each of which would, within the meaning of Part II of the 1973 Act, be a financial provision order in favour of a party to the marriage or child of the family or a property adjustment order in relation to the marriage."

(3) For section 21(a) (provisions of the 1973 Act applied for the purposes of the powers to give relief in the case of overseas divorces etc.) substitute—

"(a) section 22A(5) (provisions about lump sums in relation to divorce or separation);

(aa) section 23(4), (5) and (6) (provisions about lump sums in relation to annulment);".

(4) In section 27 (interpretation), for the definition of "property adjustment order", substitute—

" "property adjustment order" and "secured periodical payments order" mean any order which would be a property adjustment order or, as the case may be, secured periodical payments order within the meaning of Part II of the 1973 Act;"

(5) In section 32 (meaning of "family business"), for the definition of "matrimonial cause" substitute—

" "matrimonial cause" means an action for nullity of marriage or any marital proceedings under the Family Law Act 1996;".

The Finance Act 1985 (c. 54)

33. In section 83(1) of the Finance Act 1985 (stamp duty for transfers of property in connection with divorce etc.)—

(a) after paragraph (b), insert—

"(bb) is executed in pursuance of an order of a court which is made at any time under section 22A, 23A or 24A of the Matrimonial Causes Act 1973, or"; and

(b) in paragraph (c), for "or their judicial separation" substitute ", their judicial separation or the making of a separation order in respect of them".

The Housing Act 1985 (c. 68)

34. In each of sections 39(1)(c), 88(2), 89(3), 90(3)(a), 91(3)(b), 99B(2)(e), 101(3)(c), 160(1)(c), 171B(4)(b)(i) of, and paragraph 1(2)(c) to, Schedule 6A of the Housing Act 1985 (which refers to the 1973 Act), for "section 24" substitute "section 23A or 24".

The Housing Associations Act 1985 (c. 69)

35. In paragraph 5(1)(c) of Schedule 2 to the Housing Associations Act 1985 (which refers to the 1973 Act), for "section 24" substitute "section 23A or 24".

The Agricultural Holdings Act 1986 (c. 5)

36. In paragraph 1(3) of Schedule 6 to the Agricultural Holdings Act 1986 (spouse of close relative not to be treated as such when marriage subject to decree nisi etc.), for the words from "when" to the end substitute "when a separation order or a divorce order under the Family Law Act 1996 is in force in relation to the relative's marriage or that marriage is the subject of a decree nisi of nullity".

The Family Law Act 1986 (c. 55)

37.—(1) The Family Law Act 1986 is amended as follows.

(2) For section 2(1) and (2) (jurisdiction to make orders under section 1) substitute—

"(1) A court in England and Wales shall not have jurisdiction to make a section 1(1)(a) order with respect to a child unless—

(a) the case falls within section 2A below; or

(b) in any other case, the condition in section 3 below is satisfied."

(3) For section 2A(1) (jurisdiction in or in connection with matrimonial proceedings), substitute—

"(1) Subject to subsections (2) to (4) below, a case falls within this section for the purposes of the making of a section l(l)(a) order if that order is made—

(a) at a time when—

(i) a statement of marital breakdown under section 5 of the Family Law Act 1996 with respect to the marriage of the parents of the child concerned has been received by the court; and

(ii) it is or may become possible for an application for a divorce order or for a separation order to be made by reference to that statement; or

(b) at a time when an application in relation to that marriage for a divorce order, or for a separation order under the Act of 1996, has been made and not withdrawn.

(1A) A case also falls within this section for the purposes of the making of a section l(1)(a) order if that order is made in or in connection with any proceedings for the nullity of the marriage of the parents of the child concerned and—

(a) those proceedings are continuing; or

(b) the order is made—

(i) immediately on the dismissal, after the beginning of the trial, of the proceedings; and

(ii) on an application made before the dismissal."

(4) In section 2A(2), for the words from the beginning to "judicial separation" substitute "A case does not fall within this section if a separation order under the Family Law Act 1996 is in force in relation to the marriage of the parents of the child concerned if,".

(5) In section 2A(3), for "in which the other proceedings there referred to" substitute "in Scotland, Northern Ireland or a specified dependent territory in which the proceedings for divorce or nullity".

(6) In section 2A(4)—

(a) for "in or in connection with matrimonial proceedings" substitute "by virtue of the case falling within this section"; and

(b) for "in or in connection with those proceedings" substitute "by virtue of section 2(1)(a) of this Act".

(7) In section 3 (child habitually resident or present in England and Wales), for "section 2(2)" substitute "section 2(1)(b)".

(8) In section 6 (duration and variation of Part I orders), for subsections (3A) and (3B) substitute—

"(3A) Subsection (3) above does not apply if the Part I order was made in a case falling within section 2A of this Act."

(9) In section 38 (restriction on removal of wards of court from the jurisdiction), insert after subsection (3)—

"(4) The reference in subsection (2) above to a time when proceedings for divorce or judicial separation are continuing in respect of a marriage in another part of the United Kingdom includes, in relation to any case in which England and Wales would be another part of the United Kingdom, any time when—

(a) a statement of marital breakdown under section 5 of the Family Law Act 1996 with respect to that marriage has been received by the court and it is or may become possible for an application for a divorce order or for a separation order to be made by reference to that statement; or

(b) an application in relation to that marriage for a divorce order, or for a separation order under the Act of 1996, has been made and not withdrawn."

(10) In section 42(2) (times when divorce etc.proceedings are to be treated as continuing for the purposes of certain restrictions on the removal of children from the jurisdiction), for the words from "unless" to the end substitute "be treated as continuing (irrespective of whether a divorce order, separation order or decree of nullity has been made)—

(a) from the time when a statement of marital breakdown under section 5 of the Family Law Act 1996 with respect to the marriage is received by the court in England and Wales until such time as the court may designate or, if earlier, until the time when—

(i) the child concerned attains the age of eighteen; or

(ii) it ceases, by virtue of section 5(3) or 7(9) of that Act (lapse of divorce or separation process) to be possible for an application for a divorce order, or for a separation order, to be made by reference to that statement; and

(b) from the time when a petition for nullity is presented in relation to the marriage in England and Wales or a petition for divorce, judicial separation or nullity is presented in relation to the marriage in Northern Ireland or a specified dependent territory, until the time when—

(i) the child concerned attains the age of eighteen; or

(ii) if earlier, proceedings on the petition are dismissed."

(11) In section 51(4) (definitions), after the definition of "the relevant date" insert—

" 'judicial separation' includes a separation order under the Family Law Act 1996;".

The Landlord and Tenant Act 1987 (c. 31)

38. In section 4(2)(c) of the Landlord and Tenant Act 1987 (which refers to the 1973 Act), for "section 24" substitute "section 23A, 24".

The Legal Aid Act 1988 (c. 34)

39. In paragraph 5A of Part II of Schedule 2 to the Legal Aid Act 1988 (excepted proceedings)—
   (a) for "decree of divorce or judicial separation" substitute "a divorce order or a separation order"; and
   (b) in sub-paragraph (b) of that paragraph, for "petition" substitute "application".

The Housing Act 1988 (c. 50)

40. In paragraph 4(1)(c) of Schedule 11 (which refers to the 1973 Act), for "section 24" substitute "section 23A or 24".

The Children Act 1989 (c. 41)

41.—(1) The Children Act 1989 is amended as follows.
   (2) In section 6(3A) (revocation or appointment of guardian) for paragraph (a) substitute—
      "(a) a court of civil jurisdiction in England and Wales by order dissolves, or by decree annuls, a marriage, or".
   (3) In section 8(3) after "means" insert "(subject to subsection (5))".
   (4) In section 8, insert after subsection (4)—
      "(5) For the purposes of any reference in this Act to family proceedings, powers which under this Act are exercisable in family proceedings shall also be exercisable in relation to a child, without any such proceedings having been commenced or any application having been made to the court under this Act, if—
      (a) a statement of marital breakdown under section 5 of the Family Law Act 1996 with respect to the marriage in relation to which that child is a child of the family has been received by the court; and
      (b) it may, in due course, become possible for an application for a divorce order or for a separation order to be made by reference to that statement."

The Local Government and Housing Act 1989 (c. 42)

42. In section 124(3)(c) of the Local Government and Housing Act 1989 (which refers to the 1973 Act), for "section 24" substitute "section 23A or 24".

Pensions Act 1995 (c. 26)

43. In section 166(4) of the Pensions Act 1995 (jurisdiction of the court under the Matrimonial Causes Act 1973 in respect of pensions to which that section applies) for "section 23" substitute "section 22A or 23".

PART II

AMENDMENTS CONNECTED WITH PART III

The Legal Aid Act 1988 (c. 34)

44.—(1) The 1988 Act is amended as follows.
   (2) In section 1, after "III" insert "IIIA".
   (3) In sections 1, 2(11), 3(2), 4(1), (2) and (4), 5(1) and (6), 6(2)(a) and (3)(a), 34(2)(c) and (d) and (11), 38(1) and (6) and 39(1) and (4)(a), after "assistance", in each place, insert ", mediation".
   (4) In section 3(9), after paragraph (a) insert—
      "(aa) the provision of mediation;".
   (5) In section 6, after subsection (3)(c) insert—
      "(ca) any sum which is to be paid out of property on which it is charged under regulations under section 13C(5) below".
   (6) In section 15—
   (a) in subsection (1), after "(3D)" insert "and (3F)"; and
   (b) in subsection (3D), after "(3)" insert "and (3F)".
   (7) In section 16(9), leave out "and" at the end of paragraph (a).
   (8) In section 38—
   (a) in subsection (1)(f), after "legal representatives" insert "or mediators"; and
   (b) in subsection (6), after "legal representative" insert "or mediator".
   (9) In section 43—
   (a) after " "assistance" " insert ", "mediation" ";

(b) after "(3)" insert ", (3A)"; and
(c) after the definition of "financial resources" insert—
    " "family matters" has the meaning assigned by section 13A(2);".

PART III

AMENDMENTS CONNECTED WITH PART IV

The Land Registration Act 1925 (c. 21)

45. In section 64 of the Land Registration Act 1925 (certificates to be produced and noted on dealings) in subsection (5) for "section 2(8) of the Matrimonial Homes Act 1983" substitute "section 31(10) of the Family Law Act 1996 and for "rights of occupation" substitute "matrimonial home rights ".

The Land Charges Act 1972 (c. 61)

46. In section 1(6A) of the Land Charges Act 1972 (cases where county court has jurisdiction to vacate registration) in paragraph (d)—
  (a) after "section 1 of the Matrimonial Homes Act 1983" insert "or section 33 of the Family Law Act 1996"; and
  (b) for "that section" substitute "either of those sections".
47. In section 2(7) of that Act (Class F land charge) for "Matrimonial Homes Act 1983" substitute "Part IV of the Family Law Act 1996".

The Land Compensation Act 1973 (c. 26)

48.—(1) Section 29A of the Land Compensation Act 1973 (spouses having statutory rights of occupation) is amended as follows.
(2) In subsection (1), for "rights of occupation (within the meaning of the Matrimonial Homes Act 1983)" substitute "matrimonial home rights (within the meaning of Part IV of the Family Law Act 1996)".
(3) In subsection (2)(a), for "rights of occupation" substitute "matrimonial home rights".

The Magistrates' Courts Act 1980 (c. 43)

49. In section 65(1) of the Magistrates' Courts Act 1980 (meaning of family proceedings) after paragraph (o) insert—
    "(p) Part IV of the Family Law Act 1996;".

The Contempt of Court Act 1981 (c. 49)

50. In Schedule 3 to the Contempt of Court Act 1981 (application of Magistrates' Courts Act 1980 to civil contempt proceedings), in paragraph 3 for the words from " "or, having been arrested" onwards substitute—
    " "or, having been arrested under section 47 of the Family Law Act 1996 in connection with the matter of the complaint, is at large after being remanded under subsection (7)(b) or (10) of that section." "

The Supreme Court Act 1981 (c. 54)

51. In Schedule 1 to the Supreme Court Act 1981 (distribution of business in High Court), in paragraph 3 (Family Division)—
  (a) in paragraph (d), after "matrimonial proceedings" insert "or proceedings under Part IV of the Family Law Act 1996", and
  (b) in paragraph (f)(i), for "Domestic Violence and Matrimonial Proceedings Act 1976" substitute "Part IV of the Family Law Act 1996".

The Matrimonial and Family Proceedings Act 1984 (c. 42)

52. For section 22 of the Matrimonial and Family Proceedings Act 1984 substitute—

"Powers of court in relation to certain tenancies of dwelling-houses
  22.—(1) This section applies if—
    (a) an application is made by a party to a marriage for an order for financial relief; and
    (b) one of the parties is entitled, either in his own right or jointly with the other party, to occupy a dwelling-house situated in England or Wales by virtue of a tenancy which is

a relevant tenancy within the meaning of Schedule 7 to the Family Law Act 1996 (certain statutory tenancies).

(2) The court may make in relation to that dwelling-house any order which it could make under Part II of that Schedule if—

(a) a divorce order,

(b) a separation order, or

(c) a decree of nullity of marriage,

had been made or granted in England and Wales in respect of the marriage.

(3) The provisions of paragraphs 10, 11 and 14(1) in Part III of that Schedule apply in relation to any order under this section as they apply to any order under Part II of that Schedule."

The Housing Act 1985 (c. 68)

53.—(1) Section 85 of the Housing Act 1985 (extended discretion of court in certain proceedings for possession) is amended as follows.

(2) In subsection (5)—

(a) in paragraph (a), for "rights of occupation under the Matrimonial Homes Act 1983" substitute "matrimonial home rights under Part IV of the Family Law Act 1996"; and

(b) for "those rights of occupation" substitute "those matrimonial home rights".

(3) After subsection (5) insert—

"(5A) If proceedings are brought for possession of a dwelling-house which is let under a secure tenancy and—

(a) an order is in force under section 35 of the Family Law Act 1996 conferring rights on the former spouse of the tenant or an order is in force under section 36 of that Act conferring rights on a cohabitant or former cohabitant (within the meaning of that Act) of the tenant,

(b) the former spouse, cohabitant or former cohabitant is then in occupation of the dwelling-house, and

(c) the tenancy is terminated as a result of those proceedings,

the former spouse, cohabitant or former cohabitant shall, so long as he or she remains in occupation, have the same rights in relation to, or in connection with, any adjournment, stay, suspension or postponement in pursuance of this section as he or she would have if the rights conferred by the order referred to in paragraph (a) were not affected by the termination of the tenancy."

54. In section 99B of that Act (persons qualifying for compensation for improvements) in subsection (2) for paragraph (f) substitute—

"(f) a spouse, former spouse, cohabitant or former cohabitant of the improving tenant to whom the tenancy has been transferred by an order made under Schedule 1 to the Matrimonial Homes Act 1983 or Schedule 7 to the Family Law Act 1996."

55. In section 101 of that Act (rent not to be increased on account of tenant's improvements) in subsection (3) for paragraph (d) substitute—

"(d) a spouse, former spouse, cohabitant or former cohabitant of the tenant to whom the tenancy has been transferred by an order made under Schedule 1 to the Matrimonial Homes Act 1983 or Schedule 7 to the Family Law Act 1996."

56. In section 171B of that Act (extent of preserved right to buy: qualifying persons and dwelling-houses) in subsection (4)(b)(ii) after "Schedule 1 to the Matrimonial Homes Act 1983" insert "or Schedule 7 to the Family Law Act 1996".

The Insolvency Act 1986 (c. 45)

57.—(1) Section 336 of the Insolvency Act 1986 (rights of occupation etc. of bankrupt's spouse) is amended as follows.

(2) In subsection (1), for "rights of occupation under the Matrimonial Homes Act 1983" substitute "matrimonial home rights under Part IV of the Family Law Act 1996".

(3) In subsection (2)—

(a) for "rights of occupation under the Act of 1983" substitute "matrimonial home rights under the Act of 1996", and

(b) in paragraph (b), for "under section 1 of that Act" substitute "under section 33 of that Act".

(4) In subsection (4), for "section 1 of the Act of 1983" substitute "section 33 of the Act of 1996".

58.—(1) Section 337 of that Act is amended as follows.

(2) In subsection (2), for "rights of occupation under the Matrimonial Homes Act 1983" substitute "matrimonial home rights under Part IV of the Family Law Act 1996".

(3) For subsection (3) substitute—

"(3) The Act of 1996 has effect, with the necessary modifications, as if—

(a) the rights conferred by paragraph (a) of subsection (2) were matrimonial home rights under that Act,

(b) any application for such leave as is mentioned in that paragraph were an application for an order under section 33 of that Act, and

(c) any charge under paragraph (b) of that subsection on the estate or interest of the trustee were a charge under that Act on the estate or interest of a spouse."

(4) In subsections (4) and (5) for "section 1 of the Act of 1983" substitute "section 33 of the Act of 1996".

The Housing Act 1988 (c. 50)

59.—(1) Section 9 of the Housing Act 1988 (extended discretion of court in possession claims) is amended as follows.

(2) In subsection (5)—

(a) in paragraph (a), for "rights of occupation under the Matrimonial Homes Act 1983" substitute "matrimonial home rights under Part IV of the Family Law Act 1996", and

(b) for "those rights of occupation" substitute "those matrimonial home rights".

(3) After subsection (5) insert—

"(5A) In any case where—

(a) at a time when proceedings are brought for possession of a dwelling-house let on an assured tenancy—

(i) an order is in force under section 35 of the Family Law Act 1996 conferring rights on the former spouse of the tenant or

(ii) an order is in force under section 36 of that Act conferring rights on a cohabitant or former cohabitant (within the meaning of that Act) of the tenant,

(b) that cohabitant, former cohabitant or former spouse is then in occupation of the dwelling-house, and

(c) the assured tenancy is terminated as a result of those proceedings,

the cohabitant, former cohabitant or former spouse shall have the same rights in relation to, or in connection with, any such adjournment as is referred to in subsection (1) above or any such stay, suspension or postponement as is referred to in subsection (2) above as he or she would have if the rights conferred by the order referred to in paragraph (a) above were not affected by the termination of the tenancy."

The Children Act 1989 (c. 41)

60.—(1) In section 8(4) of the Children Act 1989 (meaning of "family proceedings" for purposes of that Act), omit paragraphs (c) and (f) and after paragraph (g) insert—

"(h) the Family Law Act 1996."

(2) In Schedule 11 to that Act, in paragraph 6(a) (amendment of the Domestic Proceedings and Magistrates' Courts Act 1978), for "sections 16(5)(c) and" substitute "section".

The Courts and Legal Services Act 1990 (c. 41)

61. In section 58 of the Courts and Legal Services Act 1990 (conditional fee agreements) in subsection (10), omit paragraphs (b) and (e) and immediately before the "or" following paragraph (g) insert—

"(gg) Part IV of the Family Law Act 1996".

Section 66(2)   SCHEDULE 9

MODIFICATIONS, SAVING AND TRANSITIONAL

Transitional arrangements for those who have been living apart

1.—(1) The Lord Chancellor may by order provide for the application of Part II to marital proceedings which—

(a) are begun during the transitional period, and

(b) relate to parties to a marriage who immediately before the beginning of that period were living apart,

subject to such modifications (which may include omissions) as may be prescribed.

(2) An order made under this paragraph may, in particular, make provision as to the evidence which a party who claims to have been living apart from the other party immediately before the beginning of the transitional period must produce to the court.

(3) In this paragraph—
"marital proceedings" has the same meaning as in section 24;
"prescribed" means prescribed by the order; and
"transitional period" means the period of two years beginning with the day on which section 3 is brought into force.

Modifications of enactments etc.

2.—(1) The Lord Chancellor may by order make such consequential modifications of any enactment or subordinate legislation as appear to him necessary or expedient in consequence of Part II in respect of any reference (in whatever terms) to—
(a) a petition;
(b) the presentation of a petition;
(c) the petitioner or respondent in proceedings on a petition;
(d) proceedings on a petition;
(e) proceedings in connection with any proceedings on a petition;
(f) any other matrimonial proceedings;
(g) a decree; or
(h) findings of adultery in any proceedings.
(2) An order under sub-paragraph (1) may, in particular—
(a) make provision applying generally in relation to enactments and subordinate legislation of a description specified in the order;
(b) modify the effect of sub-paragraph (3) in relation to documents and agreements of a description so specified.
(3) Otherwise a reference (in whatever terms) in any instrument or agreement to the presentation of a petition or to a decree has effect, in relation to any time after the coming into force of this paragraph—
(a) in the case of a reference to the presentation of a petition, as if it included a reference to the making of a statement; and
(b) in the case of a reference to a decree, as if it included a reference to a divorce order or (as the case may be) a separation order.
3. If an Act or subordinate legislation—
(a) refers to an enactment repealed or amended by or under this Act, and
(b) was passed or made before the repeal or amendment came into force,
the Lord Chancellor may by order make such consequential modifications of any provision contained in the Act or subordinate legislation as appears to him necessary or expedient in respect of the reference.

Expressions used in paragraphs 2 and 3

4. In paragraphs 2 and 3—
"decree" means a decree of divorce (whether a decree nisi or a decree which has been made absolute) or a decree of judicial separation;
"instrument" includes any deed, will or other instrument or document;
"petition" means a petition for a decree of divorce or a petition for a decree of judicial separation; and
"subordinate legislation" has the same meaning as in the Interpretation Act 1978.

Proceedings under way

5.—(1) Except for paragraph 6 of this Schedule, nothing in any provision of Part II, Part I of Schedule 8 or Schedule 10—
(a) applies to, or affects—
(i) any decree granted before the coming into force of the provision;
(ii) any proceedings begun, by petition or otherwise, before that time; or
(iii) any decree granted in any such proceedings;
(b) affects the operation of—
(i) the 1973 Act,
(ii) any other enactment, or
(iii) any subordinate legislation,
in relation to any such proceedings or decree or to any proceedings in connection with any such proceedings or decree; or
(c) without prejudice to paragraph (b), affects any transitional provision having effect under Schedule 1 to the 1973 Act.
(2) In this paragraph, "subordinate legislation" has the same meaning as in the Interpretation Act 1978.

6.—(1) Section 31 of the 1973 Act has effect as amended by this Act in relation to any order under Part II of the 1973 Act made after the coming into force of the amendments.

(2) Subsections (7) to (7F) of that section also have effect as amended by this Act in relation to any order made before the coming into force of the amendments.

Interpretation

7. In paragraphs 8 to 15 "the 1983 Act" means the Matrimonial Homes Act 1983.

Pending applications for orders relating to occupation and molestation

8.—(1) In this paragraph and paragraph 10 "the existing enactments" means—
(a) the Domestic Violence and Matrimonial Proceedings Act 1976;
(b) sections 16 to 18 of the Domestic Proceedings and Magistrates' Courts Act 1978; and
(c) sections 1 and 9 of the 1983 Act.

(2) Nothing in Part IV, Part III of Schedule 8 or Schedule 10 affects any application for an order or injunction under any of the existing enactments which is pending immediately before the commencement of the repeal of that enactment.

Pending applications under Schedule 1 to the Matrimonial Homes Act 1983

9. Nothing in Part IV, Part III of Schedule 8 or Schedule 10 affects any application for an order under Schedule 1 to the 1983 Act which is pending immediately before the commencement of the repeal of that Schedule.

Existing orders relating to occupation and molestation

10.—(1) In this paragraph "an existing order" means any order or injunction under any of the existing enactments which—
(a) is in force immediately before the commencement of the repeal of that enactment; or
(b) was made or granted after that commencement in proceedings brought before that commencement.

(2) Subject to sub-paragraphs (3) and (4), nothing in Part IV, Part III of Schedule 8 or Schedule 10—
(a) prevents an existing order from remaining in force; or
(b) affects the enforcement of an existing order.

(3) Nothing in Part IV, Part III of Schedule 8 or Schedule 10 affects any application to extend, vary or discharge an existing order, but the court may, if it thinks it just and reasonable to do so, treat the application as an application for an order under Part IV.

(4) The making of an order under Part IV between parties with respect to whom an existing order is in force discharges the existing order.

Matrimonial home rights

11.—(1) Any reference (however expressed) in any enactment, instrument or document (whether passed or made before or after the passing of this Act) to rights of occupation under, or within the meaning of, the 1983 Act shall be construed, so far as is required for continuing the effect of the instrument or document, as being or as the case requires including a reference to matrimonial home rights under, or within the meaning of, Part IV.

(2) Any reference (however expressed) in this Act or in any other enactment, instrument or document (including any enactment amended by Schedule 8) to matrimonial home rights under, or within the meaning of, Part IV shall be construed as including, in relation to times, circumstances and purposes before the commencement of sections 30 to 32, a reference to rights of occupation under, or within the meaning of, the 1983 Act.

12.—(1) Any reference (however expressed) in any enactment, instrument or document (whether passed or made before or after the passing of this Act) to registration under section 2(8) of the 1983 Act shall, in relation to any time after the commencement of sections 30 to 32, be construed as being or as the case requires including a reference to registration under section 31(10).

(2) Any reference (however expressed) in this Act or in any other enactment, instrument or document (including any enactment amended by Schedule 8) to registration under section 31 (10) shall be construed as including a reference to—
(a) registration under section 2(7) of the Matrimonial Homes Act 1967 or section 2(8) of the 1983 Act, and
(b) registration by caution duly lodged under section 2(7) of the Matrimonial Homes Act 1967 before 14th February 1983 (the date of the commencement of section 4(2) of the Matrimonial Homes and Property Act 1981).

13. In sections 30 and 31 and Schedule 4—

(a) any reference to an order made under section 33 shall be construed as including a reference to an order made under section 1 of the 1983 Act, and

(b) any reference to an order made under section 33(5) shall be construed as including a reference to an order made under section 1 of the 1983 Act by virtue of section 2(4) of that Act.

14. Neither section 31(11) nor the repeal by the Matrimonial Homes and Property Act 1981 of the words "or caution" in section 2(7) of the Matrimonial Homes Act 1967, affects any caution duly lodged as respects any estate or interest before 14th February 1983.

15. Nothing in this Schedule is to be taken to prejudice the operation of sections 16 and 17 of the Interpretation Act 1978 (which relate to the effect of repeals).

Section 66(3)	SCHEDULE 10	

REPEALS

Chapter	Short title	Extent of repeal
1968 c. 63.	The Domestic and Appellate Proceedings (Restriction of Publicity) Act 1968.	Section 2(1)(b).
1973 c. 18.	The Matrimonial Causes Act 1973.	Sections 1 to 7.
		In section 8(1)(b), the words "or before the decree nisi is made absolute".
		Sections 9 and 10.
		Sections 17 and 18.
		Section 20.
		Section 22.
		In section 24A(3), the words "divorce or".
		In section 25(2)(h), the words "in the case of proceedings for divorce or nullity of marriage,".
		In section 28(1), the words from "in", in the first place where it occurs, to "nullity of marriage" in the first place where those words occur.
		In section 29(2), the words from "may begin" to "but".
		In section 30, the words "divorce" and "or judicial separation".
		In section 31, in subsection (2)(a), the words "order for maintenance pending suit and any".
		In section 41, in subsection (1) the words "divorce or" and "or a decree of judicial separation" and in subsection (2) the words "divorce or" and "or that the decree of judicial separation is not to be granted."
		Section 49.
		In section 52(2)(b), the words "to orders for maintenance pending suit and", "respectively" and "section 22 and".
		In Schedule 1, paragraph 8.
1973 c. 45.	The Domicile and Matrimonial Proceedings Act 1973.	In section 5, in subsection (1), the words "subject to section 6(3) and (4) of this Act" and, in paragraph (a), "divorce, judicial separation or" and subsection (2).
		Section 6(3) and (4).
		In Schedule 1, in paragraph 11, in sub-paragraph (2)(a), in sub-paragraph (2)(c), in the first place where they occur, and in

Chapter	Short title	Extent of repeal
		sub-paragraph (3)(b) and (c), the words "in connection with the stayed proceedings".
1976 c. 50.	The Domestic Violence and Matrimonial Proceedings Act 1976.	The whole Act.
1978 c. 22.	The Domestic Proceedings and Magistrates' Courts Act 1978.	In section 1, paragraphs (c) and (d) and the word "or" preceding paragraph (c). In section 7(1), the words "neither party having deserted the other". Sections 16 to 18. Section 28(2). Section 63(3). In Schedule 2, paragraphs 38 and 53.
1980 c. 43.	The Magistrates' Courts Act 1980.	In Schedule 7, paragraph 159.
1981 c. 54.	The Supreme Court Act 1981.	In section 18(1)(d), the words "divorce or".
1982 c. 53.	The Administration of Justice Act 1982.	Section 16.
1983 c. 19.	The Matrimonial Homes Act 1983.	The whole Act.
1984 c. 42.	The Matrimonial and Family Proceedings Act 1984.	Section 1. In section 21(f) the words "except subsection (2)(e) and subsection (4)". In section 27, the definition of "secured periodical payments order". In Schedule 1, paragraph 10.
1985 c. 61.	The Administration of Justice Act 1985.	In section 34(2), paragraph (f) and the word "and" immediately preceding it. In Schedule 2, in paragraph 37, paragraph (e) and the word "and" immediately preceding it.
1985 c. 71.	The Housing (Consequential Provisions) Act 1985.	In Schedule 2, paragraph 56.
1986 c. 53.	The Building Societies Act 1986.	In Schedule 21, paragraph 9(f).
1986 c. 55.	The Family Law Act 1986.	In Schedule 1, paragraph 27.
1988 c. 34.	The Legal Aid Act 1988.	In section 16(9), the word "and" at the end of paragraph (a).
1988 c. 50.	The Housing Act 1988.	In Schedule 17, paragraphs 33 and 34.
1989 c. 41.	The Children Act 1989.	Section 8(4)(c) and (f). In Schedule 11, paragraph 6(b). In Schedule 13, paragraphs 33(1) and 65(1).
1990 c. 41.	The Courts and Legal Services Act 1990.	Section 58(10(b) and (e). In Schedule 18, paragraph 21.
1995 c. 42.	The Private International Law (Miscellaneous Provisions) Act 1995.	In the Schedule, paragraph 3.

INDEX

Generally, references are to the relevant section or Schedule number of the Act. References to the commentary to the section or Schedule are denoted by the letter 'N'. Thus the reference s.35N is to the commentary to section 35 of the Act.

[1]